Persons in Groups

Social Behavior as Identity Formation
in Medieval and Renaissance Europe

medieval & renaissance texts & studies

Volume 36

Persons in Groups

Social Behavior as Identity Formation
in Medieval and Renaissance Europe

Papers of the Sixteenth Annual Conference
of the Center for Medieval and Early Renaissance Studies

EDITED BY

RICHARD C. TREXLER

medieval & Renaissance texts & studies
Binghamton, New York
1985

Center for Medieval & Early Renaissance Studies
University Center at Binghamton
State University of New York

Library of Congress Cataloging in Publication Data
Main entry under title:

Persons in groups.

  (Medieval & Renaissance texts & studies ; 36)
  English and French.

  1. Social psychology — Europe — History — Addresses,
essays, lectures.   2. Identity (Psychology) — History —
Addresses, essays, lectures.   3. Renaissance — History —
Addresses, essays, lectures.   4. Civilization, Medieval —
Addresses, essays, lectures.   I. Trexler, Richard C.,
1932-   .   II. Series.

HM251.P4258   1985   302'.094   84-27211
ISBN 0-86698-069-5

Printed in the United States of America

Table of Contents

Contributors

Elizabeth A. R. Brown
Brooklyn College and the Graduate School, City University of New York

Peter Brown
Princeton University

Samuel Y. Edgerton, Jr.
Williams College

Sharon Farmer
Rice University

Mark Franko
Princeton University

Jennifer R. Goodman
Texas A. & M. University

Eugene Green
Boston University

Janet E. Halley
Hamilton College

Diane Owen Hughes
University of Michigan

Christiane Klapisch-Zuber
École des Hautes Études en Sciences Sociales (Paris)

Peter Marsh
Oxford Polytechnic

Timothy Murray
Cornell University

Stephen Orgel
The Johns Hopkins University

Jean-Claude Schmitt
École des Hautes Études en Sciences Sociales (Paris)

Robert B. Seaberg
Reed College

Sydel Silverman
City University of New York, Graduate School

Ronald F. E. Weissman
University of Maryland (College Park)

Introduction

The subject matter of this book, social behavior as it relates to individual and group identity formation in human beings, has as yet no discrete location in the academic division of labor. To organize a conference on this subject and to produce a book of papers from that conference was, therefore, a cross-disciplinary undertaking. Scholars from several different disciplines and with various intellectual stances came to the 1982 CEMERS conference at the State University of New York at Binghamton, which was organized by the present writer.

For some of the conferees the relation between identity and social behavior had long been a basic query of their intellectual activity, but for many others the conference provided a home for significant historical materials whose theoretical significance or context they were previously uncertain of. Thus, while the conferees might enjoy the marvelous historical evidence that showed human beings making themselves and constructing their groups in society, just what that social activity meant was a matter of debate during the conference. It remains so in this book. In publishing a number of these conference papers, we hope that readers will sense the rich variety and exchange that imbued the conference itself. This introduction aims to bring out the different approaches and points of view the authors assume in evaluating their materials.

Social behavior as a means of identity formation: this focus of our book concerns two areas of inquiry which are seldom combined in human, as distinct from animal, studies. By identity we mean that bundle of verbal and corporal statements persons and groups use to recognize one another. Identity has, of course, long been a preoccupation of humanistic scholars.

Yet it must be said that they have rarely thought of the identities of Europeans, or at least of the European elites, as the product of social behavior.

The study of persons behaving in groups, on the other hand, has a solid foundation in the social sciences, but that scholarship usually makes little reference to the personal or individual element that humanists include in their idea of identity. These areas of interest have, therefore, seldom intersected in the study of contemporary society; the combination has evoked still less interest among students of past societies. Practically no bibliography exists in the historical disciplines linking historical identities to past social behaviors.

In attempting to link these subjects, the authors of this book have one basic presumption in common: no matter what one's nation, class, status, sex, religion or age, to have an identity is, among other things, to have done things in the presence of others. We presume that actions performed in social spaces partly create and change individual and collective identities. Social spaces are, in our opinion, central to the formation, expression, and modification of individual and group identities. Individuals take action in public to make a certain image of themselves recognizable to others, and in that process they come to recognize their own person in that image. Often individuals enter into public groups to the same end and with the same effect. Through their own public identities, such groups produce not only audience- but self-recognition for the individuals who formed them.

The book begins with three theoretical statements that provide different approaches to our basic question of the relation between individual and collective identities in medieval and early modern European societies. Explorations in five different areas of social behavior follow this theoretical section. The first of these areas, that of theatrical performances, also has important theoretical implications, especially concerning the relationship between roles and identities. Subsequently, the volume explores the creation of political, social, religious, and historical identities by groups and individuals in traditional Europe.

From the beginning, the conference aimed at incorporating scholarship from outside the area of medieval and Renaissance studies. Thus two of the three introductory theoretical papers are by students of contemporary societies. Between them, these writers offer three different approaches to social behavior that may be called individualistic, collectivistic, and symbolic.

The first paper in this collection is by Peter Marsh, a psychologist of modern English society and especially of London's youth gangs. Fundamental to his ethogenic approach are two important presumptions. First, Marsh asserts that people become persons by entering into public space. Different from older psychologies that treat public groups as composed of indistinct collections of atoms, Marsh's theory rightly presumes that *people* in groups are by definition *persons*. Second, Marsh asserts that human beings have historically divided their lives into practical and expressive segments.

Through a study of the behavior of London youth groups in stadium terraces during soccer games, Marsh demonstrates his method for arriving at the meaning of those groups' expressive life. It consists in asking the actors what they meant by their behavior and analyzing their responses. In Marsh's view, the focus of the social psychologist's attention should be the performing individuals' accounts of, and thus their stated motivations for, participating in social events. Marsh finds that his youthful actors felt excluded from the institutional centers of society. Motivated by what Marsh says is the falsehood that those institutions were open, they created the gangs so as to make a place in those centers. In fact, Marsh finds that their gang behavior during soccer games does ultimately allow members to pass to adulthoods of self-worth. The youth groups of sixth-century Constantinople may also, Marsh speculates, have been similarly formed for the individual ends of their members.

Marsh's approach to his subject, which sees group activity as a response to individual needs, and his emphasis on the shaping of individual "moral careers" (Goffman) through group life within a given prestige economy, will appeal to students of European history, who already tend to emphasize individual volition and meanings as part of their ideological heritage. Marsh's approach raises problems for them as well. Medievalists and early modernists rely entirely on written sources, ones that only rarely give an account of individual career strategies. Further, these sources were overwhelmingly authored by mature males of the European political classes, and often for ceremonial purposes. They may be thought of as a continuation of that formal life in social spaces from which political males, in their legislative activities, regularly excluded the dependent classes of women, the poor, and the young. How can those dependent on written sources extract accounts of the social behavior of such dependent individuals?

A second, associated problem is raised by the fact that in his paper, Marsh views the expressive sphere irrespective of the neighborhood, sex, class, and even the age of his informers. Written sources for traditional Europe, on the other hand, usually thought of the expressive sphere of life in group-specific terms. Political males of the Renaissance called themselves "the solemn class," for example, and while they averred that in certain contexts, youth, women and the poor had a weakness for display, they nevertheless thought it best that the latter two groups, at least, limit themselves to the practical sphere and not put themselves on display. Are there in fact levels and types of display that are associated with particular groups, as our sources thought? In any case, how does a student of the past account for a political elite's group-specific understanding of display?

In her study of neighborhood display at Siena, Sydel Silverman provides one answer to this quandary by insisting that any "account" of the meaning of social behavior must begin with the power of social and political superstructures. To her, Marsh's comparison of the London toughs to the gangs of the Emperor Justinian's Constantinople would have made a significant starting point, for in Siena she found that the variety of neighborhood self-representations in the Palio increased and flourished not during the medieval republic but during the early modern period of political authoritarianism, when Siena formed part of the Grand Duchy of Tuscany.

Thus the neighborhood identities that the Sienese Palio or civic horserace even today expresses are given symbolic entities that are tolerated and even encouraged by the modern state. Through them, individual neighbors have for centuries confirmed their collective identities, no matter what their class, sex, or age. Silverman's insistence on neighborhood identities confirmed by performances is certainly in polar opposition to Marsh's toughs' shaping their individual moral careers.

By raising the possibility that individual or small-group self-fashioning might be a mere concession of modern states, Silverman makes it imperative for us to understand the relation between social behavior and political order. It is at this juncture that Marsh and Silverman can be seen to share a similar point of view. Though coming from diametrically opposed working methods, the one interested in individual, the other in collective identity, both view expression as meaningful within an overriding and inviolable political and social order. They exclude the possibility that festive behavior can subvert superstructures. That is, they do not imagine social behaviors reforming the identities of groups around and above them.

According to the Burckhardtian view of the Renaissance, that period witnessed the victory of individualism over "medieval corporatism." Despite its tenacity, such a view flies in the face of social science if only because it assumes that some historical periods are more analyzable by group or individual emphases than are others. In his paper, Ronald Weissman argues that the concept of Renaissance individualism is unsound. It is one of those historiographically applied abstractions — medieval corporatism is another — that more often obscures than illuminates the meaning of social interaction in history. Weissman suggests that we focus instead on dynamic social relations simultaneously evolving at many different levels, in the family as well as the state, the neighborhood as well as the individual, in our search for the processes of identity formation. Such an approach will produce ambiguous identities, but Weissman notes that ambiguity too is social in nature. Nor would Weissman accept the criticism that such micro-situational analyses neglect overriding political and social forces, for he insists that the acting individual manipulates, and is not just manipulated by, the social relations he enters into.

Though these authors do not use the word "theatre" in their papers, they all propound theories of social representations and methods for studying such representations. Thus the following papers, ones that deal explicitly with representing others, contain important general statements on the formation of identity in social contexts. These papers on theatre deal respectively with the use of the past, with gender representations, and with the nature of theatrical deception.

Jennifer Goodman's paper on the theatrical tournament of Arras in 1463 shows that reenacting a story in public—history masqued will be a repeated theme in this volume—was one important means by which social actors created memorable identities. The Burgundian world that for Huizinga was fancy is revealed by Goodman to have been a creative social process. To the amusement of an audience of urban denizens usually occupied with making a living, knights asked permission of the Burgundian court—playing King Arthur's—and then assumed fanciful roles that required them to conquer imaginary dangers. Goodman describes these knights as creating present and future identities through such fictionalized relivings of past realities. The knight *creatively* participates in chivalric romance, Goodman convincingly argues, "so that some small memory [might] remain" of the heroic actor. In a similar fashion and with the identical motivation *ad perpetuam rei memoriam*, Italian chroniclers recorded triumphal entries modelled on those of the Caesars.

Thus the past is an important resource for making identities in social spaces. In his paper Peter Marsh cautions that his toughs did not merely assume *roles*, because their behavior was regularly modified by their own expressive aims. Weissman too notes that individuals interpret their world on the basis of their previous participations in social dramas. Goodman shows that on a formal stage, social beings consciously incorporate great stories into their persons so as to produce a memorable identity. They do not enter into and exit from history unscathed. Human memory, as we shall see always close to dissimulation or deception, is a major theme of this book.

Mark Franko's paper on Renaissance grace and decorum takes us one step deeper into questions of theatrical representation. How are actors convincing? How did actors of this time prove to an audience that they meant what they represented? In the language of the time, grace was necessary, a behavior that seemed second nature. One had to seem one's self, even when one represented someone else. Yet contemporaries knew that second natures are learned, and nowhere more than in the dance, that never-still art of movement most demanding of artifice. How then was one to learn, and then project, a moving identity?

Franko notes the surprising fact that dance treatises of the Renaissance rarely describe or prescribe movements. Aware that dance masters of the time drew much of their pedagogy on orthodox behavior from courtesy or manners books, he searches in those texts for an explanation of the "absence of the dancing body." What he discovers is that courtesy books, all the time denouncing persons who "stand there like a block of salt," actually decry what they call gesticulation and give few guidelines on movements. Like the dance treatises, they, too, generally limit themselves to prescribing postures, that is, states of grave immobility. For the rest, the manners specialists encouraged their readers to imitate consensually-accepted, living models of grace. Thus both the dance treatises, which were supposed to teach persons how to convincingly portray others, and the courtesy manuals, which taught persons how to be themselves, ignore the details of how the graceful person, radiating *sprezzatura*, gets from one posture to another.

As Franko points out, these specialized sources, grappling as they do with the art of representation, are metaphors for larger problems of how social behavior forms identities. First, convincing an audience of one's sincerity involves learned deception. Second, unless one is to stand still, one must learn by imitating the living even when one represents a graced figure long dead, like a knight of King Arthur. Thus imitating the living to represent the dead involves subverting the latter.

What different sexes do with such memories, or were thought to do with them, is the subject of Timothy Murray's analysis of *Othello*. He shows that patriarchal Elizabethan society feared acting out the past because, given women's assumed proclivity to imitate what they saw and heard, they could create dangerous female identities in the present. The past is in fact remembered as genre or classes of moralisms through which women knew their place. Whereas women were expected merely to stand there in place of their husbands, Desdemona on hearing Othello tell stories produces an "operation of spectatorship" that has the effect of demystifying patriarchal authority. Desdemona becomes someone else. Theatre or representation, which for Murray as for other contributors to this volume is a mnemonic rather than normative type of pedagogy, can be subversive of the goals of its sponsors.

For Murray, Shakespeare's meaning in *Othello* must therefore be seen in terms of the question of the sexual character of social discourse. His paper raises a second fundamental concern as well, that of the representative character of the private, as against the public, sphere. Contrasting Desdemona's and Bianca's way of coming to terms with their lovers, Murray thinks Shakespeare makes the latter into a heroine because she will only sleep privately with Cassio and not represent herself in public as his mistress. Murray raises the question of the nature and role of the private and public spheres in identity formation and suggests that the private-public polarity is coeval with one between the individual and the social. The papers of Peter Brown and Jean-Claude Schmitt address this problem as well.

After this background in the theory and theatre of social behavior as identity formation, there follows a series of case studies, beginning with those concerning the political realm. How do rulers legitimize their authority through acting out divine history? What was the balance sheet for early modern rulers who used ceremony to increase their authority? And how did revolutionary groups legitimate themselves through public behavior? These are among the questions raised by Samuel Edgerton, Stephen Orgel, and Robert Seaberg.

Edgerton's and Orgel's papers on legitimation concentrate on the relation between visual images and political perceptions. Edgerton convincingly shows that medieval and early modern Italian states justified their judicial procedures by representing them as Last Judgments. Since the Last Judgment lay in the future, its representation in communal judicial practices had an especially coercive role. Once again, a story or event is seen as relevant to our perception and interpretation of human social actions.

Although Stephen Orgel's examination of court and city theatre during the Elizabethan age examines the political elite's attempts to justify themselves by theatrical representations, he arrives at the view that they were largely unsuccessful. He discovers that, at several levels, such representations had a subversive character, most strikingly brought out in Elizabeth's worry on being "deposed forty times" in English historical theatre. Ceremonial life did not work for Elizabeth and, in Orgel's view, was not worth the expense or the danger.

If we think back, it is clear that two different views have emerged on the relationship to social superstructures of persons forming identities in public. Marsh and Silverman at one pole see either career shaping or small-group identity reaffirmations within a model of superstructural immobility, while Murray and now Orgel at the other pole assert that superstructures were vulnerable when actors made their identities in public. How desperately, it seems, is a history of theatre or representation needed that would have this problem of edification and subversion as its central problematic.

Such a work would have to include studies of those times when revolutionaries normally excluded from the civic stage set about subverting political authority through social behaviors. Such is the brunt of Robert Seaberg's article on the revolutionary Levellers, Diggers, and Ranters in mid-seventeenth-century England. Like Marsh, Seaberg studies subjects forming groups before an audience of dominant political forces.

The first aim of any revolutionary group must, of course, be to create and perpetuate its own group identity, and Seaberg asks how each of these three groups fared on this score. He shows that the dominant public witnessed these performances in two different ways: the Levellers were the type of group that presented their images in the streets: they proudly wore green ribbons and the text of the Agreement of the People in their hats in public processions. The Ranters, on the other hand, held their gatherings in private, so that the public imagined their activities from what they heard.

Seaberg finds that the persons in groups which operated in public spaces were more cohesive: the Diggers developed the greatest solidarity or group identity because their experience in public space, which included latent and real conflict, was the most total. Seaberg further comments, as did Timothy Murray, on the sexual nature of such conflictual public representations. By showing that at times social groups seeking to disgrace the sectarians or de-form their identities dressed up as women, he again reminds us of the centrality to both audience and actors of sex and gender identity.

Nowhere is the centrality to representation of sex and other group characteristics more evident than in the papers that deal with the formation of social identities. The author of *Beowulf*, Eugene Green shows, decided who and who would not have names. Christiane Klapisch-Zuber and Diane Owen Hughes demonstrate that the authorities of late medieval times publicly categorized the good and bad, gentile and Jewish, rich and poor, young and old women of Italy by names and other physical signs. The effects on the actors themselves of the authorities' structuring of social representations is one of the interesting aspects of these papers.

Let us put Green's paper in context. We have seen the importance human beings of this age attached to the mimed story as they went about forming and subverting identities in social contexts. Green allows us to follow a past author as he assigned or failed to assign names to his characters, which amounted to furnishing future generations with a short list of individuals who because they were named could later be mimed. By remaining without names, the rest of the actors may be said to have never been formed. The social glue of a story — retinues, heralds, dependents, — Green neatly suggests, proves necessarily nameless, and in the future unemulable. Is it possible to talk of a person who is without a name in the account? Perhaps people are not persons merely by the fact of being in public, as Peter Marsh argues. To the extent that identities are produced through emulation of past figures, the literary procedure of *Beowulf*'s author constrains us to see identity as produced through the social behavior only of named heroes or villains.

Seeking to determine the relationship between social behavior and identity, Christiane Klapisch-Zuber follows Florentine women from their baptismal naming, through their dowering, their marriages, then in their actions as mother and finally as widows. Her findings are dismal. Far from the conventional picture of the fine Renaissance woman, the Florentines of Klapisch-Zuber emerge as types of dolls. They were so shuffled about among patrilineages that they were never sure of their "place" or character, in her view. This amounted to an "effacement" of Florentine women, one that resulted from a society structured so as to publicly identify men in groups. Klapisch-Zuber argues, in short, that the stage of social exchanges can be a place where identities are de-formed rather than formed or, more cautiously stated, constantly re-formed through the woman's ceaseless circulation among, and reference to, patrilineages.

Thus Klapisch-Zuber allows us to imagine one Florentine woman in ritual contexts circulated among fine male lineages and constantly marked and remarked by each. Diane Owen Hughes, on the other hand, shows us how Italian male authorities during the fifteenth and early sixteenth centuries tried to control women's behavior in public by legislating clothing: society would know what group a woman belonged to by reading her clothing. She shows that women's resistance to these sumptuary laws and to the shapes and borders of purity and pollution they implied made for constant changes in the laws.

Hughes traces the remarkable history of earrings first as used by Jews, then by prostitutes after the Jewish women themselves stopped using them, and finally by upper-class Christian women in the sixteenth-century. Religious, sexual, and status identities were implicated. Demonstrating how through this small ornamentation contemporaries read what exactly any given woman was, Hughes shows that paintings of Mary at her Purification and at Christ's Presentation responded to changing sumptuary valuations of earrings by first removing and then ultimately refitting her with these ornaments. A larger-scale history of clothing, on the Hughes model, would furnish ever-changing codes by which one could read both the statuses of those many women shuffled from ceremony to ceremony by Klapisch-Zuber's dominant patrilines, and the same women's tenacious attempts to subvert those statuses. Names, earrings, and of course many other trappings are instruments through which audiences and actors in public squares form and de-form their recognitions and images of different social groups.

The previous set of papers deals with the use of various signs in forming or de-forming individual identities in society at large. The next group examines the self-fashioning of personal and group religious identities: the universal religion of Christianity, the religion of the friars preacher, and the Reformation sect of the Familists.

Peter Brown's study of isolated early Christian groups shows how such groups and persons came to recognize themselves as Christians through the mimesis of distant holy men's reputed actions. Several papers in this collection emphasize the use of models for forming social identities, but it is Brown's paper that returns to the ancient roots of paideia, and clarifies the presumptions behind its use. He shows that precisely because the early Christian holy man was an immutable "classic," he was presumed to offer an emulator an intensely personal identification.

Brown describes the Near-Eastern holy man aping Jesus' behaviors for the benefit of his own followers, who recorded the saint's actions as if they were Jesus'. Ultimately, the minuscule distant communities of the faithful read or heard of these feats and knew themselves Christians by replicating them. The details of the saintly "declarative ceremonials," one might add, would probably have made a fledgling dancer reading the manuals of the sixteenth century envious, for the latter, as Franko's paper shows, rarely describe movements. By such imitations, Brown says, those on the margins moved toward the ineffable center of Christly behavior.

We stand, therefore, at the origins of the Christian world community, one formed by a mimesis that heightened rather than alienated individual identities. Yet intense *male* bonding was the essence of this Christian paideia; once again, gender was not an inconsequential part of the Christian identity. Brown shows that a condition of male bonding in these communities was to stylize women with the contours of the Magdalene, a figure who signified eternal danger to the male fraternity's own solidarity. In what became the Christian community, women were to have an identity only to the extent they, like the Magdalene, mourned their selves in public.

Jean-Claude Schmitt's paper shows how the practice of paideia functioned a thousand years later for one religious order built around another heroic founder: the actions of St. Dominic were consciously classicized in pictures so as to inspire individual Dominicans. In their *vitae*, Dominic's hagiographers described their father's prayer modes in words, but in the corpus of manuscripts at Schmitt's disposal, illustrators also pictured the saint performing them. As Schmitt brilliantly notes, the succession of these pictures is akin to a moving picture film, an almost live image powerful enough to move the Dominican viewers as though miming a living model.

Schmitt's study is of particular help in assessing the social quality of private in relation to public behavior, an aspect we encountered in describing Timothy Murray's evaluation of Bianca in *Othello*. Schmitt notes that the purpose of the hagiographers' pictures and texts was to furnish individual friars with authoritative ways to behave in their *private* prayers, and the events from Dominic's life shown in the images are in fact largely private in nature. Yet the prayer postures described in the texts were often said to have produced miracles, and these miracles obviously had to be witnessed by outsiders to be believable. Enter the typical "furtive witness," whose wrongdoing became the condition of establishing legitimate behavior.

Thus what the story of Dominic portrays as "private" rather than "social" behavior becomes through the legitimating witness a social context rather than a private one. No publicity, no legitimation. Peter Brown's and Schmitt's papers, as well as Eugene Green's, show that all behavior said to be legitimated by models was said to be witnessed—and thus public behavior.

Janet Halley's paper on the seventeenth-century sect of English Familists also deals with the impact of a founder on later group behavior, but in the context of the Protestant Reformation. We witness that founder's identity, and that of the group, being simultaneously asserted and negated. On the one hand, the mechanisms used by Familists to identify fellow sectarians are classical. The founder asserted that his person had become the Word, so he vaunted the silence of followers as a sign of their perfect discourse. In sect organization after the founder's death, in turn, the hierarchy distinguished between those at the top, who talk and thus represent the sect, and those at the bottom, who represent it by not talking.

Halley's analysis becomes unusual, on the other hand, when she explores the fashion in which the sectarians represented themselves in the face of outside persecution. In her phrase, authorities of the time relied on the "linguistic transparency" of their subjects, that is, they relied on their own ability to read oral performances for intent. The Familists, however, were Nicodemites. They lied to the authorities as a matter of policy, most significantly when they denounced the Familist practice of lying. They preserved their group solidarity by verbally denouncing it.

Halley's paper unifies the three contributions on religious identities around the notion of spiritual solidarities built on deceptions. Peter Brown argues that societies depending on declarative performances for identifying their constituent parts (and the Reformation period with its constant demand for testimony was certainly one of those), construct exorcistic prayers whose performance is a test of loyalty. Such prayers or testimonies were potentially subversive, however, because social performances, if inspired by the devil, could lie. Jean-Claude Schmitt's Dominicans certainly knew the medieval notions of devilishly tricking gods and saints through perfect replications of authoritative behaviors. In the Christian age, in fact, no member of the corpus mysticum was thought to be exempt from the danger of being deceived by social behavior. In the early modern period, in turn, scores of "how-to books" on deception, like the courtesy manuals that derived their inspiration from medieval courtesy literature, became available to the reading public. The religious phenomenon of Nicodemism has to be seen in this context of a fundamental, long-term association of deception with identity formation. The Familists were just one religious group whose "false" social behaviors were a condition of their social and religious solidarity.

The last two papers deal with the contribution of the dead to the formation of historical identities by the living. In reality, this theme underlies many of the papers we have already introduced. For what were Desdemona and the early Christian, the tournament knight and the reader of *Beowulf* seeking if not relations with the dead? And what did those who mimed the emulable living accomplish if not a continuation of the social behavior of the latter once they had gone? The present papers' specific quality is that they concern the relations of groups with their own dead, from the medieval

monks who lived with hallowed fellows to the grand relations of nations
with their history.

Sharon Farmer's paper on the twelfth-century ghost stories from the
French monastery of Marmoutier begins against a background of monastic
ritual as it is mirrored in the *Dialogues* of Gregory the Great: early monks
appealed to their dead brethren collectively and thus produced a collective
identity. To Farmer, the Marmoutier ghost stories reflect the emergence
of an individualized spirituality, for the ghosts of Marmoutier were often
individuals who appeared to individual monks. This meant a richer set of
networks with the beyond, including networks between individual living
and dead monks who had known or been related to each other in the *saeculum*.

Elizabeth Brown's concluding article on the French royal dead ranges
from the graves of the Middle Ages to the present-day tomb of Charles
de Gaulle. It shows that the inexpendable dead were always manipulable
for human salvation, both by the authorities who shaped the society of the
dead to foster specific social and political orders of the living, and by individual supplicants at the tombs, who sought to link themselves to the larger
living community.

Brown's subject is the formation of a French community, an identity process she studies primarily in terms of the organization and reorganization
of the French monarchs at the royal abbey of St. Denis. She shows that
societies of the dead, when concentrated in space as at St. Denis, provide
prime groups around which the living form their collective and individual
identities.

Not for nothing did one bemused Frenchman of the nineteenth century
speak of the "incests" that resulted from one such reorganization: neither
strict family genealogies nor the moral reputation of the individual dead
was of much importance for the living, whose own identity was so dependent on those hallowed shades. Brown draws our attention to the creation
of identity through the destruction and even humiliation of the historical
identities of monarchs. It is one thing to insult the living and another to
dishonor the dead, of course, but both processes commonly occurred
simultaneously. One revolutionary counsellor obviously feared living monarchists when he warned in the wake of the execution of Louis XVI and Marie
Antoinette that if the mausoleums of all the monarchs were not destroyed,
the dead kings and queens would "continue to rule over France." By destroy-
ing the mausoleums and scattering the royal remains, he meant to insult
and neutralize living monarchists as well.

But Brown does not limit her study to revolutionary desecrations. She
shows that during stable times Frenchmen had reconstructed, or constantly dishonored, the "old", to then rehonor the "new" dead. The monarchs'
rule over France constantly changed in character as visitors' behavior
changed in response to the reorganizations of the royal bones and beds.

Those reorganizations themselves in turn were certainly responses to the changing shapes of French nationhood. The eerie worship of nineteenth-century sceptics, the candles burned by the communist denizens of contemporary St. Denis before the royal saints, not to mention the only slightly less spooky national canonization of Charles de Gaulle in his village, are as instructive in their ambivalence as were the lies of Halley's Familists.

Such identity formations highlight the subversion latent in all social behavior. They show that collective and individual identities were and are created, fortified and transformed through occasionally violent but usually peaceable iconoclasm. Brown's study of social behavior at a monarchical center designed for group and personal identity formation makes us pause at such graves. Brown reminds us that remembering is a central characteristic of persons forming identities in groups.

Bringing together the common threads of this book is to summarize an infant field of scholarship. What are the principal themes of this collection of papers and what avenues for further exploration have they opened up?

The most recurrent theme in this volume is that Europeans constantly used stories about named actors as sources for self- representation. They used history in a special way, to be sure, for the messages traditional Europeans took from past persons and events were generic. That is, history was intended to teach appropriate behaviors in the present. Historical representations for the purpose of identity formation involved classifications.

Thus collective and individual actors manipulated alleged historic behaviors in their own public performances. That manipulation necessarily involved deception, which in turn seemed a necessary condition for creating identities and insuring memories, whether those identities were political, social, or religious in nature.

Are persons in groups as subversive for the living as they are to the dead? Several papers defend that proposition. They show for example how the process of identifying one's self in public involves challenging the identities of other persons and groups and even dissolving the identities of dependents. At the same time, the gender significations of different types of social behavior were found to cut across all operations of identity formation, perpetuating but also threatening male domination in traditional European societies.

Yet the emphasis on political and social superstructures posed at the beginning of this volume by Peter Marsh and Sydel Silverman cannot be ignored. Identity formation in social behavior may be interesting, indeed crucial, but it is done in public because states permit it to be. In short they posit a state that is not a work of art, not a vulnerable identity, but a presence. To what extent, after all, can political power really be subverted by performances in public? To answer that question would take another volume — one rich in papers like Robert Seaberg's — that would show the games revolutionaries play in destabilizing states. Such a volume would have as its task the study of theatre as edification and theatre as subversion.

The papers in this collection do, on balance, lend themselves to the following statement. During those centuries, identity was formed in a dynamic social process in which the miming of persons rather than the display of norms was paramount. We should not dismiss norms as fictions, even "master fictions," for Europeans traditionally praised or damned persons with reference to their relative adhesion to norms, and those judgments were themselves a form of social behavior. But this volume does suggest, I think, that while norms must be dramatically represented so as to edify, they are subverted in the showing. Identity-making buries as it creates.

RICHARD C. TREXLER

State University of New York at Binghamton
December 1984

Identity: an Ethogenic Perspective

PETER MARSH

T he term "ethogenic" social psychology is probably unfamiliar to most readers of this volume. So I would like to attempt in the first part of this chapter a brief summary of the approach and the conceptual stances it embraces. I will, in all probability, be unable to provide a clear, definitive account. But hopefully I will be able to communicate the essential features of what occasionally, and rather arrogantly, is referred to as the "New Paradigm." Later, using the unlikely example, in this context, of British soccer fans, and their aggressive patterns of group behaviour, I will attempt to show the particular relevance of the approach in understanding enigmatic social worlds and the manner in which individuals gain identity and recognition within them.

Let me start with Rom Harré, for he is responsible for the term "ethogenic." His approach is one which I share (in large part) and which I think is particularly pertinent to the title of the conference: *Persons in Groups — Social Behaviour as Identity Formation.* For it is precisely toward this issue that the approach, and our work, is addressed.

Harré and Secord's book, *The Explanation of Social Behaviour,*[1] had quite a profound impact on British social psychology in the early 1970s. Its primary function, I think, was to crystallise the discontent felt by many social scientists concerning the narrow conceptual basis of our discipline and the triviality of the experimental method which lay at the heart of publishable research. Bizarre manipulations in which "subjects" interacted with hat racks, some of us felt, could hardly reveal much about the essential features of human social existence. Social psychological theories and findings seemed to apply to very different worlds from the one I and my friends inhabited. The ways in which we interacted, carved out *our* identities and sought means of obtaining positive regard appeared to be well outside the range of our discipline's concern. And we were not, in this sense, isolated exceptions. I suppose we have a modest, though possibly egocentric notion that our theories should at least explain our *own* lives — our own individuality, our own identity. Then maybe we can try to make sense of other social worlds.

The book, *The Explanation of Social Behaviour*, whilst stopping short of providing a coherent and fully articulated alternative science, at least gave courage to those who sought to prevent social psychology from degenerating completely into a detached, sterile and essentially nonhuman discipline. Here was a framework embodying an explicit model of Man — a conception of autonomous *persons* rather than powerless subjects (or victims of biology) — a style of investigation which mirrored the ways in which we, as ordinary folk, make meaningful and rewarding our own social lives.

Rom Harré, in his latest book *Social Being*,[2] points out that social psychological theories are, perhaps inevitably, conceived within the dominant explanatory frameworks of their time. From the Middle Ages, through Hobbes, Locke and Mill to Marx and Freud we have seen the emergence of grand philosophies and their concomitant psychologies. At each moment in history such psychologies enable us not only to understand the behaviour of our contemporaries but also to "re-gloss" the activities of our ancestors — to give new meaning to their social acts. Freud's account of Leonardo da Vinci is a classic, though possibly misguided, example of such psychological time-travel. New theories, however, do not displace the old — the earlier frameworks remain as "rhetorics" — as resources for accounting. The ethogenic approach, Harré fondly hopes, reflects a dominant mode of conceiving social life in our own time. As such, he argues, it is part of a rhetoric by which that very life is created.

Harré, of course, is a philosopher first and a social psychologist second. I am *only* a social psychologist and thus have few credentials for summarising the interweaving of themes which provide ethogenic social psychology with its philosophical cloak. A considerable amount of this conceptual effort is, in any case, devoted to a systematic destruction of other psychological rhetorics — of socio-biology and behaviourism in particular. There is little point in such exercise here today. Instead let us look more positively at the basic principles and assumptions of the approach.

Human social activity can be seen as being directed, on the one hand, to material and biological ends and, on the other, to presentations of self. The principles of the former *practical order* are to be found in the causal laws of natural science, and Harré tends to place them on one side. The *expressive order*, however, provides ethogenic psychology with its prime subject material. The major focus of interest, and hence the manner in which social life is to be rendered explicable, is with how the individual creates in other members of his collective certain attitudes and expectations encapsulated in his reputation and the character attributed to him. The pursuit of such reputations, we would argue, is the overriding preoccupation of human life, and the means by which reputations are achieved are legion.

To some extent, of course, the expressive and practical aspects of human activity may be hard to separate. As Harré points out:

> ...going on strike may be both a practical activity aimed at redistributing earnings in some industry or service, and an expressive activity, an illustration of the importance of this category of work. Considered thus it could be read as a demand by the workers for the marks of respect they feel due to them, relative to that mode of work. Understanding the psychological sources of specific social activities even within the apparently uniform category of 'strikes' requires that we maintain the correct balance between the practical and expressive "motive," which may be different for each occasion.

This sense of balance is important, for one can argue that in different historical periods the relative weights of expressive and practical considerations have been quite different. The balance will also vary from culture to culture. Thus, in nineteenth-century industrial England the practical realities of day-to-day existence were so all consuming that little time or energy was available for the establishment of an expressive order for *most people*. Contrast this with, say, the European Middle Ages or with life among the Dani in New Guinea only a few decades ago, and we can see that the expressive features of social activity were far more significant, and thus must lie at the heart of meaningful explanations. The industrial life of Northern England in the reign of Queen Victoria is a problem for ethogenic theory. That period is left to Marx — philosopher of the practical order *par excellence*. Much of the rest of history, and contemporary social life, however, are such that a full appreciation of the expressive aspects of social activity is required to render such activity explicable. Concerning non-Western cultures Harré comments:

> Anthropologists give us a figure of between 8 to 10 per cent of living time devoted to sustenance of life in pre-industrial societies. That leaves a lot of social space and time for dressing up, gossiping and chasing other people's spouses.   (*Social Being*, p. 21).

The pursuit of reputation, which lies at the heart of expressive activity, is conducted within social frameworks which allow for the ritual marking of respect and contempt. (This social dynamic is, in fact, one of the very few human universals that the ethogenic approach allows.) It is assumed that private knowledge of and satisfaction in success is worthless to most individuals. The risk of public failure is accepted for the chance to bathe in the respect or admiration accorded to public success. Here respect and contempt refer not only to the attitudes and feelings of individuals but also to the more detached aspects of public ceremonial and display. Thus "marks of respect" may be afforded to a person not because a collective shares feelings or attitudes to go with such marking but because of the social demands of the occasion, the public role of the individual, etc. I am convinced, for example, that the marks of respect shown to Margaret Thatcher and Ronald Reagan have little to do with individual feelings of admiration or positive affect — they are simply ritual aspects of the macro-social frameworks which allow such individuals to occupy prescribed roles.

Where respect and contempt are institutionalised in such a manner, prestige (and its consequent contribution to identity) is said to result from "hazards." Conventional hazards might include public examinations, parliamentary elections, and so on. Each hazard is accompanied by changes in public / social reputation or what Erving Goffman refers to as "character." Individuals, however, can have many "characters." Certainly, the complexities of modern social life are such that we live in several barely overlapping social worlds interacting with distinctly separate sets of others. So, in addition to the hazards of conventional public trials, we are able to develop our "characters," our "personae," our "social identities" through the pursuit of *moral careers*.

"Moral Career" is again a term borrowed from Goffman. To my mind it is an extremely useful concept and a appropriate one in this context. It enables us to see more clearly how a concern for dignity is the dominant feature of life within social groups, and the extent to which the dynamics of groups have the clear function of supporting such preoccupations. Thus, even the most informal of social worlds will embrace tacit *role-rule frameworks*. We can identify certain positions within groups which afford a sense of personal worth, status and recognition. We can also isolate those social rules which direct, shape and render meaningful social action. That behaviour which accords with such conventions will be the subject of collective positive regard and enable vertical progress in a moral career. Social activity of a "deviant" nature — i.e. that which fails to accord with written or unwritten prescriptions within an institution, group or micro-culture, will be the subject of social sanction leading to diminished prestige or even contempt.

This kind of approach, it must be stressed, is not reducible to a simple role-theory — "a theory of internal relations between people as embodiments of *social* identities." This is because the behaviour of individuals in, and with respect to, social and public institutions is continuously modified by the *expressive* aims and activities of persons holding certain role positions.

Distinction should be made here between *personal* identity — which is the basis of individuality and human uniqueness — and *social* identity — the kind of person he appears to be as a result of the kind of role he occupies (and

I'll develop this point in a moment). An account of social life couched sole-ly in terms of the "official" (i.e. practical / functional) rhetoric of an institu-tion will be grossly insufficient for the understanding of individual behaviour.

Erving Goffman illustrates this point very nicely in his study of mental hospitals, *Asylums*.[3] Usually one would describe the activities of both staff and patients in terms of the official theory of psychiatric hospitals — that involving ideas of curing sickness, mental disorder, and so on. But such a theory is quite insufficient to provide a conceptual system for understand-ing all that happens within such an institution, particularly those activities which are to do with reputation. Ken Kesey's film *One Flew Over the Cuckoo's Nest* makes the point very cogently indeed.

Similarly, as Harré points out, to describe the London Worshipful Com-pany of Fishmongers, the descendant of a medieval guild, in terms of its original institutional function would be quite meaningless. Fish have not been mongered within the institution for centuries and it now provides for very different ceremonial and social performances.

Personal identity, then, can be seen as deriving not so much from the occupation of institutional or social roles as from the manner in which such roles are *expressed* through an individual's performances and from the man-ner in which he develops his moral career. His identity transcends his roles, and can be seen as a personal achievement. At the same time his "characters," which may be seen as a foundation for identity, remain a property of what Harré refers to as "the cluster of theories, beliefs and expectations held about him by those who have encountered him, directly or indirectly, in certain kinds of episodes." This is inescapable. The individual may choose to distance himself from any or all of the rule-systems that represent his culture. But such detachment has its price — its high social *and* practical costs.

For many people moral careers are lived out wholly within recognised institutions. Whilst the official, *functional* theory of the institution will *not* account for individual behaviour, the pursuit of a moral career will reflect the seeking after institutionally marked tokens of respect and prestige (although the *manners* in which they are obtained may be very diverse and be accompanied by any number of individual expressive performances). In many societies, however, it is possible for individuals to engage in *alter-native* moral career development, often in arenas outside of the dominant institutional framework. Respect and dignity are obtained through expressive action within arenas informally structured and created for that sole purpose.

It is here that I think the ethogenic approach has most to contribute. It can reveal the true social rationale of micro-cultures which are often deemed to be *anomic* by the society in which they arise. And since expressive action in such contexts is less clearly related to official, *practical* activities, we can view more easily the dynamics of the maintenance of dignity and social worth and the establishment of personal identities. At the heart of such alternative moral careers we will find, despite possible images of anarchy and waywardness, coherent rule frameworks which provide for social order, for the recognition of propriety and for the attribution of value to expressive performances. It is here that my unlikely example of contemporary British soccer fans might be seen to have some relevance. I would like to introduce them at this stage as a kind of case study — one which will illustrate the manner in which we attempt to understand and explain social life.

British soccer fans have been generating what have aptly been called "Moral Panics" in our society since the mid 1960s. Their activities are routinely described in the media (and by other right-thinking pillars of society) as "mindless," "thugish," "senseless" and so on. They are often viewed as perpetrators of gratuitous savagery, and as such constitute a severe threat to law and order. In dismissing such activities as *senseless*, further theorising is deterred — since a theory cannot be expected to account for that which by definition is inexplicable, is lacking in rationality or *sense*. Because of this dominant perspective it is perhaps not surprising that most psychologists have tended to view the fans' behaviour, and indeed the fans themselves, in terms of social and individual pathology.

In the discipline of sociology, only one coherent theory emerged — that of Ian Taylor. Briefly, Taylor views the aggressive activity of fans as being an attempt to regain what they saw as part of their traditional working class heritage. The game of soccer had been plucked from its social roots and taken over by bourgeois entrepreneurs who sought to "spectacularise" and commercialise the game. Football players had become remote and distant superstars — the ordinary fan no longer felt any influence over the club he loyally supported. The alienation was given vent by fighting on terraces.[4]

The theory, whilst accurately highlighting the changes within the sport, was unconvincing for a number of reasons. Above all it failed to give attention to the actual social dynamics of group behaviour on the terraces. It tried to account for the phenomenon in terms of its apparent *practical* order, avoiding completely the richness (and explanatory value) of the *expressive* order. *Our* analysis of this highly ritualised social world is couched solely in terms of key features of the expressive order — in terms of moral careers, rule frameworks, identifiable but informal social roles and symbolic tokens of loyalty, solidarity and status. Personally, I do not exclude other very different interpretations which may be offered at different levels of explanation — including those derived from anthropological and ethological theory (although I must add that Harré is far less eager to entertain such perspectives). That, however, need not detain us here.

A principal aim of the ethogenic approach is to highlight an insider's perspective — to reveal what it might be like to occupy a position within a social world from a participant's point of view. In pursuing this aim great emphasis is placed on accounts. An account may be a verbal statement offered by a participant giving description, and hence the meaning, of social activities and situations. It may also contain justifications for certain actions and rationales for particular patterns of activity. Of course, when one is concerned with phenomena which are not contemporary, then less direct evidence must be sought. For, as I suggested earlier, generating new psychological rhetorics to explain the present may enable us to view in a new light analogous events in the past. I shall expand on this point later when referring to the Circus Factions of the Roman and Byzantine eras.

Making use of an accounts methodology, and by viewing the world of soccer fans in the way that we might view our own, we find much evidence to support the idea that social action is constrained and directed by extant rule frameworks. Firstly, however, we isolate those *values* which allow for determination of prestige and social worth. Unremarkably, given the violent image of the soccer terraces, these centre around aggression, toughness and "manliness." Remember that young soccer fans, especially the more dedicated, are those who are unlikely to make much progress in the *official* careers that our society provides. Their life in school has often been a progression of humiliations and ritual affirmations of their lack of value to society. Thus they turn to alternative arenas for the establishment of a more fulfilling career. One of the skills which such individuals possess, one which has been nurtured by rejection by the educational system, is the ability to be *tough*. But for such toughness to have realisable value there must be rules to the game of being tough. There must be an expressive *order*.

Some of these rules can be inferred in quite a straightforward manner from what the fans themselves have to say. Take this example from an account offered by a fan of the Chesterfield team:

> There's an organised pattern of events, I mean, you know what is going to happen, bringing a knife, I mean, probably by your own supporters, is looked down on as being a sort of form of cowardice. There is not many people will carry knives about — there is not many who will set out to harm someone. Not many people have got that killer instinct, once you have kicked them to the floor, I mean, that's it, it is left at that and they will say, "Leave him." Someone in the group who has been fighting them will just say, "leave him, he has had enough." It is not very often it goes on to the point where he is kicked senseless.

Such an account is quite revealing. But it would be unreasonable to expect such a simple procedure to be at all exhaustive. Folk do not ordinarily go about their lives with a conscious appreciation of the rules which shape day-to-day activity. A more precise, but less direct approach is to identify examples of rule-breach. When rules are broken, the existence of the rule becomes visible through the remedial strategies members bring into the situation. Whilst rules may remain for most of the time unarticulated, a breach is a "remarkable" event — it calls for explanation.

The precise research methodology is perhaps not too important in this context. I hope it will suffice to say that using strategies based on the account collection technique, in conjunction with systematic observation and other methods, a picture of highly *ordered* conduct emerges. It is interesting to note here that football fans also have a way of referring to certain actions as "out of order." This is a particularly illuminating idiomatic phrase for it reinforces the point that there is indeed an order out of which it is possible to be.

Examination of the activities of deviants within the subculture can provide similar illumination. On the soccer terraces certain individuals are routinely referred to as "nutters." They engage in activities which are not only "out of order" but are seen, by other members, as *mad*. Thus by examining what nutters actually do, and by noting how other fans describe their behaviour, one gains a fair appreciation of what is not allowed. This knowledge of existing *pro*scriptions complements documentation of *pre*scriptions and allows for full mapping of the rule framework. In brief, one can say that the rules prescribe acts which may be endowed with meanings such as brave, manly, prepared to stand up for the group, prepared to "have a go," hostile to enemies (i.e. fans of the opposing team), loyal to one's group, and so on. At the same time, the rules specify the limits of such activities — in particular they proscribe acts which are seriously injurious, in physical terms, to one's opponents. Within this framework symbolic substitutes for physical violence are created in order that the basic values of aggressive toughness may be realised and maintained. These symbolic alternatives involve chants and songs, gestures, postures, stylised imprecations and special forms of language and non-verbal expression. These in turn provide for a highly ritualistic pattern of overt activity. The product is surprisingly bloodless (although the odd injury may be found if one looks hard and long enough. British newspapers are skilled at this; hence, the "terraces-running-with-blood image").

I should mention, at this point, one rather unfortunate by-product of this social order — unfortunate, that is, from the social researcher's point of view. To understand what this problem is, consider what has been established so far. Young fans seek alternative social worlds to the dull, unrewarding, "official" weekday world which provides them only with a sense of valuelessness and rejection. The soccer terrace microculture is created to provide for more rewarding moral careers in which the hazards are now fights and displays of daring and courage. These are easily dealt with and can provide them with the basis for personal worth and esteem. To maintain such a rewarding system, rules are negotiated which constrain the potentially bloody outcomes in such careers through the introduction of symbols and ritual. Fights are now "safe," but continue to play a vital role in the maintenance of dignity. This is the problem. You can't walk into your local pub and, turning to a group of friends, announce that you have just successfully entered into a highly orchestrated, symbolic agonistic encounter with a fan of the rival team. Instead you want to announce that you have "kicked the shit out of him." So what happens? Fans, quite simply, enter into a conspiracy to deny the existence of social order — to subscribe to the idea that at each moment one is risking one's life in the pursuit of group solidarity, for this is what being a *Man* is all about. The naive researcher who listens to the social talk of fans without a coherent theory regarding the motives or illocutionary force of such talk, will be a very confused individual.

The football fan himself, however, is able to entertain quite happily this duality of perspective. On the one hand he is in possession of sufficient social knowledge to appreciate both the nature and the function of the rule framework. On the other, in order to render routine events in his life as "remarkable," he creates a *rhetoric* of violence, one which has much in common, in fact, with the outsider's perspective. This aspect of the inside rhetoric aids and abets an *illusion* of violence. It is within this illusion, however, that selves are presented and personal identities established.

The *chronological* and *developmental* aspects of moral careers are perhaps easier to determine, for they are visible to even the most casual, but regular, observer.

Young boys, around the age of 9 or 10, begin their moral careers as "Novices" or, in the fans' terms, as "little kids." At most soccer grounds they take up positions at the front of the terraces — often on the wall which separates the enclosure from the pitch. Their dress is fairly unremarkable except for symbols of allegiance such as scarves and favours. Their activity level is also quite low. But what is most striking is the fact that very little attention is paid by them to the game itself. Instead, their interest is focused away from the pitch and back onto other older fans on the terraces, for their's is essentially a learning role — a social apprenticeship.

Towards the back of the terraces are assembled a group of far more energetic and distinctively dressed fans. It is to members of this group that the media refer with great regularity using terms such as "hooligan," "savage," "thug," etc. Being more neutral social scientists we refer to them as the *Rowdies*. (I should add at this point, for those not familiar with British soccer grounds, that the terraces I am referring to are those located behind the goals. The home fans are allocated one of these areas, and consider it to be a sacrosanct territory — one to be defended at all costs from invasion by rivals. Fans of the visiting team are confined in the area at the other end of the pitch.)

The Rowdies group provides for the first major "promotion" in the moral career of the aspiring soccer fan. Having spent a year or so "hanging around" as a "little kid," and having gained sufficient social knowledge (of things like chants, gestures and *style*), a Novice may relocate himself on the terraces, adopt the distinctive "gear" of the Rowdy and seek more substantial recognition within this much more structured group.

There are no special initiation rites for marking entry into this new group, but particular performances are now required of those who are to win any kind of social status or recognition. A number of definable role positions are also available within the Rowdies, whereas the Novices group contains little or no opportunity for such social identities. We discuss the roles much more fully in our book *Rules of Disorder*[5] — here I might just mention one or two. There are, for example, "Chant Leaders" — those individuals who initiate and "conduct" the highly stylised chants or songs, the majority of which are concerned with expressing hostility toward the opposition rather than support of one's own team. Achieving the position of a Chant Leader involves "hazarding" of a rather special kind. One has to be able to carry the group along. To sing out the first line of a chant or song and to find that nobody is with you results not only in embarrassment but also in derision and loss of prestige. But those with the "bottle" (what Americans call "heart") can find themselves in high esteem, enjoy considerable status and begin to carve out a very special identity.

A second highly significant role is that of "Aggro Leader." Here I must explain the term "Aggro" for it is a peculiarly British expression. It derives, really, from the word "aggravation" and is used, particularly by members of youth cultures, to refer to a wide range of conflicts, fights or, more generically, "bother." The characteristic feature of aggro, however, is that it is conducted very much within the kinds of rule framework that I have been describing.

The aggro leader, then, is an individual who is capable of instilling sufficient confidence into his fellow fans that they will follow him into running battles with the opposition or, more rarely, with the police. The aggro leader should not be confused, however, with a "good fighter." Because of the special nature of aggro he might never have to do any fighting at all in order to achieve such a reputation. Rather he must be skilled in those rhetorical skills I mentioned earlier, whereby mundane events are rendered remarkable — as "bloody" and dangerous — as routine acts are recast as courageous and manly.

The Rowdies group presents opportunities for fans with different kinds of aspiration to become, perhaps for the first time in their lives, "someone special" — to achieve a personal identity founded on the social identities for which the micro-culture provides. There is, however, a further stage in the moral career — a further sub-grouping to which the most successful fans might aspire. This group we call the "Graduates," although often the culture provides its own appellation. At Oxford United's ground, for example, they were called the "Town Boys."

The Graduates group comprises those members of the terrace culture whose reputations are so firmly established that they can rest on their laurels. No longer do they have to wear the symbolic dress of the Rowdy — scarves tied around the wrist; thin T-shirts even in the depths of winter — the heavy boots, and skinhead style hair cuts. In fact, they look as unremarkable as any other young men in their early 20s. But they are clearly revered, respected and *identified* by the groups around them.

Finally, their moral careers over, older fans drift away from the soccer terraces into marriages, mortgages and, with difficulty, a steady job. Keen observers in the ethogenic mould, however, will often observe their embarkation on new careers in, say, the darts team of that other timeless British institution — the local pub.

What we have here in this all-too-brief sketch of the social life of football "hooligans" is, through an ethogenic analysis, a reasonably clear example of how group activities serve in the establishment of personal identities. Let us consider the various components involved.

Firstly, we can see how certain social collectives come into being for the primary purpose of providing arenas for expressive order. In my example a *practical* order is difficult to discern. Our attention is therefore necessarily drawn to the features of the expressive order which provide for social identities, for marking of respect, for reputation and the recognition of personal worth. *Personal* identity comes about within such a context as the individual works through his social projects — as he progresses through a moral career. This development of a personal history and of a reputation as a unique, worthwhile person (what football fans would call "a good old boy") is the fruit of such projects. And it is these which give rise to personal identity — to a sense of being an *individual*. This is made very clear, I think, in a short extract from an account provided by a Southampton fan called Kevin. Kevin, at the age of 20, had "graduated" in the terrace culture:

> I think when you actually get to know the group of people that you go to the football with or actually know socially you don't need to conform to the expected standard. I mean you can be more of an individual because people accept you for an individual *rather than just one of the boys*.

Kevin's personal identity, his sense of being *an* individual, comes about only because his *social* identities have been clearly marked and have provided the fundamental rewards which are the prerequisites of positive self regard. He no longer has to conform to what he describes as the "expected standard" *solely because* his acceptance of that standard, and his competence in the roles and actions prescribed by that standard, are no longer questioned by other members of his collective. He can be different only because his fundamental *sameness* is firmly defined.

I suggested earlier that the ethogenic perspective we offer is not one which need be limited to contemporary social life or to apparently deviant sub-cultures within our technologically developed communities (although I think the approach can be particularly illuminating in such areas). No, it is, I think, a style of social psychology which, although a product of its own time (in Harré's sense), can be used to reinterpret social phenomena at earlier points in history. One such phenomenon which has interested me, princi-pally perhaps because of my interest in contemporary soccer hooliganism, is that of the Circus Factions—the Blues and Greens of Rome and Byzantium.

As most of us are aware, the hippodromes of Rome provided for the ex-citing spectacle of chariot racing. Each of four major teams of charioteers rode in a particular colour and of these the Blues and Greens came to dominate the field. Associated with each of these teams were rival groups of highly vociferous fans—the Circus *Factions* who tended to upset folk very much in the way that our soccer fans do now. Pliny, for example, was moved to write of this "fanaticism":

> Fancy such influence and power wielded by one worthless shirt, not merely among the common crowd, which is more worthless even than that, but even among some men of taste. When I see this sort of person so insatiably fond of a sport which is so empty, meaningless and repetitive, I must admit to a feeling of pleasure that the pleasure is not for me. (*Letters* IX. 6)

This is very much the kind of sentiment you can find in British newspapers today and indeed among some of my fellow academics who think that soc-cer is a game for people with brains in their feet. But having said that, I think that the Romans probably engaged less in the "moral panics" which so beset us today and even recognised the expressive order which underlay such activities and recognised the social value that such order might have—as a safety valve or as providing less *destructive* opportunities to frustrated youth.

So we can look back to the Circus Factions and now maybe challenge the merit of those theories which sought to explain this phenomenon solely in terms of its practical/functional or instrumental aspects. Some writers have suggested, for example, that the pattern of behaviour was essentially political and that disturbances among the factions were sparked off by such immediately practical problems as increases in the price of corn, etc. From *our* standpoint, however, such theories are unconvincing since they fail to account for the highly *ritualised* features of the social action and pay little attention to the expressive functions. Alan Cameron, however, Professor of Latin at Columbia University, formerly at London University, comes much closer to our style of analysis in his book, *Circus Factions*.[6] It is he who sees an immediate parallel with our understanding of the contemporary soccer world. Like us he also views the relationship between behaviour and the particular *setting* as relatively unimportant — football fan behaviour, for example cannot be explained solely with reference to the sport itself. He says:

> It is clear from the evidence that there is a direct connection between the games and faction misbehaviour just as there is between the football stadium and soccer hooliganism today. But in neither case is the violence to be explained solely in terms of the excitement generated by the charioteers or footballers. Other factors are certainly involved. In both cases there is undoubtedly a ritual element.... The games can serve as a field where the youth who leads an otherwise ordinary and unexciting life can prove himself a man by fighting ... for an hour he can be an object of fear to all those who cross his path. The problems and anxieties that dog his everyday life will be dissipated in the excitement.   (pp. 295–96)

We are encouraged to see Professors of Latin adopting a similar perspective in their analysis of historical events to that which we seek to apply to contemporary social phenomena. I am reasonably sure that many other rather enigmatic patterns of group behaviour throughout history could be re-glossed in this way, a more realistic appreciation of their true social function thus being realised. This in turn should, of course, influence current social science theorising. It might help dispel further the rather fanciful idea held by many sociologists that the social "problems" which beset us today — *youth problems* for example, are essentially novel products of 20th century capitalist society. It might help us appreciate the timeless nature of significant expressive orders and the crucially important function they have always played in allowing people in groups, eventually, to become individuals through their own social work.

To end, let me just summarise the case I have been struggling to make:

Personal identity — that is, the given permanence and discernible uniqueness of human individuals, is an indisputable *fact* of the world.

Personal identity is not, however, something that is *given* (other than in the rather trivial sense that we recognise each other as distinct persons through our perception of each other as individual and continuously animated *bodies*).

Personal identity is something which is *worked* for — is undertaken as a *project* — and thus patterns of complex social interaction can be understood in terms of such projects.

These projects involve, first, the establishment of social identities. Such is the flexible nature of our societies that where limited opportunities for social identity exist within the "official" culture, alternative sources may be found in "unofficial" cultures.

Having established social identities which provide for reputation, dignity and recognition, *personal* identity can be achieved through giving individual expression to required role performances. We can also bend the rules a little, but first those rules have to be learned through conformity. To be individuals we have first to be "one of the boys."

Notes

1. Harré, R. and Secord, P. *The Explanation of Social Behaviour* (Oxford: Blackwell) 1972.

2. Harré. R. *Social Being* (Oxford: Blackwell) 1981.

3. Goffman, E. *Asylums* (Harmonsworth: Penguin) 1961.

4. Taylor, I. 'Soccer consciousness and soccer hooliganism' in S. Cohen (ed) *Images of Deviance* (Harmondsworth: Penguin) 1971.

5. Marsh, P., Rosser, E. and Harré, R. *The Rules of Disorder* (London: Routledge and Kegan Paul) 1978.

6. Cameron, A. *Circus Factions: Blues and Greens at Rome and Byzantium* (Oxford: O. U. P.) 1976.

At the Intersection of Anthropology and History: Territorial Festivity in Siena

I f historians and anthropologists are increasingly taking each other's work seriously and borrowing, selectively, in both directions, they remain practitioners of very different kinds, still rather mysterious to each other. These comments on one anthropologist's excursions into the use of history for the construction of social theory are offered in the interest of illuminating this promising intersection of disciplines. Drawing from a comparative study of competitive festivals throughout Central Italy, this paper focusses on the *palio* of Siena during the "long" sixteenth century, the period of its origin.

The study grew out of a concern with a central theoretical issue in contemporary anthropology: are symbolic forms best understood, in the first instance, through their internal logic or meaning, or through external conditions in which they are grounded? Crudely put, this is the debate between symbolists and materialists. An anthropologist's basic questions have to do with the nature of human variability; one's areal specialty serves mainly as a source of raw material to draw on in engaging those questions. My source was Central Italy, and the palio of Siena—which began to attract the attention of anthropologists in the 1970s—appeared to me an opportunity to explore that important issue. Various anthropological analyses were being published that proposed to deduce, through ethnographic observation, the symbolic meaning of the palio: one using a combination of psychoanalytic and Levi-Straussian terminology,[1] a second using a Geertzian concept of "cultural performance,"[2] a third addressing the internal logic of the festival as a "template."[3] My own theoretical inclination was, rather, to begin by inquiring into the political-economic context in which the cultural forms occur. This meant, first, starting not with the palio but with the social units enacting it, namely the *contrade* of Siena, territorial organizations of a particular type. Second, it meant that the problem had to be phrased historically: under what conditions did this kind of territorial organization emerge; what processes account for its perpetuation or change; and finally, what role did the palio and other cultural forms play in that historical trajectory?

For an anthropologist, however, the principles identified in any one case cannot be thought of as unique to it. I therefore attempted to mark out the structural similarities between the palio and certain other festivals in the region, defining a model of Central Italian urban festivals that take a particular form: ritualized competition among territorial or other divisions within an urban-centered unit, phrased in metaphors emphasizing the civic identity of the overarching unit and of the divisions within it. Within this general model, two different patterns of festival competition were found to exist in the region: one based on territorial units, the other on nonlocalized social or economic categories. The study then undertook intensive analysis of two "type cases" exemplifying the two patterns, Siena and Gubbio, utilizing a combination of historical and ethnographic approaches. The general aim was a comparison of the social, political, and economic implications of territorial and categorical organization of festivals. The present discussion is limited to the territorial pattern as manifested in Siena.

Two general hypotheses guided the study. First, that competitive festivals emerge and persist as a function of the relationship among polities at different levels of organization, such that there are state interests in strengthening the units that compete in festivals. Second, that such festivals are a function also of the socioeconomic composition of the units competing in them, such that these units crosscut, bypass, or obscure the lines of strategic class interests.

The language of "hypotheses" and "comparative" study should not be interpreted as claims for a method of controlled experiment or the anthropological version of experiment — testing for statistically significant correlations among variables. I am not proposing the scientism of the so-called cross-cultural method in anthropology, in which a worldwide sample of societies is selected on the assumption that each case is an independent, ahistoric example of human variability, and in which the complexities of ethnographic data are disassembled and coded as variables. At the same time, I would not endorse the view of those ethnographers who, like some historians, insist upon the incommensurability of their case with any other. This use of hypothesis and comparison is a search for structure, generality, or consistency within the plethora of detail in ethnographic and historical data, and an attempt to discipline interpretations and push them forward. In my opinion, it is an application of the scientific method, in which social science principles guide the search for pattern in the data through a process of moving back and forth between the general, comparative statements and the rich details of particular cases. It is, however, also a social science that requires history. To seek principles of order within the data means to try to state the conditions under which certain phenomena occur, and the search for specifiable "conditions" demands historical depth. Historical data provide for the anthropologist not "a chronicle of what happened" (as F. G. Bailey has said) but clues to regularities — by showing them operating over time and in relation to changing conjunctions of circumstances.

My initial explorations into the historical literature on Siena led to an analysis of the palio that I have presented elsewhere.[4] It took as its starting point not the festival but the social units competing in it, the contrade, treating them as part of a history of territorial organization within the city. The modern Sienese contrade are particular kinds of local divisions, marked by a high degree of corporateness, internal organization, and autonomy with reference to certain functions. The problem was then rephrased as: what are the structural implications of divisions of this kind, and what conditions may account for them? From this viewpoint, the antecedents of the seventeen contemporary contrade, identified by totemic symbols, appear first as festival organizations, probably emerging out of confraternities, in the last quarter of the fifteenth century. They became conspicuous during the sixteenth century, participating in a variety of festival events. They coexisted with smaller local units descendant from the medieval contrade (the 42 *compagnie*) until the mid-seventeenth century, when the totemic contrade became the locality terms used almost exclusively in documents referring to administrative as well as ritual functions. Their number and their boundaries continued to fluctuate, however, until in 1729 — following recurrent territorial disputes — the 17 modern contrade were fixed by an official decree.

In this view, the significance of the palio emerges in the fact that it was the major function of the contrade and, as such, a focus for their identity and continuity and a stimulus to their formal organization. The contrade preceded the palio as functional, symbolically identified units and their functions always went beyond the palio itself, but the palio became an instrument of their continued vitality.

My first hypothesis suggested that strong corporate divisions within the commune were fostered by the Tuscan state as part of a process of emasculating the commune. The historical work showed that, in fact, following the conquest of the Republic after 1555, the Medici governors of Siena actively fostered the contrade, ordering the staging of contrada-organized festivity on any occasion lending itself to public celebration of the new state and its rulers. Richard Trexler's study of ritual in Renaissance Florence allows us to place the developments in Siena in a larger historical context.[5] Trexler traces a transformation in Florentine public festivals beginning in the late fifteenth century and suggests that this was a process whereby the rulers brought marginal social groups and neighborhood organizations onto the center stage of ritual, enlisting them as allies in the task of "dismantling or reorienting the major urban festivals ... so as to weaken their ... civic character."[6]

The transformation under the Medici of Siena's major public festival, the Assunta on August 15, is a case in point. Under the Republic, this festival was a demonstration of the political supremacy of the Sienese state, celebrating Siena's triumph over the Florentines at Montaperti in 1260 by giving thanks to the Virgin for her special protection and dramatizing the submission of the hundred-odd dependent communities of the Republic. Within this festival organized by the civic administration, the totemic contrade of the early sixteenth century had an occasional and subordinate role; then, after 1546, contrada festival events subsided. Following his conquest of the Republic, Cosimo I set August 18, 1558 as the date for his taking formal possession of Siena, and he ordered that the Assunta festival be held in homage to him, forbidding the political expressions but calling for contrada-organized bullfights and races. In 1560, he decreed that the Sienese bring their wax offerings to Florence on the day of the Assunta to demonstrate their submission; then, he came to Siena on August 25, directing that the contrade hold a bullfight "as is customary for the festival of August." From then on, the contrada events became central to the Assunta festival.[7] The commune as a political entity was represented only as a shell. A new balance was struck: while the Medici state turned the festival into a statement of its own supremacy, it tolerated the Sienese use of a religious "submission to the Virgin" as a metaphor for their memory of autonomy. The contrade served both sides; they became both allies in the glorification of the Medici and distinctively Sienese "statelets" perpetuating the cultural forms of autonomy.

The Medici were directly implicated in the development of the contrada-based palio itself. For instance, the July palio originated in 1592, ordered by the Grandduke to commemorate the installation of the Medici dynasty.[8] The Medici governors also set the forms of contrada competition, outlawing bullfights in 1590 (in conformity with a ban by the Council of Trent) and in the seventeenth century increasingly encouraging horse races in substitution for buffalo races.[9]

Clearly, however, the Sienese nobility had as much a stake in the contrade as the Medici princes. Early on, each contrada had prominent Sienese families among its leading citizens or "protectors." Until the commune took on a major role in organizing and financing the palio in the early nineteenth century, the noble protectors were the main source of support of their contrade, as well as their leaders and representatives. The palio became (as it still is today) an event that attracted the most stellar visitors and afforded the Sienese nobility advantageous connections — their reputations enhanced by this public evidence of their control of and intimacy with their plebs. The value of such connections went beyond prestige; they translated into good business for the great bank of Siena — the Monte dei Paschi, founded in 1472 and its fortunes linked to the rise of the territorial states.

The interest of the local upper class in the contrade bears upon my second hypothesis, which focussed on the contrade as *multiclass* territorial divisions. Subsequent study confirmed the significance of this factor for the entire historical trajectory of the contrade. The contrade each incorporated the range of socioeconomic diversity in the city, and in each one the "protectors" retained dominance, which went along with an insistence upon an ideology of egalitarianism and patterns of cross-class intimacy within the contrada. There is abundant evidence that the contrade became, in fact, a counterforce against class-based alliances, as well as a favored form of celebration of the current political order.

Although the data take us beyond the time frame of this discussion, it would be fair to say that every government of Siena from the Medici on, and the local upper class in every period, supported the contrade and saw them as a stabilizing force. The survival of the contrade throughout the vicissitudes of Sienese and Italian politics over four centuries, indeed their favored status under one political order after another, derives, I think, from their combination of structural and symbolic characteristics. On the one hand, they were rarely seen as a threat; not only did their multiclass makeup underwrite the *status quo*, but their very localism and their trappings of autonomy made them ready symbols of the popular will, whose support could be valuable. On the other hand, they offered a treasury of symbolic material, which could lend itself to a multitude of purposes. Their color combinations, numerology, mythology, and customs could be attached to a great variety of meanings, and the contrade as such could represent the Sienese soul, civic liberty, resistance to the Florentines, democracy and popular initiative, law and order, familism, love of country, or any number of the ideals emphasized by different political programs.

Yet there remains still the question of Siena's uniqueness among the cities of Central Italy: what is it about Siena that accounts for the uninterrupted continuance there of the palio-contrada complex? I believe at least a part of the answer is in the presence of the Monte dei Paschi. It was the wealth of the bank that underwrote the costs of the palio, whether indirectly through the noble "protectors" of the contrade or directly through grants to the commune and the contrade. The seat of the Monte dei Paschi's far-reaching network of operations has always been the city of Siena. The bank wove its public image inextricably with the image of Siena, especially the prime symbol of Siena, the palio. Not only did the wide appeal of the palio serve in the forging of the bank's expansion, but the bank's charter as a "public-interest" institution required that it disburse a portion of its profits for charitable and public purposes, mainly to Sienese institutions. The bank became a direct benefactor of the palio, a role that proved critical in the survival of the festival.

The use of historical material in this analysis is quite different from that of historians, and some methodological comments may be in order. It must be emphasized that this is an anthropological, not a historical, study; the selection of material was dictated by an anthropological problem, not by the historical record itself. Since the anthropologist cannot transform himself into a historian, he must depend upon the integrative work of historians, particularly when the processes of interest to him require coverage of a long time span. However, historians may not have produced the kinds of syntheses the anthropologist needs, and he may then have to supplement the secondary sources with archival work, however inept he may be at it. An immediate difficulty he faces is that, since the problem has come out of a discourse extraneous to the historical record, the relevant data are not likely to be found in rich sources coherently addressing the problem but will be dispersed and fragmentary. My own approach has been to enter into the historical material—both secondary and primary—much as an anthropologist in the field: beginning with a survey of the terrain and then looking for key informants and key clusters of events, evaluating information as I would evaluate it if it came from living informants, following clues, and relying a good deal on a fieldworker's intuition.

Such historical work is, in fact, much like fieldwork in another way: the data do not present themselves in the terms of analysis but must be recast into those terms. Neighborhoods are not described in the historical record as "discrete" or as having "fluid boundaries"; but neither are they in the field. As in fieldwork, the anthropologist delving into history must probe for bits of evidence on the way things were—especially by looking at what actually happened in known instances—and then piece the bits together into patterns. The patterns obtained in the material under study must then be translated into concepts; in the case of anthropological concepts, these are shorthand ways of talking about regularities found through continual comparison of the full range of cases that we have information on (i.e., the whole cross-cultural record). Historians who wish to use social-science concepts need to understand this process in order to learn how to make the translations in reverse. Concepts like "family," "peasant" or "network," for example, carry theoretically loaded meanings and cannot simply be superimposed upon descriptive data.

What I am arguing for here is not an eradication of the differences in perspective and method that separate history and anthropology, but rather a collaboration entailing learning on both sides.

Notes

1. Alan Dundes and Alessandro Falassi, *La Terra in Piazza: An Interpretation of the Palio of Siena* (Berkeley and Los Angeles: University of California Press, 1975).

2. Alice Pomponio Logan, "The Palio of Siena: Performance and Process," *Urban Anthropology* 7 (1978): 45–65.

3. Don Handelman, "The Madonna and the Mare: Symbolic Organization in the Palio of Siena." In *Spectacle — An Anthropological Inquiry*. Edited by Victor Turner and Masao Yamaguchi. Tokyo: Sanseido, 1983, pp. 153–84.

4. Sydel Silverman, "On the Uses of History in Anthropology: The Palio of Siena," *American Ethnologist* 6 (1979): 413–36.

5. Richard C. Trexler, *Public Life in Renaissance Florence* (New York: Academic Press, 1980).

6. Ibid., p. 506.

7. Giovanni Cecchini, *Palio e contrade nella loro evoluzione storica* (Siena: Monte dei Paschi, 1958), pp. 70–78.

8. Ibid., p. 82.

9. Giulio Pepi, *Le contrade e il Palio* (Siena: La Diana, 1967), p. 63.

Reconstructing Renaissance Sociology: The 'Chicago School' and the Study of Renaissance Society

RONALD F. E. WEISSMAN

What do historians study when they seek to understand Renaissance society? Three areas of sociological inquiry have dominated the field: studies of corporate groups, of individualism, and of class. In one or more of these units of analysis, historians have located the "center" of the society of the Renaissance, both in terms of method of analysis, and of perceived social reality. The first two concepts, corporatism and individualism, represent the polarities of much traditional Renaissance sociology. At one extreme stands Burckhardt's heroic individual, freed from the constraints of group loyalty, obligation, and custom. At the other extreme stand the tightly knit clans, families, and guilds into which many historians have seen Renaissance society fragment. Debates about the degree of individualism, the causes of weakened corporate solidarity, and the mechanisms that are alleged to have transformed Renaissance society from corporate to individualist in form, still occasion much controversy. Other historians have stressed the importance of stratification. For many years in Italy, and more recently in England and the United States, historians have suggested that class dynamics determined the fundamental structure of Renaissance society.

All of these approaches have sought the underlying category or classification that provides the key to the social world of the Renaissance. In the process, historians have elevated categories such as class or corporation to the status of ideal types or philosophic Universals. But as claims for the importance of class, corporatism, or individualism grow, the meaning of such terms often becomes increasingly difficult to determine, and the range of phenomena ignored by those making such claims becomes broader as well.

Renaissance stratification studies offer an excellent example of the difficulties of contemporary Renaissance sociology. Few historians doubt the importance of economic or prestige differentials in shaping Renaissance identities. But students of Renaissance society disagree about the relative importance of class — defined in terms either of "objective" economic relations or subjective consciousness — or other modes of stratification. Modes of stratification were simultaneous and varied in the Renaissance. Groups segmented along the lines of class did not always overlap well with groups partitioned along lines of prestige or political power. The notorious difficulty in identifying unambiguously the patriciate in fourteenth and early fifteenth century Florence (where stratification studies are well advanced), given different distributions of power, political clout, and economic resources, alerts us to the weakness of viewing Renaissance society principally in terms of one-dimensional stratification systems.[1] Even when social stratification is relatively well-articulated, it does not convey all of society's key processes, especially because emphasis on conflict and competition between groups and classes may lead to a neglect of important conflict within such groups. Some historians have recognized the fluidity of Renaissance allegiances to groups, but have sought, nevertheless, to make abstractions such as groups the analytic units of preference.

I argue for a redirection of Renaissance sociology that focusses not on groups, but on that very social fluidity (which, alas, is often confused with individualism) that makes the study of corporate groups and ideal types so problematic. What Renaissance sociology requires is a more pragmatic, Nominalist approach to the study of society. While I do not deny the heuristic utility of categories such as class, corporation, or Renaissance individualism, I suggest that a more appropriate unit of analysis for studying Renaissance society is neither the individual nor the group, but rather, the *social relationship* that links individuals to each other and to groups. This unit of analysis is, I believe, able adequately to encompass both patterns of group affiliation and the nebulousness of Renaissance social relations.

In suggesting the primacy of studying social bonds over individuals or groups I hope to call attention to the importance of the Chicago School of Sociology, a tradition of inquiry that owes its origins to a group of philosophers and students of social organization active six decades ago at the University of Chicago, the most important of whom were John Dewey and George Herbert Mead.[2] Mead, in particular, deserves note, for it was he who defined the key concepts that have animated virtually all research in the Chicago tradition. This tradition, known today as Symbolic Interactionism, enjoys an important place in current sociology and anthropology, especially for students of social identity, group process, and microsocial behavior. The interactionist tradition is, however, relatively unknown to social historians, most of whom have relied explicitly or implicitly upon

Functionalist or Marxist modes of social analysis.[3]

For Marxists and Functionalists, the constituent elements of society are groups or classes, the groups through which individuals are assumed to form their social identity. Functionalists view society as a system of inter-related parts, a system which operates to maximize its own survival. Social survival may be viewed as the minimization of social conflict or the max-imization of the integration of the parts of the social system, or the attain-ment, in Talcott Parson's term, of an equilibrium state among the levels of a social system. For Functionalists, identity formation is typically viewed as a process of passive socialization, the acquisition of previously existing group characteristics, a relatively automatic process. Personal identity is, in large part, composed of group norms, values, psychological traits, and goal orientations all of which serve to maximize social integration. How these teleological patterns and goals are established and transformed is, of course, usually quite difficult to specify.

For Marxist sociology, "society does not consist of individuals; it expresses the sum of connections and relationships in which individuals find themselves."[4] But for Marxists not all relations are equal. Relations of economic production and exchange determine patterns of social structure, social conflict, and individual identity. All are shaped by interests in and rights to power, usually control of economic resources. Changes in identi-ty are normally the result of changing relations among classes, usually cor-responding to periods of consciousness-raising coexisting with periods of class conflict.

The symbolic interactionist approach to the study of society stresses social relations and linkages and, in so doing, differs from other schools of social inquiry in the following ways:

First, society is viewed as process, not structure. It is found in its behaviors, its conduct, rather than in its systems of stratification.

Second, the processual nature of society occurs through its social in-teraction. Like Marxism, interactionism takes as its object of study social relations. Unlike Marxism, interactionism does not elevate, on an a priori basis, the importance of any particular kind of social rela-tion such as relations of production or economic exchange.

Third, for the interactionist, while functional or institutional groups and social classes serve as significant reference groups, they are not the primary units of analysis. The primary unit of analysis is the social relation linking individuals, for it is individual interaction that mediates or underlies what is perceived as group interaction or group identity. And this is especially true of Renaissance corporate groups, member-ship in which often required sponsors, i.e., personal relations.

Forth, identity, or to use Mead's term, the self, is not the product of Marxist power relations, dominant groups, or functional needs. Nor is the "self" an aggregation of personal *attributes* such as age, level of wealth, or occupation. The self is located in its *relations* and only emerges in its relations with others. The self is less a structure or a static collection of qualities than it is the intersection of one's key interactions.

Fifth, the "social reality" studied by interactionists is viewed as being necessarily subjective, since all behavior, all interactions, have at their heart subjective, interpretive processes. Individuals act towards the world on the basis of the meanings that they give to the world. Socially constructed meanings and expectations are central to social analysis. Most Symbolic Interactionists reject the existence of so-called "objective social facts."

Sixth, unlike deterministic traditions, Symbolic Interactionism views individuals as much manipulators of social relations as manipulated by them.

The philosophy of George Herbert Mead, summarized in his lecture notes published as *Mind, Self, and Society*[5] in 1934, centers on the premise, shared with his colleague John Dewey, that man constructs his society on the basis of his use of significant symbols. By communication, by sending, perceiving, and interpreting gestures, man interprets and structures his relations with others based on his prior interactions.

Mead's concepts and social-psychological models offered evocative, but at base, vague insights about the nature of the interaction process. Later interactionists such as Herbert Blumer, Anselm Strauss, and Ralph Turner developed methods of social analysis based on Mead's initial insights, expanding, in particular, on the nature of interaction and its importance in the development of self and society. Contemporary Interactionism has attempted to define more precisely how society is organized around its interaction processes, and how those processes aid identity formation. In clarifying Mead, Interactionists emphasize the following:

the interactions that form society constitute networks of relations. During interaction, individuals exchange and interpret symbols and interpret the meaning of their interaction with the world. Shared interaction networks and shared meanings derived from common or similar interactions constitute common social worlds;

any given interaction is influenced by the entire network of relations and by the social worlds in which each individual is involved;

individuals interpret their world through interaction situations, that is, in terms of meanings derived from current and prior interactions. One's place in an interaction network is critical in forming interpretations and expectations. Meaning is thus situational.

How might an Interactionist approach the study of Renaissance society? Two concerns are paramount: the pattern of interlinkage existing among the inhabitants of Renaissance communities, and second, the meanings individuals derived from their interactions with each other. In order to distinguish the interactionist approach to the study of Renaissance society and behavior, I will use interactionism to critique one of the most venerable and enduring interpretations of Renaissance society, Renaissance Individualism.

The formulation of Alfred von Martin remains a classic statement of Renaissance Individualism, and echoes of his interpretation resonate throughout contemporary Renaissance studies. Von Martin attributed the growth of individualism to the development of Renaissance capitalism.[6] Trade and the growth of a money economy weakened traditional personal bonds to lineage and corporate groups within Italian city states. In the tradition of Marx, it was assumed that impersonal, bourgeois relations based on cash transactions replaced relations based on personal obligation. Social atomization replaced an organic social order. The middle class townsman, no longer bound by the older corporate and organic constraints of clan and guild, was free rationally and ruthlessly to pursue individual and private goals.

While this argument, for the interactionist, has the virtue of emphasizing the importance of social linkages, it makes untenable theoretical assumptions about the priority and importance of economic relations over all other social relations, and assumes that economic exchange relations condition but are not conditioned by the remainder of one's social network. Economic activity and economic change may, ultimately, transform other social relations. This should, however, be considered a research hypothesis, not a scientific law. From an interactionist perspective, no form of social relation is necessarily prior as a conditioning factor of or cause of other social relations. It is true that in some modern societies, where personal contacts are widely separated from each other, and where economic associations do not follow ties of kinship, friendship, or residence, economic exchanges may be less likely to share the cultural meanings of other forms of social exchange, or to be constrained by social relations more generally. But the existence of elements of a capitalist economic order in Renaissance Italy does not necessarily imply anything about the nature of social relations in the Renaissance. Indeed, traditional patterns of social relations may themselves serve to place constraints on what are commonly perceived to be the "purely" economic activities of the Renaissance economy. Throughout Mediterranean Europe, capitalism has developed by taking advantage of, rather than subverting, traditional social linkages to family, neighborhood, patronage clique, and community. In the process, capitalism became something very different from the rationalizing and socially atomizing corrupter of traditional social relations envisioned by those who view capitalism as a Marxist or Weberian ideal type.[7]

Viewed from the tradition of Chicago sociology, the key assumptions required to validate the economic individualist interpretation of the Renaissance are difficult to maintain. Interactionism does not accept the necessarily "rationalized" or impersonalized nature of social relations implicit in idealist notions of what "Capitalism" necessarily entails. If one examines the actual transaction networks that shaped Renaissance capitalism, as historians are now beginning to do, one finds such networks categorized by complex ties to friends, family, and neighbors. And, if one examines the *meaning* of economic relations for those most mercantile of Renaissance merchants, the Florentines, one discovers how the perceived demands of kinship and friendship permeated all spheres of economic life. Rather than establishing the constraints of the rest of the social system, Renaissance capitalism was itself constrained by the complexity of Renaissance social ties. Whether discussing the choice of business partners or the extension of credit, Florentines such as Paolo da Certaldo, Leon Battista Alberti, and Giovanni Rucellai all rejected the possibility of operating on "pure" economic grounds. The demands not only of blood but also neighborliness and community sociability had in some real, demonstrable fashion to be honored in all exchanges, and, in this way, social relations themselves placed strong bounds around the supposed "economic rationality" of Renaissance society.[8] Rather than derive the nature of social relations from the "necessary" implications of a vague concept such as "Capitalism," historians should examine the actual social linkages through which Renaissance business was actually conducted, and examine how these interlinkages affected the meaning of economic relations for Renaissance society. In a quite idealistic fashion, Renaissance historians tend to derive the social order from abstractions such as individualism and capitalism, rather than understand the meaning of such abstractions from *within* the social order.

In our attempt to define, to categorize, to stratify, or to emphasize the dominant importance of particular types of social relations, as proponents of class theory, economic individualism, or corporatism do, we lose sight of a key facet of Renaissance identity that has often been confused with individualism: the problem of social ambiguity. As students of historical sociology, we seek to make sharp distinctions, to discern clear patterns of fragmentation and alliance. But in the process of seeking to impose clear distinctions on Renaissance society, we often lose sight of the sense of confusion and ambiguity that had its important role to play in shaping the Renaissance sense of self.

I would argue that central to the problem of urban life in the Renaissance was the interpretive and interactive process of untangling the complex web of obligations engendered by overlapping, conflicting, simultaneous commitments to family, neighbors, political allies, competitors, friends, associates, clients, and patrons. The Renaissance urban community should be studied by viewing different forms of social relations together, instead of treating individual types of relations, including abstract relations such as group loyalty, as separable from a complex whole. When relations are viewed together, what emerges is an awareness of the complexity of social ties. If anything, the Renaissance town suffered from too much community, rather than from individualism or anomie. In a society whose social relations were overlapping, in a society in which intense loyalty continued to be demanded by one's intimates and associates and of them as well, the problem of managing commitments to diverse groups and individuals was not without significance. One's own sense of doubt and conflict, one's sense of the difficulty in honoring competing commitments, was mirrored in one's expectations of how others would interact with oneself. Such a sense of conflicting loyalty, of identity obscured, is found throughout Renaissance literature, from Boccaccio to Machiavelli. Renaissance diaries and memoirs, in particular, all devote considerable attention to the problem of the behavior required to satisfy and validate diverse commitments. But this ambiguity, expressed in the Renaissance's fascination with the etiquette of social interaction, with manners, loyalty, love, and friendship, is obscured by traditional Renaissance sociology. How can one intepret, let alone perceive, the ambiguity of social categories when one's sociology is dependent upon taxonomy, distinction, and categorization?

In arguing for a new sociology of the Renaissance, I believe that we must advance beyond the idealistic and theoretical categorizations that have traditionally been the stuff of Renaissance studies. Such a new sociology would focus on the twin processes of social interaction and social signification, on the actual relations and the perceived meanings of Renaissance social life. Only by viewing all social relations simultaneously — as they in fact were lived — and only by examining social relations as interrelated processes through which Renaissance townsmen gave real meaning to their lives will we move beyond the idealistic structures of traditional Renaissance studies.

Notes

1. On the difficulties of identifying the patriciate and the need for complex, multi-level analysis, see Gene A. Brucker, *The Civic World of Early Renaissance Florence* (Princeton: Princeton University Press, 1977), chapters 1 and 5, and Samuel Kline Cohn, *The Laboring Classes in Renaissance Florence* (New York: Academic Press, 1980), chapter 2.

2. On the Chicago School of Sociology and the Interactionist tradition, see Herbert Blumer, *Symbolic Interactionism: Perspective and Method* (New York: Prentice-Hall, 1969); Berenice Fisher and Anselm Strauss, "Interactionism," in *A History of Sociological Analysis*, ed. Tom Bottomore and Robert Nisbet (New York: Basic Books, 1978), pp. 457–98; Bernard Meltzer, John W. Petras, and Larry T. Reynolds, *Symbolic Interactionism: Genesis, Varieties, Criticism* (London: Routledge & Kegan Paul, 1975); Anselm Strauss, ed., *George Herbert Mead on Social Psychology* (Chicago: University of Chicago Press, 1964); Jonathan H. Turner, *The Structure of Sociological Theory* (Homewood, Illinois: The Dorsey Press, 1982), pp. 305–85; and J. David Lewis and Richard L. Smith, *American Sociology and Pragmatism: Mead, Chicago Sociology, and Symbolic Interactionism* (Chicago: University of Chicago Press, 1980).

3. The Symbolic Interactionist tradition, to the extent that it is known at all by social historians, is known largely through the work of Erving Goffman, and through Peter Berger and Thomas Luckmann, *The Social Construction of Reality* (Garden City: Doubleday, 1966).

4. Karl Marx, *Grundrisse*, trans. David McLellan (New York: Harper and Row, 1971), p. 77. This, as far as it goes, is a quite acceptable formulation of the In-teractionist position. However, most Interactionists reject as a priori prejudices the remainder of Marxist analysis, particularly emphases on group ('class') rela-tions, and the assumptions that economic relations and conflictual patterns are in-herently prior to all other interactions and are therefore somehow socially fundamental.

5. George Herbert Mead, *Mind, Self, and Society* (Chicago: University of Chicago Press, 1934).

6. Alfred von Martin, *Sociology of the Renaissance* (New York: Harper and Row, 1963 [1932]), pp. 1–11.

7. Peter and Jane Schneider have gone so far as to label Mediterranean capitalism "broker capitalism" because of its reliance on traditional modes of social organiza-tion. *Culture and Political Economy in Western Sicily* (New York: Academic Press, 1976), p. 11.

8. See my *Ritual Brotherhood in Renaissance Florence* (New York: Academic Press, 1982), chapter 1.

Display, Self-Definition, and the Frontiers of Romance in the 1463 Bruges Pas du perron fée

JENNIFER R. GOODMAN

... you noble princes and knights, barons and squires of renown, not long ago something very strange took place, hereabouts, in the land of the high and victorious prince, the Duke of Burgundy. A poor knight, led astray in a wasteland ... in doubt of what would happen to him wandering around by night in an unknown place, came upon an obstacle in the form of a boulder ... from the boulder hung a horn of brass, which gave him to understand that ... he should blow the horn twice and at the third blast he would receive an answer.... The knight ... brought the horn to his mouth and ... made the hill and valley echo.... Then, all at once, as if he had sprung up from underground, a strangely shaped dwarf appeared, dressed all in cloth of gold, but with a very sullen air about him.[1]

This romantic scene introduces not a romance, but a fifteenth-century tournament record, that of the *Pas du perron fée* of Philippe de Lalaing.

On April 28, 1463, Philippe de Lalaing, a knight of the court of Philip the Good of Burgundy, inaugurated a *pas d'armes* for the entertainment of his sovereign lord and the visiting dowager duchess of Bourbon, Duke Philip's sister. Philippe de Lalaing's *Pas du perron fée* (the Joust of the Enchanted Rock) recalled the achievements of his famous elder brother, "the good knight" Jacques de Lalaing, as well as other Burgundian *pas d'armes* of its period.

The *pas d'armes* itself has been defined by Larry Benson as a species of tournament, "almost as much masque as tournament," "in which a knight sets himself up at a given spot ... and offers to joust all comers."[2] Benson surveys the *pas* familiar in romance, from the *Joie de la court* episode in Chrétien de Troyes' *Erec* to the *pas d'armes* of Alexander the Orphan in Malory's *Book of Sir Tristram*, which lasts for an entire year. Boucicaut's 1390 *pas d'armes*, held over thirty days at St. Englebert near Calais, undoubtedly helped to bring this style of joust further into fashion. The year-long *Pas de la fontaine aux pleurs*, Jacques de Lalaing's memorable effort in this direction, is chronicled in Jacques' chivalric biography.[3]

To the specialist in fifteenth-century chivalry, the *Pas du perron fée* may seem to differ little from other Burgundian tournaments modeled on the *pas d'armes* — the *Pas de l'arbre d'or* or the *Pas de la dame sauvage* — unless in its comparatively modest and manageable outline. Philippe de Lalaing's joust was not remarkable in the annals of Burgundian chivalry for the fame of its participants, although they were illustrious. Its accounts reveal no special magnificence of occasion, though, as this essay demonstrates, it was a magnificent event. Its nineteenth-century editor remarks of the story around which the *pas d'armes* was built that, *"elle ne mérite pas l'analyse."*[4] Today, this tournament can prove useful to scholars precisely because of its fictional design. It shows how a fifteenth-century Burgundian knight chose to define himself within the pattern of late medieval romance. The analysis of this neglected and unlikely material, neither history nor fiction, can benefit students of history, literature and society.

The two main accounts of the *Pas du perron fée* occur in *Bibliothèque nationale* manuscript Français 5139 (*anciens fonds*), edited by Félix Brassart in 1874, and in British Library manuscript Harley 48, folios 54–78.[5] Both record the *"fiction"* of the *pas d' armes* — the story on which the tournament is based. Their detailed accounts of the tournament show the enactment of this *fiction* by and before the ducal court. Brassart chose to edit the B. N. manuscript because of its possible association with Limbourg Herald and its possibly fuller treatment of the joust. The student of late medieval romance may prefer the narrative of the B. L. text. This paper can happily make use of both versions.

The *Pas du perron fée* was based, as its B. L. manuscript record states, "sur ungne fiction de phae;" we might translate the phrase as "upon a fairy-tale." The Burgundian knight-errant Philippe de Lalaing represented himself for the purposes of the event as a prisoner of an all-powerful enchantress, rather like a benevolent Morgan le Fay, who has locked him in her magic boulder (*le perron fée*), not to win release until he has faced the knights of Philip the Good in the lists.

The two tournament records might easily be combined to form a single romance. The text edited by Brassart opens the narrative with the disoriented Philippe de Lalaing blowing a horn after sunset outside the enchanted rock

and the knight's debate with an impertinent dwarf—the romance's characteristic challenge to adventure. The Harley manuscript account cuts from its
introduction evoking the Nine Worthies and Jacques de Lalaing to a conversation between the prisoner knight and the *Dame du perron fée* herself.

> It happened one day that this lady went to see the good knight, and
> said to him, "Sir Philip, you are my captive, as you know, and you
> cannot leave this place without my permission."
>
> And he answered, "Madam, that is so; but when it pleases you,
> your ladyship and courtesy will take pity on me, to which I plead
> humbly, for you know and see that I am at an age where, if there
> is any good in me, I should frequent the places where other knights
> prove themselves...."
>
> When the lady heard him speak so well and graciously, moved by
> pity and courtesy—and not wishing to gain the reputation of being
> cruel—she said to him, "Sir Philip, I know by report your prowess
> and that of those from whom you are descended, so I will set you
> a task, and if you wish to leave this prison you must perform for my
> love a *pas d'armes*, ... and if you accomplish it with honor, I promise
> you that I will release you completely from prison, but if you don't
> want to do this, you will stay here forever."
>
> When this good knight heard the offer the lady was making him,
> he was happy as possible, for she was speaking to him of the thing
> he loved doing most in the world.[6]

The passage suggests the elegant detail of the narrative, and also reminds
the modern reader of the fifteenth-century jouster's delight in his own ath-
letic performance. The Harley manuscript maintains the fiction of the knight
as prisoner throughout the preliminary stages of the tournament and even
the actual joust. Only on the completion of the *pas d'armes* will the knight
be released to rejoin the court.

Brassart is hardly unorthodox in reading this tale as a standard episode
from romance. In texts contemporary with the *Pas du perron fée*, sorceresses
like Morgan le Fay constantly capture knights in order to exact chivalric
and frequently amorous forfeits.[7] Still, its matter-of-fact presentation gives
this semi-fictional sketch peculiar force and interest. This is a romance with
living characters, written for, by and around the actors who appear in it.
Indeed, the sole unidentified figure may remain the lady who directs the
action, *la dame du perron fée*. Hardly evident in Brassart's text, in the Harley
manuscript account she discusses her plans with Philippe de Lalaing at
length, consoles him for delays in scheduling the joust, and is last seen sharing wine and spices with him to celebrate his release from twelve days of
jousting, successively, "with lance and sword; with lances, in war harness,
and with lances and jousting gear, against sixty-four opponents."[8] Whether

a figment of Philippe's imagination or a well-known lady who chooses to remain anonymous, the *dame du perron fée* maintains a *dangier* and charm of her own. In practical terms, her role in shifting the responsibility for the joust from Philippe de Lalaing and the Duke of Burgundy to herself seems crucial to the fictional design of the *pas d'armes*.

Whatever imaginative preliminaries the accounts present, the first public event of the pas remains the announcement of Philippe de Lalaing's challenge at the court of Philip the Good. This could not have been the impromptu presentation the tournament record describes; court protocol would demand that every step be choreographed in advance. Nevertheless, the ritual of the romance required the Duke, like his model King Arthur, to be taken by surprise. The court's banter with Limbourg Herald, who pronounced the challenge, reflects a well-simulated astonishment.

> And then the Duke asked Limbourg where this magic rock was, and said he'd never heard of any fairy lady ... and that he thought the days of King Arthur were coming back. And the others said the same. "I don't know what's going on," said Limbourg, "but I can tell you that the lady is full of honor and goodness and that she speaks very good French...."[9]

Philippe de Lalaing's challenge was offered formally, first to the senior members of the court who must approve the program of the joust, and then to the knights for their acceptance. In the Harley manuscript account, the knights' responses are solicited in a second scene, in which the lady's dwarf berates the courtiers. His style of abuse has been made familiar by the dwarfs and *demoiselles maledisantes* of romance.[10] This scene invited the courtiers who take up Philippe's challenge to step into the romance themselves. This "audience participation" ratified Philippe de Lalaing's presentation of himself as the imprisoned knight, and, reciprocally, confirmed the Duke of Burgundy in his favorite role as a new King Arthur. While the initial *fiction* of the *pas d'armes* focuses on the challenger, this episode reminds the reader that the tournament remained a corporate enterprise.

The joust itself, moved from Brussels to Bruges by the ducal itinerary, opened on April 28. In the great market square, the citizens had made room for the spectator stands, lists, and the *perron fée* itself, in all its gold, silver, red and blue splendor.

> ... at the far end of the space there was a rock fourteen to fifteen feet high, made with skill, well and agreeably worked and painted in several colors; gold, silver, blue, black, red, and more....[11]

Three shields, to represent the three events of the *pas d'armes*, hung from the rock beside the horn of brass. The *perron* was guarded by the dwarf, in his coat of blue-tinted cloth of gold, and four griffins — men in griffin costume, to be precise — chained to the rock. These griffins, on cue, swung open the marvelous rock to allow Philippe de Lalaing to appear magically in the lists. Now display takes its place as a primary effect of the tournament. The records both set down the trappings of each jouster in fascinated heraldic detail.

> The third comer on that day was my lord Anthony, Bastard of Brabant, who called himself "the Disorderly Knight," accompanied by a great troop dressed as unbelievers, and within, wild men on foot, and also well escorted by knights and squires. And his horse was trapped in blue velvet edged with gold thread and tears, all covered with silver bells made like big pears, and on the horse's crupper, a very large silver bell, and on his helmet he had a tuft of down, and on top of that a crimson crest loaded with goldsmiths' work. Then they fought and the said knight gave his required twenty-seven sword-blows, and the said de Brabant gave twenty-four.[12]

Each knight attempted to impress his special character on the spectators. The *pas d'armes* may center itself around Philippe de Lalaing, but his opponents refuse to reduce themselves to nonentities. Most of all, through the successive jousts, the image of this new Round Table acting as a unit to display its military prowess flaunts itself before us.

As the joust ends, once again the two records diverge. The closing ceremonies as the lady frees Philippe de Lalaing from the *perron* are succeeded by his entertainment at her lodgings.[13] This will be the reader's last sight of the lady in whose name this complex ritual was performed. Of all the major participants, she alone refuses to take her bow at the final celebratory banquet. Brassart suggests that she is represented in the *entremés* — a centerpiece of a galley captained by a lady. He hints at some gallantry on the part of the duke; Harley 48 implies that Philippe de Lalaing is taken with the lady himself.[14] Any literal courting remains elusive, submerged in the public aims of the *pas d'armes*. The lady elects to preserve her incognito from outside spectators, if not from the Burgundian court. She commissions Philippe de Lalaing to deliver the prizes at the banquet. In a charming touch, each participant is awarded a badge to wear in commemoration of the event. Brassart's text records the quatrain inscribed on each jouster's favor. The resplendent Anthony, Bastard of Brabant, received one proclaiming:

> It is your glory and great treasure
> To have a heart noble in intent,
> And that your hope is brighter
> Than a rare jewel set in gold.[15]

This gesture unites the corporate aspect of the joust with the personal element once more. These badges are, at the same time, signs of group activity and individual trophies.

Brassart's text ends with these quatrains. Harley manuscript 48 chooses to finish with a dance led by M. de Ravestain. This performance is naturally the most elegant possible; *"et mieulx ne l'eut su faire, car mon dit seigneur de Ravestain estoit tenu pour l'un des bien danssans du royaulme de france...."*[16] The three major awards of the tournament are then presented to three of the most eminent participants, M. de St. Pol, M. de Ravestain, and Jacques de Luxembourg, to no one's surprise, not even the winners', "for these were not the first prizes that had ever been given to them."[17] Plan and custom carry through to the end.

This essay has already suggested several ways of interpreting Philippe de Lalaing's *pas d'armes*. The joust remains, first of all, a major sports event, anticipated eagerly by participants and spectators. The records of the *Pas du perron fée* also underline the importance of display in the tournament. Indeed, the *fiction* of the *pas d'armes* may be seen as a special form of display. In it, Philip the Good's court portrayed itself as a center of romance, investing itself with the magic as well as the moral authority of King Arthur's Round Table.

These observations might apply to many fifteenth-century tournaments. The special interest of the *Pas du perron fée* lies in its focus on the individual knight's creative participation in chivalric romance. The two records chart the distance Philippe de Lalaing and his comrades chose to venture into the world of romance. The quest for identity is now considered a major theme explored in the later medieval romance. Philippe de Lalaing's joust preserves one knight's ritual of self-definition within the collective chivalric fantasy of the Burgundian court. He transforms himself into a Fair Unknown, the captive of an elusive enchantress, into a tireless and formidable antagonist testing the knights of the court in their turn, and, at last, into the proven champion returning to his fellows from the frontiers of romance. Philippe de Lalaing does all this, Harley 48 reports, "so that some small memory may remain of him." He deserves to be better remembered.

Notes

1. Félix Brassart, ed., *Le Pas du Perron Fée* (Douai: L. Crepin, 1874), pp. 40–41. "... o! vous nobles princes et chevaliers, barons et escuiers de grant pris, est advenu chose très estrange, cy entour, ès pays du très hault et très vittorieux prince, le duc de Bourgoingne, que ung povre chevalier, fourvoiré en unes landes se trouva, sur le serain et après soliel escons, entre deux grans et larges estans plains d'eaue. Donc luy ... finablement doubtant de son aventure d'aller ainsi vaucrant par nuit en lieu non congneu, trouva ung obstacle fait en manière d'un perron, et ... audit perron, pendoit ung cor d'araing, qui donnoit à entendre ... que, ... il boutast et sonnast le cor à deux poses, et la troisième, il s'apercheveroit de response.... Ledit chevalier ... mist le cor en sa bouche, et ... en fist retenter montaigne et valée....

Lors tout prestement, comme sesours fust par dessoubz terre, s'aparu un nayn d'estrange fourme, vestu toutesfoies estoit de drap d'or, maiz portant chière très refrongié." Unless otherwise noted, all translations quoted in this essay are those of the author.

2. Larry D. Benson, *Malory's Morte Darthur* (Cambridge, Mass.; Harvard University Press, 1976), pp. 182, 179.

3. See Georges Chastelain, *Chronique de Jacques de Lalain; Chronique du bon chevalier Messire Jacques de Lalain, frère et compagnon de l'ordre de la Toison d'or* in *Collection des chroniques nationales françaises*, 41, ed. J. A. Buchon (Paris, 1825). Jacques' chivalric biography also gives biographical particulars on his brother Philippe (ca. 1430–65). See also Brassart, pp. 21–24, and, for Jacques, Benson, pp. 179–83.

4. Brassart, p. 2.

5. For Brassart, see note 1 above. I am grateful to the officers of the British Library for permission to quote from my transcription of B. L. MS. Harley 48. The manuscript also contains a *Livre de l'instruction d'un prince*, two pieces on the funeral of Richard Duke of York, and a copy of Anthony Woodville, Lord Scales' 1465 letter of challenge to the Great Bastard of Burgundy. For other copies of both tournament records, see Brassart, pp. 14–21.

6. B. L. MS. Harley 48 fol. 55r. All quotations from this text are based on my own transcription of the manuscript. The use of i, j, u, and v, and the punctuation, have been modernized. "Advint ung jour que celle dame alla visiter ce bon chevalier & lui dist, 'Mesire phillipe vous estes mon prissonier comme vous saves et de ce lieu ne poves partir sans mon congie.' & y respondi, 'Madame, il est ainsi, mais quant il vous plaira vostre seignieurie & courtoissie me fera grace, a laquelle je en suplie humblement, car vous savez et voyez que je suis en age, s'il y avoiet quelque bien en moy, de me trouver es lieux ou les aultres chevaliers se occupioit....' Quant la dame l'ouy si vertueusement et gracieussement parler, meue de pitie & courtoissie, sans voulloyer aquerre la renommee destre cruelle, lui dit, 'Mesire Phillippe, je congnoies asses par renommer vostre bonne chevallerie et de ceux de qui vous estes issus, que je vous feray ung jeu parti, est si vous voullez issir de ceste prison, il faut que serves pour l'amour de moy ung pas d'armes ... et se vous l'achevez avec honneur, je vous assure sur ma foy que je vous aquiteray entierement hors de prison, et se ainsi ne le voullez faire, vous i demourez a james.' Quant ce bon chevalier entendi l'offre que la dame lui faisoiet, il vut telle joye que plus ne povoit, car elle lui parloiet de la chosse du monde quil l'aymoit mieux a faire."

7. For instances of this in an Arthurian text contemporary with the *pas d'armes* examined here, see *The Works of Sir Thomas Malory*, ed. Eugène Vinaver (2nd ed.; rpt, Oxford: Clarendon Press, 1973), I: 256–58; II: 510–12, 553–55, 597, 638–44. The final pages lead up to the joust of Alexander the Orphan mentioned on page 2 above.

8. Brassart, p. 3.

9. B. L. MS Harley 48, fol. 57r. "Et puis demanda le duc a lembourc ou estoiet ce peron phae & en quel pais et quil nau ouy james parler en son temps que dame phae eussent pais & qu'il pensoient que l'entencion temps revenoiet comment il sensoit du temps du roy Artus. Et parreillement les aultres disoient. 'Je ne say que c'est,' dist lembourc, 'mais tant vous dy je que la dame est plaine de grant honneur & bonte et qu'elle parle ung tres biau francoys.' "

10. For impertinent dwarfs and *demoiselles*, see Malory, I: 296–313; II: 462–71. The impertinent dwarf has a long history dating back at least to Chrétien de Troyes' *Chevalier de la charrette* where one drives Lancelot's infamous cart.

11. Brassart, p. 50. "et au bout d'icelles clousteres, avoit ung perron de xiiij à xv pies de hault, fait par artiffice, bien et gentement ouvré et painst de diverses coulleurs tant d'or d'argent, d'azur, de noir, de rouge comme d'aultres." See also Caxton's reference to the "perron" at which Lancelot and Tristram duel, Malory, II: 568–69.

12. Brassart, p. 58. "Le troisième entrant, pour celluy jour, fu messire *Anthoine, bastard de Brabant*, qui se nomme *le chevalier desroyé*, acompaignié d'une grant gent en habit d'increduli, et dedens, hommes sauvages à piet, et aussi bien accompaignié de chevaliers et escuiers. Et estoit son cheval houchié de velours bleu bordé de fil d'or et de lermes, et tout chargié de campennes d'argent, en fachon de grosses poires, et sur la croupe du cheval, un cloqueste d'argent bien grosse, et dessus son harnais de teste, avoit une touffe de duvet, et dessus une creste de cramoisi chargié d'or-faverie dorée. Le chevalier et ledit Brabant coururent, sans rompre lance. Puis combatierent, et acomply ledit chl^r son nombre de xxvij coups d'espée, et ledit de Brabant xxiiij."

13. B. L. MS. Harley 48, fols. 74v–75r.

14. See B. L. MS. Harley 48, fols. 74v–75r; Brassart, p. 14.

15. Brassart, p. 85. "Ce vous est gloire et hault trésor / D'avoir le ceur en noble entendre, / Et dont plus cler vous est l'atendre, / Que precieuse pierre en or."

16. B. L. MS. Harley 48, fol. 77r. "and none would have known how to do it better, for my said Lord of Ravestain was considered as one of the best dancers of the kingdom of France. . . ."

17. B. L. MS. Harley 48, fol. 78r. "Car se nestoit pas la premiers pris qui leur eussent este pressentez. . . ."

Renaissance Conduct Literature and the Basse Danse
The Kinesis of Bonne Grace[1]

MARK FRANKO

T he inference that individual human identities were to some degree fashioned by standards of group behavior in the Renaissance may be drawn from the title of this conference — Persons in Groups, Social Behavior as Identity Formation. The tyranny of the group in imposing a fantasmatic institutionalized identity upon the individual is nowhere more evident than in conduct literature: while sometimes considered to describe "precious" behavior, courtesy books from Castiglione to Faret actually encode a sociology of action and reaction that may be patterned into Codes. By Codes I mean systemic forms of theatricality, referred to as grace in the Renaissance, which provide conventional responses or "solutions" to ever new and various stimuli. It is my contention that the theory of social grace was not modeled on the dance but elaborated through it and that the practice, or rather art, of grace in courtly society, as courtesy books represent it, was also primarily kinetic. Sixteenth-century manuals of good behavior reveal the influence of the Italian courts on the nobility and upper bourgeoisie of France, Burgundy and Holland; grace was the goal of Castiglione's courtier, Erasmus' multi-class child, Guazzo's conversant and Arbeau's law student-dancer. I shall therefore draw on all of the above writers in profiling the theoretical body which emerges as exemplary to the European consciousness of formalized social behavior devolving from the courts.

The interrelationship of Renaissance courtly dance and courtesy theory is a commonplace of dance history. "L'histoire de la danse," writes Françoise de Ménil, "on ne saurait trop le répéter, est l'histoire des moeurs."[2] The present paper grew out of a need to challenge the easy circularity of

this copulative in order to answer two questions: how can we account for
the lack of descriptions of movement in early dance treatises and how can
the quasi absence of the dancing body, once problematized, lead to a
clarification of the enigma of grace?[3] I have chosen the basse danse as exemplary because its practice extended from the Italian courts of the fifteenth
century through the Burgundian school to the French bourgeois Arbeau
who revived it in 1588.[4] The following analysis of discourse on *externum
corporis decorum* in courtesy books reveals the operation of two opposing Codes,
one of posture and the other of gesture, which structure the choreography
of the basse danse as a kinetic model of grace.[5]

Let us first examine the postural Code of the pose. In courtesy books,
the normative body is represented frontally in an erect posture. Proper erect-
ness is a mean between rigidity and lethargy. "Resupinare corpus," writes
Erasmus, "fastus indicium est: molliter erectum, decet" (*E*, A.7). For Guazzo
"s'ha a comporre tutto il corpo in maniera, che non paia nè tutto d'un pez-
zo intiero, nè tutto snodato" (*G*, 81v). The mean is also expressed as a state
of balance: "Corpus igitur aequo libramine sit erectum" (*E*, B.7). The face
is the privileged locus and the epitome of posture. Faret describes
countenance as "une juste situation de tout le corps.... Mais elle reçoit
toute sa perfection des mouvements du visage.... Et certes on peut dire
que c'est le visage qui domine au maintien extérieur ..." (*F*, 195). Of all
facial features, the eyes receive the utmost attention. "Ut ergo bene compositus pueri animus undique reluceat, relucet autem potissimum in vultu,
sint oculi placidi, verecundi, compositi ..." (*E*, A.3). Axiomatization of
the glance ("sint oculi placidi, verecundi, compositi") becomes a model for
axiomatization of body posture as a whole ("ut ergo bene compositus pueri
animus *undique reluceat*"). Similarly, deviation from the ocular Code con-
taminates the appearance of the whole. "Incompositi gestus non raro vi-
ciant, non solum oculorum, verum etiam totius corporis habitum ac for-
mam" (*E*, A.4).

The correct form of the glance is arrived at in two ways. It is suggested
by reference to Tradition. "Picturae quidem veteres nobis loquuntur, olim
singularis cuiusdam modestiae fuisse, semiclusis oculis obtueri quem admodum apud Hispanos quosdam semipetos intueri blandum haberi videtur
et amicum" (*E*, A.4). The modest gaze is not turned inward. It is directed
at the interlocutor. "Oculi spectent eum cui loqueris, sed placidi simplices-
que, nihil procas improbumue prae se ferentes" (*E*, C.7). Modesty has its
own degrees of intensity directly proportionate to the gloriousness of the
whole body. " ... Mirentur alii tu te bene cultum esse nescias. Quò maior
est fortuna, hoc est amabilior modestia" (*E*, B.4).[6] The modesty of the look
fulfills a dissimulated deictic function. In being attentive, it is sufficiently
uncompelling to allow the other's gaze a certain liberty. In this sense, the
look is an ostensibly passive gaze which stages the body to be viewed. It

corresponds to the feminine glance in the basse danse as Arbeau describes it. "Et les damoiselles avec une contenance humble, les yeulx baissez, regardans quelquefois les assistans avec une pudeur virginale" (*O*, 30v). The look is also, however, a glance sufficiently focused to constitute the vanishing point, as it were, of the perspective within which the interlocutor's attention is captured or engaged, prolonging the contact. In this sense, the look is an active glance staged by the body. It corresponds to the male's glance in the basse danse, "la vheue asseurée." In other terms, the dance analyses the double function of the glance into distinct sexual roles.

The correct glance is also arrived at by an enumeration of every possible predication of what it should *not* be: "[oculi] ... non torui quod est truculentiae non improbi, quod est imprudentiae: non vagi ac volubiles, quod est insaniae ..." (*E*, A.3). In this perspective, "mediocritas" is nothing but the suspension or neutralization of perverse or erroneous attitudes.[7] All precepts follow the same procedure of elimination. Calviac writes, "la tête ne doit estre ni trop baissé [a sign of laziness], ny trop haut [a sign of arrogance]" (*H*, Xiiij). The correct carriage of the head mirrors that of the eyes and of the body in general. "Mais se doyt tenir droict et sans effort, car cela ha bonne grâce" (ibid.). Avoidance of lateral movements of the head also lends precision to the correct bearing. "Et ne faut point aussi que sa teste pande d'un costé ny d'autre dessus son corps, à la mode des hypocrites ..." (ibid.). Each facial feature is both metaphor and metonym of the same postural mean. As for the eyebrows: "sint exporrecta supercilia, non adducta, quod est tortuitatis: non sublata in altu, quod est arrogantia: non in oculos depressa, quod est male cogitantium" (*E*, A.4). As for the cheeks: "inflare buccas fastus indicium est, easdem demittere, est animum despondentis ..." (*E*, A.6). As for the lips: "os nec prematur quod est metuentis alterius halitu haurire, nec hiet, quod est morionum, sed leniter osculantibus se mutuo labris coniunctum sit" (*E*, A.6). The same principle of moderation between two extremes applies equally to the rest of the body. For example, "humeros oportet aequo libramine temperare, non in morem antennarum, alterum attollere, alterum deprimere" (*E*, A.7).

Just as the eyes are exemplars of correct posture, the hands are an antimodel embodying all the mistakes to which other body parts are prone. Physiognomy treatises also fulminate against hand movement. "Celuy qui s'esmeut de legier, et en parlant joüe des mains, est mauvais fol, et deceveur. Et celuy qui parle sans mouvoir ses mains est de grand entendement, est sage et preud'homme."[8] The gestures which civility prohibits are fast, unexpected, brief, repetitive and suggestive or mimetic. Erasmus will refer to them as gesticulation or agitation. While there are no explicit desiderata for the quality of permitted gestures, we may deduce that they are by opposition slow, smooth and separated by pauses and halts. Gestures of the hands are undesirable as they may be used to represent "quelque vicieux désir, ou deshonneste conception"(*T*, 33v). Indeed, it would seem that arm and hand movements have no place in the social dance of the Renaissance which was institutionalized as a form of *bienseance*. Most current reconstructions of historical dance are performed according to this premise. Tuccaro writes, "le bal et la danse qu'on faict sans gestes et mines, est une certaine espece separee des autres ..."(*T*, 41v). However, we shall see that a form of permitted idiosyncracy, originality or gesture within the systemic does exist, corresponding roughly to what Stephen Greenblatt has called "individual self fashioning."[9]

If we turn to Arbeau's description of the basse danse we can ascertain the pertinence of civility's Code of the pose for this dance type. Arbeau compresses the precepts of physical measure into two phrases applying to all the dances of his repertory: "Ayez la teste et le corps droit, la vheue asseuree ..."(*O*, 63v–63r). The head is mentioned first, confirming its independence from the body as transcendent element of the series. The role of the face and eyes as model is iterated by a semanticization of the glance ("asseuree") which differentiates "droit" from Capriol's description of himself before he danced as "quasi une buche de bois"(*O*, 2r). The precepts of physical rectitude, while calling for an immobile stance, preclude rigidity. "Vos mains soient pendants, non comme mortes, ny aussi pleines de gesticulations ..."(*O*, 63 r). Posture approximates adherence to an imaginary center constantly remeasured between inflation and deflation. The role of the negative proposition (neither, nor) is to represent posture as a transitional moment between action and its arrestation, in which stillness is not yet motion but no longer immobile.[10]

After the reverence, the basse danse consists in walking hand in hand with the partner (*simples* and *doubles*) with nine halts for movements in place (*branle* and *reprise*).[11] "Les marches et mouvements ... de la basse danse sont pesants et graves"(*O*, 40r). They should be performed "marchants honnestement avec une gravité posée"(*O*, 30v). For the *simple* the dancer steps forward on the left and steps together with the right foot. In the double he takes three consecutive steps forward (left, right, and left) before stepping together with the right. There is nothing in the description which would distinguish the *simple* or *double* from walking in everyday life. Indeed, Arbeau warns that the steps should not be so big as to deform the erect posture of the upper body. "Et se fault donner garde de faire les annonces des pieds si grandes qu'il semble qu'on veuille mesurer la longueur de la salle ..."(*O*, 28v). In sum, the steps of the basse danse exhibit the dancer's probity to all present by circulating two or three times through a room. The step together reminds the onlooker that the walking body is a moving posture.

The basse danse, however, is not complete if it is not followed by the faster and lighter *tordion* or *tourdion*. The *tourdion* is a slightly less energetic version of the other major French Renaissance dance, the gaillard. "Le tourdion n'est autre chose qu'une gaillarde par terre"(*O*, 29v). Since the movements of the *tourdion* are hopping and jumping, we will study its intertextual connections with civility's gestural Code. The movements of the *tourdion* complete the basse danse in that they exemplify the body as product or, in other terms, they naturalize the Code of the pose. Having *bonne grâce* consists precisely in the acquisition of this naturalness. First we will give a brief description of the choreography.

The *tourdion* or gaillard consists in what are called "les cinq pas": three hops, a jump and a pose. The hops come in a variety of forms ("greve," "ru de vache," "entretaille," "pied croisé," "marque talon") because while one leg hops the other can swing front, back or sideways or else tap the floor or actually switch places with the hopping leg. Since these steps may be done either on the right leg or the left, the variety of combinations is enormous. The jump ("sault majeur") may be complicated with leg beats in which case it is called a "capriole." The landing of the jump is held as a pose ("position" or "posture"). The jump and the pose together are considered a unit called "clausulam" or "cadance." The five steps are repeated *ad infinitum* but the first three and, to a lesser degree, the fourth, may be varied at each repetition. The dance therefore requires considerable mental preparation and concentration if one is to introduce variations.

If the first part of the basse danse in Arbeau's description is a paradigm of probity, the gaillard recalls the unrefined popular dance of the day. "Ceulx qui dancent la gaillarde aujourd'huy par les villes, ilz dancent tumultuairement, et se contentent de faire les cinq pas et quelques passages sans aulcune disposition et ne se soucient pourveu qu'ilz tumbent en cadance . . ."(*O*, 39v). Once again Arbeau is reviving, if not a forgotten dance, a forgotten manner of dancing. "Du commencement on la dançoit avec plus grande discretion"(ibid.). Indeed, dances characterized by hopping and jumping were singled out by Renaissance polemicists for special blame. A reformist moral theology in the sixteenth century equated agitated movement with madness. Just as measure and moderation were qualities of prudence or judgment in the Renaissance sociolect, the polar opposite of measure was not evil but a form of imprudence characterized as vanity, passion or madness.[12] In Tuccaro's *Trois Dialogues* Roger Cosme attacks the dance as a mad agitation: "Qui est celuy qui sans passion considerant l'agitation des personnes qui dancent avecq une telle et si grande diversité de mouvements, ne s'esmerveille de la folie de tels hommes et femmes qui s'y delectent, et ne les fuye comme personnes folles et du toute insensees?"(*T*, 18r–19v). Lambert Daneau criticizes the dancer as being temporarily deprived of prudence, a faculty of judgement which allows us to regulate the "honnêteté" of our own actions. He also blames the form of the dance which is "non convenable à gens modestes, graves, et de sens rassis"(*D*, 14). The problem which form presents to stable judgement is that of diversity; first of all, the diversity of dances: "la forme est fort diverse. Car il y a branles, et encor de mille sortes, des bals, gaillardes, pavannes, courantes, voltes, et infinies autres façons"(ibid.). The problem of diversity is also one of steps and, as such, is peculiar to the gaillard: "car pour tout c'est un art de sçavoir faire des cinq pas, et les diversifier ..."(*D*, 16). Within each step bodily movement is diversified as well and, seemingly, at odds with itself:

> ...il faut bien qu'il y ait quelque autre espece de folie, c'est à dire, defaut de sens et de prudence, qui les fait sauteler et se tourmenter (*D*, 15).

Jumping combined the agitation of constant movement, an indication of madness, with the physical inflation of vanity or vainglory. By jumping, the body would seem to increase its height and volume. If the diversity of leaps, hops and jumps, "des sauts perilleux et autres mouvemens estranges et bateleresques" in Montaigne's words, were attributes of madness, the act of walking evenly and in a straight line was one of the descriptive systems of prudence. "Comme elle [la Nature] nous a fourni de pieds à marcher, aussi a elle de prudence à nous guider en la vie."[13] It is therefore not fortuitous that the basse danse, being composed primarily of sober "non-imitative stepping" as Curt Sachs phrased it, could represent virtue and accede to a form of "legalized" dancing. How is it possible then that the *tourdion* or gaillard could be part of the basse danse? We will seek the answer in civility's gestural Code.

Although civility places strict limits upon physical movement, it does contain a gestural Code. The gestural Code is intimately related to dissimulation and to nature as well as to the aesthetic enigma of grace. Erasmus states the theory of gesture as follows: "...contra [gestus] compositi, quod natura decorum est reddunt decentius: quod vitiosum est, si non tollunt, certè tegunt minuuntque"(*E*, A.4). Gesture, first of all, exercises a corrective or masking function. Its most frequent masking function in *De civilitate morum puerilium* is turning away. "Si aliis presentibus incidat sternutatio, civile est corpus avertere"(*E*, A.5). Turning away is complemented by a series of subsequent attenuating gestures.

> ...Mox ubi se remiserit impetus, fignareos crucis imagine, de in sublato pileo resalutatis que vel salutarant vel salutare debuerant ... pueri est aperire caput"(*E*, A.5).

Yawning is another facial deformation which gesture may make amends for. "Si fors urgeat oscitatio, nec datur averti, aut cedere, strophio volané tegatur os, mox imagine crucis obsignetur"(*E*, A.6). Laughter is another involuntary act which threatens to deform the poise of the face and, indeed, of the whole body. Erasmus flatly prohibits the latter eventuality. "Cachinnus et immodicus ille totum corpus quatiens risus, quem ob id Graeci συγκραχσιον appellant, nulli decoris est atati, nedum pueritiae"(ibid.). Here again, a deviation from prescribed posture is a sign of vice. "Sic autem vultus hilaritatem exprimat, ut necoris habitum, dehonestet, nec animum dissolutum arguat"(ibid.). Vice is identified with error and virtue with knowledge. There are nevertheless corrective gestures for the laugh that might overpower composure. "Et si qua res adeo ridicula inciderit, ut volentibus eiusmodi risu exprimat, mappa manuué tegenda facies" (*E*, A.6–A.7). An equivalent series of coded gestures applies to nasal excretions:

> A naribus absit mucoris purulentia, quod est sordidorum ... strophiolis excipere narium recrementa decorum, idque *paulisper averso corpore*, si qui adsint honoratiores. Si quid in solum deiectum est, emuncto *duobus digitis* nasa, mox *pede proterendum* est"(A.4–A.5, my emphases).

Similar instructions can, on occasion, find their way into Arbeau's rules for dancing as well. "... Crachez et mouchez peu, et si la nécessité vous y contrainct, torné le visage d'aultre part et usez d'un beau mouchoir blanc..."(2O, 63r).

There is, however, a second aspect to the gestural Code. "[Gestus] compositi, quod natura decorum est reddunt decentius...." Quintilian makes an equally cryptic comment in his discussion of oratorical action. "Decor quoque a gestu atque motu venit."[14] We have progressed from grace as an overall effect of corporal propriety to grace as a specific attribute of movement. "Du côté du sujet," writes the twentieth-century esthetician Raymond Bayer, "la grâce est esthétique de *l'aisance* ... Elle est faite d'une technique de la surêté intérieure."[15] Apart from the often cited mistakes, the only major error or vice that requires concealment is the visibility of the behavioral Code as Code. The role of grace is to conceal coded behavior with a natural appearance. Gesture affords the diversity without which the Code of civility would become predictable, visible and thereby discredited. Lack of moderation in the application of civility's precepts can be as great a fault as lack of measure itself. Arbeau remarks that the dance "apporteroit mespris a celluy qui comme un pillier de salle y seroit trop assidu"(*O*, 5r). Gesture or movement, in other terms, is the prism through which all other precepts can be bent: the rules of its use defy codification.

> Elles [les civilités] ont quelques formes penibles, lesquelles, pourveu qu'on oublie par discretion [discernement], non par erreur, on n'en a pas moins de grâce. J'ay veu souvent des hommes incivils par trop de civilités et importuns de courtoisie (*M*, I, XIV, 46–47).

Erasmus' "natural" gesture which produces grace, like Castiglione's famous *sprezzatura*, can only be defined negatively as that which is unaffected. It is a "je-ne-sais-quoi." One must "usar in ogni cosa una certa sprezzatura, che nasconda l'arte, e dimostri cio, che fisa, e dice, venir fatto senza fatica, e quasi sensa pensarvi. Da questo credo io che derivi assai la gratia ..."(*C*, 65–66). Though naturalness is a carefully contrived appearance of non-assiduity, the natural gesture cannot be coded as uncoded without defeating its own purpose. "Non v'accorgete, che questo, che voi in M. Roberto chiamate sprezzatura è vera affettatione? perche chiaramente si conosce, che esto si sforza con ogni studio mostrar di non pensarvi e questo è il pensarvi troppo"(*C*, 68). Precepts may stipulate a given posture, but the end product escapes definition. "Toutes les bonnes parties que nous avons alleguées, sont tres-considerables en un Gentilhomme, mais le comble de ces choses consiste en une certaine grace naturelle, qui en tous ses exercices, et jusques à ses moindres actions doit reluire comme un petit rayon de Divinité ..."(*F*, 26–27). Instruction is ultimately a matter of imitation. "Tout le conseil qui se peut donner en cela, c'est que ceux qui ont un bon jugement pour reigle de leur conduite, s'ils ne se sentent douez de ce sublime don de nature, taschent du moins a reparer ce manquement par l'imitation des plus parfaits exemples, et de ceux qui auront l'approbation generale"(*F*, 27). Courtesy books initiate an unending process of mastery of the body through imitation; the courtier imitates him who is most successful at transcending collective control and who therefore extends the boundaries of the permissible by appearing natural. Just as each bodily feature perfects its bearing by modeling itself on the composure of the body as a whole, the general composure is made up of the harmony of individual features. The same procedure holds true for the "social body." Conformity results in a confusion between biology and the law in that regulation and spontaneity seem to presuppose one another. Failing genius, one conforms to the divine aptitude in others. So, writes Guazzo, "si veste della cognitione di se stesso per mezo della civil conversatione..."(*G*, 70r). Civility functions as an institution, a self-perpetuating ideology in practice, in that each deviation from the Code which falls short of brilliant transgression is noticed by others and discreetly brought to the attention of the uninstructed. "Finalmente ci contentiamo," writes Guazzo, "di sottoporci alle communi opinioni, e ci veniamo a ravvedere di qualche nostra imperfettione, la quale ci sforziamo di correggere secondo il giudicio altrui"(*G*, 71v). Because movement is said to reflect simultaneously a perfect conformity to a norm of propriety and the flowering of an innate quality (prudence as individual nature or "complexion"), it is unrepresentable. Therefore, the specificity of the dancing body in dance treatises is also passed over in silence.

But movement is not unrepresentable solely because its role is to naturalize the pose. It is not sufficient in the system of civility that physical discipline be made to appear spontaneous according to what Bayer calls "l'esthétique de la résorption des contrôles"(*B*, 171). "Le domaine," writes Bayer, "de la spontanéité soudain s'élargit, et la *sprezzatura* y fait entrer tous les contrôles. C'est la vigilance, à son tour, qui devient spontanée ... le contrôle, transfiguré, vient jouer de verve avec la verve"(*B*, 167). We do not agree that the control Code of the pose is literally transfigured any more than we agree with the opposite extreme as Pierre Legendre expressed it: "le contraire de l'orthodoxie est la folie."[16] Grace witnesses to the clandestine reintroduction of madness into the system. Grace is the dissimulation of artifice behind a second nature manifested as movement. Arbeau tells us that the gaillard must be danced by someone who already possesses the qualities necessary for its performance. "La gaillarde est appellée ainsi parce qu'il fault estre gaillard et dispos pour la danser..."(*O*, 40v). Similarly, when Arbeau's student Capriol first hears of the jump one must perform in the gaillard, the "capriole," he underlines his own natural predisposition to the step in an onomastic code: "J'apprendray volontiers ceste capriole puis qu'elle porte mon nom"(*O*, 48r). The dancing body is absent from dance treatises because movement, being by definition a product of the genius or inspiration of a unique personal nature, cannot be analysed. It is not sufficient to speak of a natural versus an acquired gesture in order to elucidate the system. A last example from Pierre Charron serves to illustrate this conclusion. Charron posed the possibility of a hyperbolically natural gesture which might transcend the distinction of the natural versus the acquired gesture.

> Comm'il y en à, qui ont des contenances, gestes, et mouvements artificiels et affectés, aussi y en a, qui en ont de si naturels et si propres, qu'ils ne les sentent, ny ne les recognoissent point, comme pencher la teste, rincer le nais. Mais tous en avons, qui ne partent point de nostre discours, ains d'une pure naturelle et prompte impulsion, comme mettre la main au devant de nos cheutes.[17]

The three types of gesture correspond to three degrees of propriety:

> Distinction de la vraie prudhommie, en vertu naturelle et en vertu acquise: il y a encore une troisième composée des deux; ce qui constitue trois degrés de perfection. Pour achever cette perfection, il faut la grâce de Dieu ...(*S*, II, III, 73).

The synthesis of the natural and the acquired echoes on the religious context of the term grace as a form of the marvelous. Arbeau will also implore the grace of God to come to the aid of earthly grace in the final line of *Orchesographie*.

By focusing on the kinesis of grace we in no way mean to homologate civility with an aesthetics. The pragmatics of gesture in dancing suggest a bridge between a ritualized exercise and a crucial improvisation. It has not been the aim of this paper to treat the kinds of persuasion which civility is designed to exert.[18] We have aimed to show that the kinetic profile of persons in courtly or court-oriented groups in the Renaissance is basically inter-mimetic. Furthermore, the hyperbolically "natural" gesture presupposes mimesis within a social class of mythical beings as a condition of unrepeatability and social uniqueness. It is a kind of universal act *in re* proceeding from and only bestowed upon the "godly." It should be considered as a chapter in the as yet unwritten history of kinetic theatrical theory in the Western tradition.

Notes

1. The courtesy books and dance treatises to which we will refer will be abbreviated in the text as follows:

O: Thoinot Arbeau, *Orchesographie. Et Traicte en Forme de Dialogue, par lequel toutes personnes peuvent facilement apprendre et practiquer l'honneste exercice des dances* (Lengre: Jehan des preyz, 1589; rpt., Bologna: Forni Editore, 1969).

H: Claude Hours de Calviac, *La civile honesteté pour les enfants avec la manière d'apprendre à bien lire, prononcer* ... (Paris: 1560).

C: Baldesar Castiglione, *Le Parfait Courtisan du Comte Baltasar Castillonnois*, trans. Gabriel Chappuis (Lyon: Jean Huguetan, 1585). Bilingual edition.

E: Desiderius Erasmus, *De civilitate morum puerilium per Des. Erasmum Roterodamum, Libellus nunc primum et conditus et aeditus* (London: W. de Worde, 1532).

F: Nicolas Faret, *l'Honeste Homme ou, l'art de plaire a la cour* (Paris: chez Jean Brunet, 1639).

G: Stefano Guazzo, *La Civil Conversatione del Signor Stefano Guazzo Gentilhuomo di Casale di Monserrato divisa in quattro libri* (Vinegia, Presso Altobello Salicato, 1586).

D: Lambert Daneau, *Traite Des Danses, Auquel est amplement resolue la question, a savoir s'il est permis aux Chretiens de danser* (Lyon: Jean Beraud, 1579).

T: Archange Tuccaro, *Trois Dialogues de l'Exercice de Sauter et Voltiger en l'Air, avec les Figures qui servent a la Parfaite Demonstration et Intelligence Dudit Art* (Paris: 1599).

2. Françoise de Ménil, *Histoire de la danse à travers les âges* (Paris: Alcide Picard et Kaan, 1906), p. 160.

3. I treat these questions more fully in *Renaissance Dance Theory, c. 1420–1589: an Intertextual Model*, forthcoming in 1984 (Birmingham: Summa Publications).

4. Arbeau's *Orchesographie* is the single most informative document on dance technique in the French sixteenth century. Some American dance historian-reconstructors tend to eye Arbeau with diffidence as they measure his distance from the Italian and Burgundian schools of the late fifteenth century when the basse danse enjoyed its heyday. It is rarely acknowledged that since Arbeau was born in Dijon (1520)

and died in Langres (1595) he was close to the Burgundian tradition. It is never-theless true that no comparable document on sixteenth-century Parisian court dance exists with which Arbeau's choreography might be compared. Certain French dance historians, on the other hand, appear to be assimilating Arbeau's dances to "danse populaire," thereby conveniently erasing dance as a courtly or court-oriented phenomenon. See, in particular, Michel Guilcher, "L'interprétation de l'or-chésographie par des danseurs et des musiciens d'aujourd'hui," in *La Recherche en Danse* 2 (1983): 21–32.

5. For background on the basse danse see Ingrid Brainard, "Bassedanse, Bassadanza and Ballo in the 15th Century," in *Proceedings of the Second Conference on Research in Dance* (New York: Congress on Research in Dance, 1970), pp. 64–79, and, Daniel Heartz, "The Basse Dance. Its Evolution circa 1450 to 1550," in *An-nales Musicologiques. Moyen Age et Renaissance*, T. VI (1958–1963), pp. 287–340.

6. Erasmus considers clothes as an extension of the body. "Vestis quodàmodo corporis corpus est, et ex hac quoque licet habitum animi conicere" (B.3). Arbeau writes in the same vein, "quand vous danserez en compagnie ne baissez point la teste pour contrerooler vos pas et veoir si vous dansez bien" (63v).

7. It is important to note that virtue in courtesy books is "defined" in two ways. It may be defined tautologically as techniques for the production of its appearance. The technical term for virtue in both civility and dance is measure. Virtue may also be defined negatively as the avoidance of its contrary. This definition is equally circular. In this case again, being virtuous and acting appropriately are one and the same, or, as Cicero stated, "quod decet honestum est, et, quod honestum est, decet." *De Officiis* (Cambridge: Harvard University Press, 1975), I XXVII (94), p. 96.

8. I.G.G.D.L.L.:R, *Traicte' de la Phisionomie, c'est a dire, la science de cognoistre le naturel et les complexions des personnes* (Paris: chez Michel Daniel, 1619), p. 5.

9. See *Sir Walter Ralegh, The Renaissance Man and His Roles* (New Haven and Lon-don: Yale University Press, 1973) for a discussion of the relationship of "individual self fashioning" to the roles which society imposes on Renaissance man (especially pp. 33–40).

10. This physical dynamic is essential to the aesthetics of Renaissance dance. See my "The Notion of *Fantasmata* in Fifteenth-Century Italian Dance Treatises," forthcoming in *Dance Research Annual* XVII.

11. I am relying here solely on Arbeau's description of the basse danse. The limita-tions of this paper do not permit a detailed comparison of different states of the basse danse. Moreover, as Ingrid Brainard points out, the step combination of the Italian and Burgundian basse danse of the fifteenth century "is still valid in the sixteenth-century dance books by Antonius de Arena, Thoinot Arbeau and others..." op. cit., p. 66.

12. Michel Foucault has identified two points of view on madness in the Renaissance. One is the tragic experience of madness of which dancing as a delirium of perpetual motion would be an example. The second kind of representation of madness is a critical and moral one in which madness is the disorder of vanity and vainglory. See *Histoire de la Folie à l'âge classique* (Paris: Gallimard, 1972), pp. 13–55.

13. Michel de Montaigne, *Essais* (Paris: Garnier, 1962), III, XIII, p. 526. This work will henceforth be referred to as *M*.

14. Quintilian, *The Institutio Oratoria of Quintilian* (Cambridge: Harvard Univer-sity Press, 1969), XI, III (68), p. 280.

15. Raymond Bayer, *l'Esthétique de la Grâce* (Paris: Alcan, 1933), p. 209. This work will henceforth be referred to as *B*.

16. Pierre Legendre, *La Passion d'être un Autre. Etude pour la Danse* (Paris: Seuil, 1978), p. 55.

17. Pierre Charron, *De la Sagesse* (1601; rpt. Geneva: Slatkine Reprints, 1968), I, VI, pp. 32-33. This work will henceforth be referred to as *S*.

18. I address myself to this question in "The Role of Action in Stefano Guazzo's Theory of Conversation," forthcoming in *Communication and Cognition*. Proceedings of the Colloquium "Music, Reason and Emotion" (Ghent: 1984).

Othello's *Foul Generic Thoughts and Methods*

TIMOTHY MURRAY

I would like to preface my discussion of *Othello*'s foul generic thoughts and methods with a brief consideration of the sociological importance of genre. In "Shakespeare and the Kinds of Drama," Stephen Orgel suggests that genre was an important method of identity formation in Renaissance England. He writes that "the genres for such Renaissance critics [as Scaliger and Sidney] were not sets of rules but classifications, ways of organizing our knowledge of the past so that we may understand our relation to it and locate its virtues in ourselves. The ancient world, says Scaliger's *Poetics*, is not a world of monuments. It is real and recoverable, and the process of creation is also a process of re-creation."[1] And Barbara Lewalski, in her foreword to Rosalie Colie's *The Resources of Kind: Genre Theory in the Renaissance*, writes that "Miss Colie persuades her audience to acknowledge their constant and inevitable dependence upon genre (kind) for any apprehension of reality in life as in literature, and then displays how genre functions as a mode of communication — a set of recognized frames and fixes upon the world. In this perspective genre is not only a matter of literary convention ... but also a myth or metaphor for man's vision of truth."[2] Generic thought of the Renaissance is thus a method of recovering and classifying past thoughts and virtues — it is a tool for an archeology of knowledge not to be revered as monumental, but to be re-formed, re-cast, and re-created in the text.

Yet we now might want to question the merits of such an archeology: is its knowledge real and recoverable — mimetic — as our Renaissance forefathers so wanted to believe, or is it only figural and representable, always lamenting the process of re-presentation as one prefigured by the limita-tions of re-creation, prefigured by signs of loss? And what about the relation of gender to genre? Does genre's function as the myth of "man's vision of truth" mean the loss of woman?

Thomas Rymer probably would have suggested that these questions pertain not to generic method, the value of genre, but to generic classification, the attribution of genre. In his diatribe against *Othello*, for example, Rymer criticizes Shakespeare for playing free and loose with the generic purity of tragedy. Rymer focuses less on the tragic flaw *of the hero* than on the flaws *of the play's action*. He writes that "the foundation of the play must be concluded to be monstrous; and the constitution, all over, to be most rank, 'foul disproportion, thoughts unnatural.' Which instead of moving pity, or any passion tragical and reasonable, can produce nothing but horror and aversion, and what is odious and grievous to an audience."[3] In Rymer's view, the foundation of *Othello*, the structural core of the play, is an aberration of tragedy because it shows more horror than pity. According to such logic, moreover, this aberration permeates the reception of the play as well as its production. Any performance of *Othello* would enact the re-creation of thoughts unnatural in the minds of the audience.

Rymer's criticism of *Othello* for not having a therapeutic effect on its audience may say more about certain Renaissance notions of theater — as a genre — than about this particular play's failure. In the following pages, I would like to discuss how a study of *Othello*, in view of genre as well as gender — what I will call "generic" considerations — shows Rymer's horror and aversion to be endemic to particular Renaissance concepts of theater, both as systems of classification and as methods of pedagogy, which is to say, as forms of identity formation.

The threat of mimesis, especially its threat to a particular woman, is the focus of the first act of *Othello*. Othello attributes the source of Desdemona's love to his storytelling which he confesses to have had the effect of a love potion on Desdemona. To Brabantio, moreover, Desdemona's seduction can mean only disproportion and thoughts unnatural:

>   she, in spite of nature,
> Of yeers, of country, of credit, everything
> To fall in love with what she feared to look on!
>   (I.iii.96–98)

Here Brabantio relates his loss of Desdemona to her subliminal overcoming of all civilizing codes, to her confused feminine desire for a black Moor whose appeal seems to lie less in the form of his fearful image than in the subconscious magic of his fantastic tales. Othello defends himself, however, by citing the force of Desdemona's own theatrical spectacle:

> These things to hear
> Would Desdemona seriously incline;
> But still the house affairs would draw her thence;
> Which ever as she could with haste dispatch,
> She'd come again, and with a greedy ear
> Devour up my discourse. Which I observing
> Took once a pliant hour, and found good means
> To draw from her a prayer of earnest heart
> That I would all my pilgrimage dilate,
> Whereof by parcels she had something heard,
> But not intentively. I did consent,
> And often did beguile of her tears
> When I did speak of some distressful stroke
> That my youth suffered. My story being done,
> She gave me for my pains a world of kisses.
> She swore in faith 'twas strange, 'twas passing strange;
> 'Twas pitiful, 'twas wondrous pitiful
> She wished she had not heard it; yet she wished
> That heaven had made her such a man. She thanked me,
> And bade me, if I had a friend that loved her,
> I should but teach him how to tell my story,
> And that would woo her. Upon this hint I spake.
>
> (I.iii.144–65)

In Othello's mind, his story elicits a chain of responses from Desdemona that generates a theatrical performance of its own. The image of Desdemona and her greedy ear entices him into a repeat performance of the details of his wanderings. Desdemona's subsequent caresses (or Quarto "sighs") bearing both maternal and sexual warmth along with her wily wish that heaven had made her such a man comprise Othello's proof that he was not the sole performer on this stage of love. Her suddenly inconstant behavior, produced by the sight and story of Othello, is cited in the play by her husband, her father, and Iago as the ocular proof of her feminine capriciousness. Still underlying the patriarchal mistrust of Desdemona is not only the public belief in her inconstancy as a female but also, and perhaps most importantly, the boldness of her own theatrical performance in the wake of the Moor's storytelling. The source of male fear, then, might be said to be the power of mimesis: Desdemona's seduction of her desirous beholders.

This fear was prevalent in Renaissance England. Theater, as a generic institution symbolic of beholding and cultural differentiation, was shunned by some as the source of social mimetic impurity giving rise to "fears of mixture and disrupted male identity."[4] Tracts documenting the paternal fear of public theater describe theatrical beholding in terms virtually

synonymous with Brabantio's and Othello's accounts of the visual seduc-
tiveness of Desdemona. To cite one example, William Rankins writes of
theater as a visual

> labyrinth where lodged these monstrous minotaures, had many winds
> and *turnes fit for a mind* (as they terme it) *Male*content, to walke never
> content: wherein manie things able to intice a pleasant eye to beholde
> or an open eare to delight.... I shall tell you of things *strange* to con-
> sider, but more *strange* to behold, no less true than *strange*, yet not so
> *strange* as damnable.[5]

What is strange, turning, and *male*content in *Othello* is the operation of spectatorship. Desdemona's response to what " 'twas strange, 'twas passing
strange" results in Othello's perception of her as the personification of
theatricality:

> You did wish that I would make her turn.
> Sir, she can turn, and turn, and yet go on
> And turn again.
>
> (IV.i.252–54)

Desdemona's early visual doting on Othello even turns back on the Moor.
His inconstant behavior results from what he sees as his wife's theatrical
feigning. Othello himself personifies by his seizure, his impassioned actions, and his erratic turnings the imitation of the theatrical inconstancy
he so fears. His loss of self-control in the face of the theatrical Other causes
Othello to commit thoughts and deeds exemplifying the antitheatrical fears
of dramatic mimesis. His desire for spectacle and the contagion of his
beholding result in the dissolution of the self, leadership, and hierarchical
status.

The critics of the public stage condemned the generic attraction and imitation of theatrical storytelling for its unconscious force. Stephen Gosson
writes that "those impressions of mind are secretly conveyed to the gazers,
which the players do counterfeit on the stage ... the expressing of vice by
imitation brings us by the shadows, to the substance of the same."[6]
William Prynne identifies this mimetic substance as the "execrable precedents
of ancient, of moderne Play-poets, and Players witnesse, who have been
so deeply plunged in this abominable wickednesse, which my Inke is not
black enough to discypher."[7] To a certain extent, the feared blackness of
Othello, also that of "the black and witty" Desdemona, is a metaphor of theater.

The horror of Othello, in this context, lies not so much in the generic
impurity of the tragic hero or action as in the threat of theater's societal
black death, "by meanes of which," complains Prynne, "both Governours,
Government, Religion, and Devotion are brought into contempt."[8] To
reconsider the archeological significance of *Othello*, I would ask us to ques-

tion what it means for the play's generic structures to be, as Lewalski would have them, "a metaphor for man's vision of truth." Although *The Moor of Venice* concerns man's vision, the play hints at the blackness of truth, not its virtue.

The antitheatrical writers thought that theatrical blackness infects morals as well as actions. Moreover, because the opponents of theater considered women's morals to be the most susceptible to the theatrical blemish, writings against theater worked to conflate notions of gender with the genre of theater. The fundamental antitheatrical argument calls to mind Desdemona's purported inability to shun mimesis:

> ... those Buxsome and Bountifull Lasses ... usually were enamoured on the persons of the younger sorts of Actors for the good cloaths they wore upon the Stage, beleeving them realy to be the persons they did only represent.[9]

The antitheatrical prejudice held that women were less capable than men of distinguishing between a theatrical sign and its counterfeited signified. To a female beholder, the argument goes, parts and titles manifest their bearers rightly. This antitheatrical assumption was also an archeological notion. Wouldn't women necessarily be susceptible to fictional princes and lords because of their social conditioning and "subjection to the male conscience"?[10] The antitheatrical certainty of women's trust in mimesis stems from the patriarchal training of women to believe in the signs of patriarchy and to live as the signs of men. Women were (and still are) encouraged to efface themselves for the potency of their significational function as representations of their men. This adage of woman as a mirror of patriarchy is pronounced clearly by Othello in his plea to the Duke:

> I crave fit disposition for my wife,
> Due reference of place, and exhibition,
> With such accommodation and besort
> As levels with her breeding.
>
> (I.iii.233-36)

Like Caesar in *Antony and Cleopatra*, Othello understands a woman's exhibition to be part and parcel of patriarchal place and breeding. Her disposition is a sign of the potency of her father's or husband's place and exhibition.

Disposition, I might add, here suggests moral comportment as well as social standing. Brabantio's charge that Desdemona has sullied herself by denigrating his name foreshadows the source of jealousy in the play. Cassio's plaint to Desdemona provokes her to perform a name other than Othello's. She promises to

> perform it
> To the last article. My lord shall never rest;
> I'll watch him tame and talk him out of patience;
> His bed shall seem a school, his board a shrift;
> I'll intermingle everything he does
> With Cassio's suit. Therefore be merry, Cassio,
> For thy solicitor shall rather die
> Than give thy cause away.
>
>   (III.iii.21–28)

Othello feels that Desdemona's significational switch as Cassio's mouthpiece levels both her breeding and his due reference of place — his bed becomes a school and his board a shrift! Indeed, Desdemona talks Othello out of patience. Her method produces his madness.

Othello's jealousy stems from his failure to accept the fluidity of what we now might call "levelling" signification. Woman is, as Iago would say, *but a sign* capable of operating simultaneously on multiple levels of representation (including her own). Such inconstant signification levels the mimetic function of a fixed hierarchy of signs. As Iago explains, "A slipper and subtle knave, a finder / of occasion, that has an eye can stamp and counterfeit / advantages, though true advantage never present itself" (II.i.241–43). Such a realistic approach to representation naturally undermines the Venetian faith in a rigid order of patriarchal hierarchy in which signs always present their true advantage.

The male anxiety caused by this reality may explain, at least partially, the Renaissance mistrust of female spectatorship, of women's possible acknowledgment of sign systems that demystify patriarchal mimesis. Consider Desdemona's method in receiving Othello's threatening story of the handkerchief. Confronted with Othello's familial memory of the magical webbing, Desdemona first deflects the memory with rhetorical questions: "Is't possible?" "Indeed, Is't true?" (III.iv.68,75). She then counters the Moor's passion with a celebrated challenge marking the methodological gap between them, "Why do you speak so startingly and rash?" (III.iv.79). Finally, Desdemona drives her husband mad by countering his demand for optical proof (his mimetic bias) with a peculiar and idiosyncratic turnabout. "This is a trick to put me from my suit" (III.iv.88). Here the handkerchief, like Othello's bed, becomes a double sign of the husband and the lieutenant. Practised in her method, Desdemona excels at reordering fixed sign systems to attain her personal goals.

The difference between Othello's and Desdemona's methods may be the fundamental generic distinction of the play. Whereas Othello habitually restricts himself to universals and generalizations, especially in his representations of women, Desdemona fragments and reorders signification; whereas

Othello thinks through magic and passion, Desdemona is given to argumentative lucidity and logical discourse. Her flexible reading of the handkerchief is one of many examples of her method.

Throughout the drama, Desdemona displays an alertness to the play of language by vigilantly reading and rereading signs, by interpreting events for her own understanding and for the calm of her lodging. In Act 3, scene 4, she spars with the punning clown and counters his nonsense with a demand for the discovery of meaning ("can anything be made of this?"). In Act 3, scene 3, she rationally dismisses Othello's emotional "pain upon my forehead" by explaining: "Why, that's with watching; 'twill away again." Their different reactions to theatrical puzzles, moreover, are most dramatically displayed in Act 4's bedroom scene. In response to Othello's whimpering cries of "your mystery, your mystery," Desdemona seeks the signification of his declaration:

> Upon my knee, what doth your speech import?
> I understand a fury in your words.
>
> (IV.ii.31–32)

Desdemona demonstrates her flexibility with language by recognizing speech as a performative sign of the locutor's behavior, as well as speech as the agent of words. While Othello acts out the passion of his words, Desdemona tries to reorder his performance into controllable discourse.

Still, we need to be more precise about the *genderic* significance of Desdemona's sensitivity to method. What about Iago's excellence at significational seeming? And where does Desdemona as a female worker of words stand in relation to Iago? Like the ancient, Desdemona uses words counter to her own meaning, "I do beguile / the thing I am by seeming otherwise" (II.i.120–21). But Desdemona out*man*euvers Iago in the *man*ipulation of method for self-discovery. In Act 2, scene i, her seeming packs a strong genderic wallop. She humorously dismisses Iago's jokes degrading women as inaccurate, "O heavy ignorance. Thou praisest the / worst best" — 'O most lame and impotent conclusion. Do not learn of him, Emilia, though he be thy husband." Differentiating between wives and husbands, Desdemona emphasizes another genderic difference in the play. To Iago, his humorous maxims contain, no doubt, much ironic truth. The Moor's wife, however, reclassifies the maxims (a genre of truth) into "old fond paradoxes to make fools laugh i' th' alehouse." This testy put down is more than evidence of generic mixture in the play (from tragedy and comedy to maxim and paradoxical proverb). It suggests the generic implications of the play's archeological methods. Desdemona implies that sexist maxims — or any generic models framing clearly definable truths — are impotent and archaic, more appropriate for an old man's alehouse than for a theater sensitive to genderic signification.

Yet, the fraternal bond of the alehouse scores the tragic blow in *Othello*. Othello suspects Desdemona, not Iago, of being seemy. As a woman, Desdemona is especially susceptible to the antitheatrical prejudice against feminine self-fashioning, sexual frankness, and the re-presentation of words. As Iago describes woman, her words and actions are always duplicitous:

> You are pictures out of door,
> Bells in your parlors, wildcats in your kitchens,
> Saints in your injuries, devils being offended,
> Players in your housewifery, and housewives in your beds.
>
> (II.i.109)

Ironically, Desdemona's method enacts Iago's words. She does claim to go to bed for work ("His bed shall seem a school"). In the thoughts of Othello, moreover, she rises for play ("my wife is fair, feeds well, loves company, / Is free of speech, sings, plays and dances" [III.iii.184–85]). Othello readily confuses Desdemona's generic method with his notion of her gender. When she is working he thinks that she is playing.

In her unique attempt to reorder the linguistic play of her house, Desdemona commits the representational actions of a whore. In Act 2, scene 3, she mixes the scene of her bed with that of the public hall by appearing in her night clothes to inquire, "what is the matter, dear." Also, exactly like Bianca, she leaves her private quarters to seek "where Lieutenant Cassio lies." Conversely, when Desdemona is not in public quarters, men other than her husband seem to have relatively easy access to her private space. Although her meetings with Iago and Cassio in private places in the Citadel are innocent enough in the minds of the players, they could turn abnormal in the eyes of the beholder. Merely the sight of Cassio leaving Desdemona's side is enough to spark confused suspicion in Othello.

Desdemona's generic fate is to have her "body and beauty," her "well-painted passions," interpreted with suspicion by the cultural codes of man. The performative behavior of Desdemona meets readily with the same suspicion that theater's opponents expressed for actors dressed in women's array. In Prynne's words:

> this putting on of woman's array must needs be sinfull, yea abominable; "because it not onely excites many adulterous filthy lusts, both in the Actors and Spectators; and drawes them on both to contemplative and actuall lewdnesse ..." but likewise "instigates them to self-pollution ... and to that unnaturall sodomiticall sinne of uncleanesse.[11]

Similarly, to Othello, Desdemona's self-discovery is their self-pollution. "O thou weed, / Who art so lovely fair, and smells't so sweet, / That the senses ache at thee, would though hadst never / been born!" (IV.ii.66–68). Othello's quick condemnation of what he beholds as Desdemona's "uncleaneness," moreover, is so similar to the antitheatrical censure of theater for being feminine that he confuses Desdemona's generic method with his belief in her genderic fickleness. In one of the most shocking moments of the play, Othello spurns Desdemona with revealing words: "keep it as a cistern for foul toads / to knot and gender in turn thy complexion" (IV.ii.60–61). Being obsessed with Desdemona's gendering, Othello is capable only of foul thoughts in hearing her plea as the "solicitor" of Cassio's favors.

Ironically, in her strongest statement of self-defense, Desdemona utters language that almost ensures the possibility of her beholders' confusion of generic method with genderic behavior. When relying on her powers of persuasion during the moving bedroom scene with Iago in Act 4, Desdemona states in her defense: "I cannot say 'whore.' / It does abhor me now I speak the word" (IV.ii.160–61). Just as Desdemona saw Othello's passion acted out through his words, her misogynous beholders hear her admit her speech (ab-hor) to be the performance of the word (whore) which she just denied being able to utter. This paradox is the horror of *Othello* felt so keenly by Thomas Rymer, who complains that "no woman bred out of a pigsty could talk so meanly."[12]

Such aversion to Desdemona's speech needs to be understood in a broad generic sense — archeologically as well as tragically. Perhaps we should think of Desdemona as a female scapegoat who is sacrificed by an antitheatrical and misogynous society for being a visible woman exercising flexible and rational methods contrary to the fearful norms of patriarchy. But, in conclusion, permit me to extend Rymer's plaint of "foul disproportion." Our ways of generic classification can seduce us into critically satisfying assertions like Edward A. Snow's thesis that "the tragedy of the play ... is the inability of Desdemona to escape or triumph over restraints and Oedipal prohibitions that domesticate women to the conventional order of things."[13] Still, any summary of the play's disproportion as the return of woman to the conventional order of things loads the tragedy on only *one* bed, which perspective signals, in Lewalski's terms, "man's vision of truth."

There remains at the conclusion of the play a concealed but radical woman's vision of things, maintained by Bianca, the true whore missing from the tragic loading of the bed. The traces of this vision derive from Bianca's public disclaimer of the patriarchal social structure (in comparison with Emilia's compromised woman-to-woman disclaimer, which has made her a feminist hero to some critics). In Act 4, scene 1, Bianca refuses Cassio's demand to take out the work in the handkerchief and issues him an ultimatum — that he visit *her* on *her* terms or have no woman at all. Consider the generic implications of Bianca's threat. She changes the scene of whoredom (of "gendering") from her public displays in the streets to the discovery of her own place and space. Her subjective existence, moreover, is no longer contingent on her penetration and occupation by phallic heroes. She pronounces her willingness to live separately, if need be, from the significational and performative space of her white knight Cassio. Bianca is the *only* woman in the play to proclaim openly and publicly her indifference to patriarchal beds and the magnetic webbing of heroic representation. As suggested by her easy show of paleness in regarding Cassio's wound, she may even have relaxed the painting of her face, the male sign of her previous public self. The "gastness of her eye" suggests Bianca's acknowledging horror of phallic aggression in the streets, of which she has been a cheap whorish victim.

Herein lies the generic disproportion of *Othello*. Bianca's discovery of a female life "as honest" to her self makes her readily suspected of performing violence on her male counterpart. Iago is able to capitalize on her new feminism by associating it with the actor's ability to change faces, to practice "hypocrisie." But Bianca's generic separatism is more threatening to Venice than is her suspicion as an actress. Her assertion of ontological Otherness threatens the patriarchal dependence on her presence as an engine for social definition through generic differentiation. Bianca no longer honors the signs of either whore or virgin. She will not be bought, conquered, or penetrated for some hero's assertion of self.

But, tragically, Bianca's indifference to man's vision of truth and subjectivity provokes a classic response. In the play, the male reaction displaces Bianca nominally and generically from her rightful home to their legal confines. Iago's final command to Bianca, "I charge you go with me" once again forces her to lie in the bed of patriarchy. In another context, that of the play's critical reception, Shakespeare's literary solicitors either forget Bianca or cite her as yet another example of the tragic whore. In essence, Bianca stands out in the play as an index and obscure prologue to the history of foul generic thoughts.

Notes

1. Stephen Orgel, "Shakespeare and the Kinds of Drama," *Critical Inquiry*, 6 (1979), 115.

2. Rosalie L. Colie, *The Resources of Kind: Genre-Theory in the Renaissance*, ed. Barbara K. Lewalski (Berkeley: University of California Press, 1973).

3. Thomas Rymer, "A Short View of Tragedy," in Alvin Kernan's edition of *Othello* (New York: Signet, 1963), p. 194.

4. David Leverenz, "Why Did Puritans Hate Stage Plays," *The Language of Puritan Feeling: An Exploration in Literature, Psychology, and Social History* (New Brunswick: Rutgers University Press, 1980), p. 35.

5. William Rankins, *A Mirror of Monsters* (London: Printed for I.C. for T.H., 1587), F3, sig Biv, my emphasis.

6. Stephen Gosson, *Playes Confuted in Five Actions*, reprinted in Arthur F. Kinney, *Markets of Bawdrie: The Dramatic Criticism of Stephen Gosson* (Salzburg: Institut für Englische Sprache und Literatur, Universität Salzburg, 1974), pp. 192–93.

7. William Prynne, *Histriomastix* (London: Printed by E.A. & W.I. for Michael Sparke, n.d.), p. 211.

8. Ibid., p. 124.

9. *The Actor's Remonstrance or Complaint for the Silencing of their Profession, and Banishment from their Severall Play houses* (London: Printed for Edw. Nickson, 1643), p. 6.

10. Juliet Dusinberre, *Shakespeare and the Nature of Women* (London: MacMillan, 1975), p. 93.

11. Prynne, p. 208.

12. Rymer, p. 198.

13. Edward A. Snow, "Sexual Anxiety and the Male Order of Things in *Othello*," *English Literary Renaissance*, 10, No. 3 (Autumn 1980), p. 407.

The Last Judgment as Pageant Setting
For Communal Law and Order
In Late Medieval Italy*

SAMUEL Y. EDGERTON, JR.

T he great Dutch historian, Johan Huizinga, observed that an outstanding characteristic of the "Waning Middle Ages" in Western Europe was the propensity of Christian peoples to convert every political idea, no matter how abstract, into a pictorial image. Perhaps never before or since the fourteenth, fifteenth, and sixteenth centuries, has the popular conceptualization of every-day social values and moral issues been so related to the sense of sight, or better, dependent on the ability to translate what one sees in the visual world into symbolic personifications and hierarchical pictorial arrangements in the imagination.

This deeply-imbedded Christian association of pictorial imagery with the divinely revealed lessons of sin and salvation was effective right from the beginning for converting the pagan barbarians and bringing order to European peoples after the fall of the Roman Empire. Again, during the slow evolution of Western Civilization from agrarian / feudal to mercantile / urban, the use of pictorial imagery proved just as effective in establishing the very notion of *civitas*, by setting before peoples' eyes a vivid comparison between their own earthly cities and the vision of the City of God in heaven. Indeed, just as compelling as the necessity for worldly security and economic opportunity among the people of the Middle Ages, was the need to believe that the city of man on earth could become a New Jerusalem where human beings might safely work for heavenly redemption. For this reason especially, the authorities in the budding medieval cities sought to link the notion of civic law and order on earth to the divine promise of hell or heaven in the hereafter.

For the Christian faithful in the Middle Ages, no picture was more indelibly impressed upon the imagination, nor more awesome, than that of the *Last Judgment*. It was most vividly imaged, even before artists reckoned with it, in the Scriptural words of the apostles Matthew and John. John's spectacular picture of the apocalypse, as recorded in the Book of Revelation, that is, of Jesus seated on an emblazoned throne, surrounded by the four "living creatures" amongst psychedelic colors and terrible sounds, was at first the more intriguing to artists. However, by the thirteenth century, John's mystical vision gave way to Matthew's more rational representation of Jesus seated simply as king and judge, with Mankind on trial as if in a court of law; the innocent souls at his right hand admitted to heaven; the guilty souls at his left condemned to hell (Matthew 25: 31–46):

> When the Son of Man shall ... sit upon the throne in all his glory. And before him shall be gathered all nations. And he shall separate them from one another as the shepherd divideth his sheep from his goats. And he shall set the sheep on his right hand, but the goats on his left. Then shall the King say unto them on his right hand, Come ye blessed of my father, inherit the Kingdom prepared for you from the foundation of the world. ... Then shall he say to them on the left hand, depart from me ye cursed, into the everlasting fire prepared for the devil and his angels.

The reason for this shift in emphasis is not hard to understand. With the increase of urbanized society, the need for legal institutions also grew, and especially divine legitimation of these institutions. Thus, the vision of the Last Judgment was more and more transformed into the image of a supreme judicial court, a kind of heavenly finale to the legal proceedings daily carried on by the earthly judges in the city halls of the great urban centers of Europe, as shown in the early sixteenth-century woodcut in figure 1, from Jean Milles de Souvigny's *Praxis criminis persequendi*, Paris, 1541, a French treatise on criminal law.[1] In fact, Jan van Eyck or some Flemish painter close to him surely made this association in a splendid panel now in the Prado, Madrid, where God the Father is seated on an elaborate Gothic throne. Beside Him, as "associate justices", are the Virgin Mary and St. John the Evangelist. Before God, standing outside the "bar" just as would have been constructed in any fifteenth-century European courtroom, are two groups of litigants, representing the indicted souls of all Mankind, receiving their verdicts just like defendants in an earthly trial.

This new *Last Judgment* iconography was already well-established in the portal sculpture of many of the great urban Gothic cathedrals in France by the mid-thirteenth century. In Italy, it made its appearance most dramatically in the ca. 1306 fresco of Giotto, for the interior entrance wall of the Arena Chapel in Padua. However, I illustrate another, later *Last*

Fig. 1. *Anonymous French woodcut artist,* A Sixteenth-Century Criminal Court; *from Jean Milles de Souvigny,* Praxis criminis persequendi..., *Paris, 1541, fol. 56r.*

Fig. 2. Fra Angelico, The Last Judgment, painted wood panel, ca. 1440, San Marco Museum, Florence; Photo courtesy of Alinari-Art Resource.

Judgment by Fra Angelico, a much smaller wooden panel of ca. 1440 now in the Museo San Marco in Florence (figure 2). In both of these we may briefly review the by-now standard elements of what I call the *juridical*, as differing from the *apocalyptic* Last Judgment.

First, we see Christ in the center and seated in the dominating position. Apostles, saints, elders, and angels are grouped symmetrically below and at either side of the Saviour. At Jesus's feet two angels trumpet up the dead from their tombs, calling for their souls to appear before the throne of God to be judged. At Jesus's right hand, depicted palm up, the saved souls dressed in gleaming white ascend into paradise. At His left, shown palm down, the damned are dragged screaming into a darkened hell. It is interesting how Fra Angelico updated the traditional, hierarchical composition with the application of linear perspective without changing any of the essential elements of Matthew's gospel description. Furthermore, in Fra Angelico's painting, we see how the elected souls, to the Saviour's right, advance through a lovely, flowering meadow and enter heaven through a lofty gate in a crenelated wall. This gate and wall look remarkably similar to the actual gates and walls of Quattrocento Florence. In other words, the painter wanted to make a visual association in the viewer's imagination between the secular city on earth, ever aspiring to keep its citizens free of sin, and the New Jerusalem, the heavenly home of the successfully saved. Fra Angelico, we know, was a Dominican monk living in the convent of San Marco in Florence. His mentor and prior of San Marco at that time was Fra Antonino Pierozzi, better known as St. Antonine since his canonization in the sixteenth century. St. Antonine dedicated himself to improving the morals of his fellow-Florentines, and he often attacked from his pulpit the vainglory of women, especially if they bleached their hair, or let it hang long so as to tempt and cause evil thoughts in men.[2] We may note that on the heavenly side of the *Last Judgment*, all the women have their hair either neatly braided or their heads covered, while on the hell side, several of the damned women wear their long blond tresses loose. In two instances black demons even pull the women into hell by grabbing their hair.

Between the Trecento and Cinquecento in Christian Europe, juridical Last Judgment iconography was so fixed in the popular imagination that artists could take its composition for granted as a convenient form for expressing pictorially all sorts of political messages. For example, after the fall of the Duke of Athens's tyrannous government in Florence in 1343, an artist in the circle of Taddeo Gaddi painted a fresco showing St. Anne, on whose feast day the Duke was overthrown, as a gigantic figure enthroned like Christ the Judge in the center. Beside her is a model of the Palazzo Vecchio, the chief government building in Florence which the Duke had usurped and from which he was finally driven. At her favored right, St. Anne restores the colors to the people and priors of Florence, while with her left hand, turned palm down again, she dismisses the evil Duke, who skulks away amid the shattered symbols of his disgraced office.

More than a century later, the painter Sandro Botticelli represented still another Florentine political crisis in the format reminding of the *Last Judgment*, this time the spiritual upheaval caused by Savonarola. This abraded picture now in the Fogg Museum at Harvard, was painted by Botticelli about 1495, during the time that the charismatic Dominican preacher was driving Florence into a puritanic theocracy. The painter showed Christ Crucified with the penitent Magdalene at the foot of the cross to His right. Also at Jesus's right he showed the unmistakable skyline of the city of Florence. Further to His right, sits God the Father, the source of light for the whole scene. At Jesus's other hand, however, the entire sky is filled with a gigantic pall of black smoke, in the midst of which demons and flaming torches fall upon the earth. On the ground below still at His left, an avenging angel strikes a miniature lion, the symbolic *marzocco* or emblem of the city of Florence. Botticelli's right-left pictorial sermon is clear: Florence can only be saved from damnation through public atonement of her citizens, just as Mary Magdalene begged for mercy at the foot of the cross. Savonarola's promise that Florence could then become New Jerusalem is signified by the silver lining to all the dark clouds which threaten the city to the Saviour's left.

Perhaps the earliest application of the *Last Judgment* composition to the cause of Italian republicanism was made by Giotto in a now-lost fresco painted in the Palace of the Podestà (the later Bargello) in Florence about 1325.[3] The artist apparently conceived the idea of personifying the political abstraction "communal good," combining the appearance of Christ and secular ruler. The image proved popular, and we have a more elaborated version of Giotto's idea extant on the walls of the Palazzo Pubblico or city hall of Siena, the well-known *Allegory of Good Government* painted by Ambrogio Lorenzetti in the late 1330s (figure 3). While many modern scholars, especially Nicolai Rubinstein, have analyzed this intriguing fresco, and have identified all the individual figures and the meaning of its allegory, no one so far has pointed out how neatly this painting takes propaganda advantage of its artistic *composition*.[4] Let us examine this design, from the viewpoint of a contemporary Trecento observer, in whose imagination the imprint of the Last Judgment was already indelibly imbedded. First, we notice that the principal and largest figure, the personified Good Government seated like a *Maiestas Domini* among the colors and emblems of Siena, is off-center to the viewer's right. The reason for this asymmetric emphasis would have been perfectly comprehensible to the Trecento viewer; the artist simply wanted to reserve more space to the right hand of Good Government and less to his left, in other words, to stress the beneficent aspects of Good Government's rule as allegorized in the figures to his right, and

Fig. 3. Ambrogio Lorenzetti, Allegory of Good Government, *fresco, ca. 1337, Sala dei Nove, Palazzo Pubblico, Siena.*

to add, literally, a more sinister note to the less pleasant aspects of Good Government's rule at his left. Seated on both sides of Good Government like the apostles in a standard *Last Judgment*, Ambrogio painted female personifications of six cardinal Virtues; or rather, he depicted the five usual Virtues: Fortitude, Prudence, Magnanimity, Temperance, and Justice, then adding an unusual figure of Peace and an extra figure of Justice. Justice in fact is at each end of the composition, both to the right and left of Good Government. At Good Government's right her figure looms larger than any other save that of Good Government himself. This grand female presides over her symbolic scales (which are actually held by Wisdom above Justice's head). They are perfectly balanced because she holds the pans at equal levels with her hands. In these pans are other little allegorical figures representing the Aristotelian-Thomistic notions of Distributive and Commutative Justice. Below this ensemble sits another female figure labeled Concordia who holds a rope, one end of which hangs from Justice's scales and the other extends to the right hand of Good Government, passing through the hands of a group of men representing the honest burghers of Siena. The rope, of course, is a pictorial pun on the word *concordia*; the good men "with the rope" — *con corda* — thus prosper in harmony with Sienese Good Government. Exactly half-way between Justice and Good Government to the latter's right reclines the conspicuous figure of Peace. She is almost in the center of the whole fresco, and her emphasized position between Justice and Good Government surely was meant by the artist to indicate her importance, second only to that of Justice, as the chief virtue of good government. Turning our attention now to the narrowed left-hand side of Good Government, we see Justice's shrunken twin holding a sword which she props on a severed human head balanced on her knee. At her feet are a number of bound prisoners guarded by soldiers. The conspicuous rope which binds the prisoners' hands was probably intended to contrast with the rope of "concord," and thus to stand for just the opposite, or "discord." Justice on this side therefore represents the unpleasant but necessary function of Good Government to prosecute and punish criminals. Trecento viewers would have readily related the plight of the bound prisoners in this picture to that of damned souls in hell, in the same location in standard *Last Judgment* scenes.

In fact, so useful for the purposes of prosecuting criminals was the poignant imagery of the *Last Judgment*, that public court rooms were sometimes constructed architecturally to replicate its composition. In early sixteenth-century Pistoia near Florence, for example, the still extant podestà's court in the Palazzo Pretorio had a bench specifically reserved for defendants to sit on as they awaited trial and verdict. Significantly, it was placed to the left of the judges' podium. In this same respect, fifteenth-century artist Pedro Berruguete painted a series of panels on the *Life of St. Dominic*, now in the Prado. In one panel (figure 4), he depicted *St. Dominic Presiding over*

Fig. 4. Pedro Berruguete, Saint Dominic Presiding over an Auto-da-Fé, *painted wood panel, ca. 1480, Prado Museum, Madrid; photo courtesy of Alinari-Art Resource.*

an Auto-da-Fe. Here we see what was in all likelihood a true likeness of a fifteenth-century inquisitional court.[5] The painting shows an out-of-doors trial of heretics before the Saint who presides over his fellow judges according to the by-now familiar *Last Judgment* seating arrangement. What is even more significant, however, is that the guilty heretics are being punished, by garroting and burning, once more at the left-hand side of the judges. The artist has also depicted the poor defendants in this trial wearing yellow capes inscribed "condemned heretic," and foolscaps bearing images of devils. Yellow was a color often associated with deceit and cowardice, and real-life wrongdoers were frequently forced to wear such embarrassing clothing in public, especially the foolscap or *mitra*.

Trecento painters frequently borrowed from the imagery of local criminal prosecution in order to make their representations of the hell side of *Last Judgment* pictures more realistic and frightening. The Sienese artist Taddeo di Bartolo painted a particularly obscene version of the inferno inside the Duomo of San Gimignano, where he showed the devil defecating sinners from his anus. These appear, emerging from Satan's behind, naked and wearing only *mitres* on their heads inscribed with their sins, just as real-life miscreants in Siena or San Gimignano were often forced to parade through the streets also without clothes except for the identifying foolscap. Similarly, Giotto, in his Arena Chapel *Last Judgment* from the beginning of the fourteenth century, depicted a number of sinners in hell hanging, some with ropes around their necks as from the conventional gallows, and others more unconventionally. One man hangs by a rope attached to his teeth. Another woman is suspended by her own long blond hair. Two others, a man and a woman, hang upside-down; he by a rope tied to his penis, and she by a hook in her vagina. In the urban communes of medieval Italy, as everywhere else in Christian Europe, capital punishment by hanging was deemed more humiliating than decapitation, and it was therefore generally reserved for lower-class crimes and criminals. Giotto's message to his upper-class Scrovegni patrons was poignant. Hell knows no social distinctions; aristocratic sinners will be humiliated and degraded in the devil's pit no differently than the most vile denizens of the secular cities are regularly tortured and publicly executed under earthly criminal law.

In Florence, the building which most symbolized the criminal prosecution system at work was the Bargello (literally "home of the jailer"), the headquarters of one of the city's three police departments, where criminals were tried, tortured, jailed, and frequently executed.[6] This grim, fortress-like building stood as the antithesis to the Cathedral, for just as the latter edifice was filled with images of the good people of Florence, depicted in complimentary poses and ascending into heaven, so the Bargello walls were covered with effigies of the bad, often shown hanging ignominiously upside-down or in some other degrading pose. In fact, it was statutory law in the

SIGNIOR MIO
GIESV.CHRIS
TO ABI MISE
RICHORDIA
DELANIMA
MIA·

A vij ore di notte eimpiccato a le finestre del
Potesta ein sep oi r ura il di S. Maria maddalena·

Fig. 5.   Anonymous Italian artist, The Execution of Rinaldeschi, *painted wood
panel, ca. 1505, Stibbert Museum, Florence.*

city that any person defaulting on his debts and in contempt of court have
his likeness caricatured in such an insulting manner on the street facade
of the building. By being thus exposed in public, the culprit was made to
suffer not only *de facto* humiliation among his former friends and neighbors
but *de jure infamia*, an actual condition in law which deprived him of all
his former civil rights, even implying this same disgrace for all eternity in
hell.[7] Furthermore, in order to enhance and increase this visual association of the secular penal code with the eternal punishments of hell, the
municipal authorities began in the late Quattrocento to hang criminals directly out of the Bargello windows. Figure 5 is a detail from an anonymous
painting of the early Cinquecento, depicting the execution of one Antonio
di Giuseppe Rinaldeschi in 1501. Rinaldeschi was so sentenced for throw-
ing a piece of horse-dung at a painting of the Virgin Mary. Thus it was
especially appropriate that he, who had blasphemed a sacred image, have
his own image shamed, an "image for an image" as it were. Even though
Rinaldeschi came from a moderately noble family, his sin of wrath was

punished by his being hanged publicly from Florence's architectural symbol of hell on earth.[8]

The usual place of criminal execution in Florence, however, was, as in nearly every medieval city, outside the walls. This followed a very ancient custom once again reinforced by ubiquitous *Last Judgment* imagery. For just as sinners in hell were often depicted as the devil's excrement, so the Commune symbolically "defecated" its guilty criminals by expelling them from the city by way of a tortuous circuit through the street to the place of execution. Old maps of Florence show this site just to the east, near the Arno where the present-day Viale della Giovane Italia intersects with the Lungarno. Later, about 1530, the place of execution was moved to what is now the Piazza Beccaria where it functioned until 1786 when capital punishment was abolished in Florence, and the Piazza renamed for Italy's great enlightened penal reformer.

During its heyday, however, the old *Pratello della Giustizia*, as the place of execution was called, was the goal of a most melancholy journey which took the criminal several hours and kilometers around the streets of Florence from the Bargello, exposed to the jeering populace, and often *attanagliato sul carro*, that is, branded with red-hot pincers as he rode in the tumbril on the way to his death. Finally, the lugubrious cortege would enter a narrow street just behind Santa Croce, still aptly named the Via de'Malcontenti, and then out a gate in the urban walls known as the *Porta della Giustizia*. At this point the tumbril would halt for a moment of spiritual respite at a little chapel especially built just without the gate and a few meters away from the scaffold on the *Pratello*. This chapel belonged to the lay-confraternity of Santa Maria della Croce al Tempio, known as the "Black Brotherhood" because the *fratelli* by custom wore black cassocks and kept their faces completely covered under black pointed hoods. It was the Christian charity of these brothers that they accompany and comfort the condemned criminal during his final moments from the Bargello to the *Pratello*. Inside their chapel where they took the *afflitto*, the "afflicted" as the condemned was euphemistically called in the old records, there was an altarpiece before which the brothers knelt with their charge in order to offer up last prayers. The altarpiece contained a painting still extant, and it was done by no less than Fra Angelico. It is a large panel now housed in the San Marco Museum, but had been originally commissioned for the Tempio Confraternity sometime around 1440 as a devotional image to comfort condemned criminals. The subject shows Christ just taken down from the Cross, His lifeless body being lamented over by His mother Mary and a number of other saints. The whole scene takes place in a meadow just outside a city depicted with crenelated walls, looking uncommonly like Florence itself. Indeed, this similarity was very much intended. Fra Angelico wished to remind the poor *afflitto* that the Saviour too had suffered a fate like the one he was about to suffer, and just as Jesus died bravely and with decorum in order to save Mankind, so the criminal should meet his death on the gallows just as resolutely, in hopes that Jesus would be sympathetic, and at the Last Judgment might offer some mercy to his miserable, sin-stained soul.

Certainly, one of the most compelling notions in Christianity is that no matter how heinous the crime, or how deserving the criminal might be of his corporeal punishment, Jesus might still offer salvation to his soul precisely because of his physical suffering on the scaffold, which the criminal must accept as penance due for his crimes. This hope of redemption at the Last Judgment seat is what the brothers of Santa Maria della Croce al Tempio held out to the poor condemned as he awaited execution. By reassuring him of this possibility, they were able to reduce his terror and give him courage to face the hangman. Also, their ministrations helped educate the populace not only about the wages of sin, but in that most beautiful act of Christian charity according to the Gospel of St. Matthew: "When I was in prison, ye comforted me ... because ye have done this to the least of these my brethren, ye have done this unto me."

By the sixteenth century, however, the naive idea that the secular city could replicate on earth the City of God, was greeted with increasing cynicism. And nowhere did the old notion collapse more totally than in Florence. In 1530, the very pope in Rome, Clement VII, himself a Florentine, subjugated his native city with Spanish mercenary troops, thus ending forever the Florentine republic, with its futile Savonarolan dream of becoming a sin-free New Jerusalem. By no coincidence, Michelangelo Buonarroti, also a citizen of Florence, painted his own titanic *Last Judgment* in the Sistine Chapel in Rome not long after the republic's collapse. The artist, an ardent admirer of Savonarola, left his home in bitterness, never to return again. Indeed, Michelangelo's *Last Judgment* is one of the last grand representations of this subject, which began to lose popularity as a political vehicle in Italy during the sixteenth century. While Michelangelo's fresco still follows the traditional form of the juridical Judgment, its content, insofar as its political intention was concerned, is quite different from Fra Angelico's of a century earlier. In the latter, as well as in his *Lamentation* for the Tempio Brotherhood, Fra Angelico was expressing the notion that judgment and salvation in heaven were intimately connected with one's behavior on earth as institutionalized by the communal authorities. In Michelangelo's *Last Judgment*, on the other hand, there is not a single reference to any contemporary political institution. In fact, the artist depicted saints as well as sinners in the nude, implying that all souls before the Judgment Seat are completely free of the taboos and social pressures that constrained them in life. Michelangelo's *Last Judgment* is thus representative of the new reformation attitude toward heavenly redemp-

Fig. 6.   Michelangelo, Saint Bartholomew; detail from the Last Judgment, *fresco, ca. 1538, Sistine Chapel, Vatican City; Photo courtesy of Alinari-Art Resource.*

tion in the sixteenth century, that salvation was less a matter of being a good citizen of the community, even as prescribed by the Church, and more of individual soul-searching and direct communion with God. It has recently been demonstrated that Michelangelo's *Last Judgment* does not emphasize the damnation of all Mankind, as has often been claimed, but is actually a pathetic plea for Michelangelo's own individual soul.[9] This is evident when we understand the meaning of the flayed skin which the figure of St. Bartholomew holds in his hand to the *left* of Christ (figure 6). This is not Bartholomew's skin, since the nude saint quite obviously has his own intact. It represents, of course, the *artist's* skin, as is clear from the inclusion of his inimitable features on the flayed face. St. Bartholomew not only holds Michelangelo's skin to the left of Christ the Judge, but he dangles it menacingly over the yawning pit of hell, depicted with such *terribilità* below.

The meaning of Michelangelo's striking signature here derives from a popular story of the late Middle Ages, the moralized legend of the Persian king Cambyses who condemned a corrupt and unjust judge to be skinned alive. The son and successor to this judge was then made to sit on the judge's throne, covered by the skin of his father, as a constant reminder of the father's sin and the judge's duty to be ever just and righteous. This story was adapted and Christianized in the *Gesta romanorum*, a book of subjects for sermons written in the fourteenth century and subsequently published in numerous editions thereafter. The Christian lesson taught by this story was that the unjust judge's skin symbolized his sin, which, when removed, represented his expiation and redemption, and, quoting directly from the *Gesta romanorum*, "Christ not only gave his own skin for us in the seat of His Cross, but also His life."[10] Michelangelo's flayed skin thus too represents his sin which he offers for mortification in hell. By its figurative removal, he offers painful penance, as he begs for mercy at the Last Judgment throne.

The image of judge in association with anatomical flaying was widespread in early Christianity. A catacomb painting in Rome, for instance, shows Christ in the guise of a philosopher-surgeon presiding over the dissection of a human cadaver.[11] This tradition carried on in the Middle Ages in the imagery of both law and medicine. Another woodcut from the already mentioned, sixteenth-century *Praxis criminis persequendi* illustrates how autopsies in homicide cases be performed in open court before the judge. An arrangement very similar was also used in the medical schools for carrying out anatomy lessons, as represented on the title page of the most popular anatomical treatise of the fifteenth and early sixteenth centuries, the *Anathomia* of Mondino de'Luzzi (Mundinus), as published in Venice in 1493/4. The judge-like professor is shown in the upper center, reading from his text and residing over the dissection.[12] Once again the ancient image of Christ as *iudex in cathedra* has lent its visual authority to a secular occupation.

Michelangelo himself was a skilled anatomist, carrying out numerous disections in order to improve his drawing of the human body.[13] In his time, the most convenient source of human cadavers for medical anatomy was the public gallows — the bodies of hanged criminals. In Rome, the pontifical authorities were surprisingly liberal, allowing such bodies to be turned over periodically to the physicians. In Florence, the Tempio Brotherhood, the lay-confraternity whose charity it was to comfort condemned criminals and then to see that they received decent Christian burial, nonetheless openly cooperated with the medical profession in this traffic. In fact, during the reign of Duke Cosimo I in Florence, the Tempio Brothers even supplied cadavers to artists!¹⁴

It is an interesting fact that Michelangelo, while he lived in Rome, was also a member of a confraternity whose charity it was to do exactly as the Tempio in Florence, to offer spiritual comfort to condemned criminals. This was the Brotherhood of San Giovanni Decollato. Michelangelo's involvement with the confraternity began in 1514, then grew distant, but toward the end of his long life, there is no doubt that the aging artist's increasing obsession with his own death drew him closer to the charitable ideals of San Giovanni Decollato. In 1564, when he finally died at the age of 89, the brothers of this confraternity, solemnly dressed in black cassocks with hoods covering their faces, carried the artist's body in a funeral procession through the streets of Rome before its final interment in Florence.

Some fifteen years before his death, Michelangelo began carving one of his most moving sculptures, the unfinished *Pietà* now in Florence. This work was apparently intended to stand over his own tomb. Once more the artist included his self-portrait, for we see him, characteristic flattened nose and all, standing as the old man behind Christ and holding His body just taken down from the Cross. Michelangelo has here represented himself as either Nicodemus or Joseph of Arimathea who, like the brothers of San Giovanni Decollato, once volunteered to tend the corpse of a humble criminal just executed on Calvary, and to give His body a decent burial.¹⁵ In fact, the cassock and cowl which the artist depicts himself wearing is quite like that worn by the brothers of San Giovanni Decollato in sixteenth-century Rome.

About the same time that Michelangelo began this *Pietà*, the pensive sculptor came into contact with Dr. Realdo Colombo, the famous anatomist who had succeeded Vesalius in the anatomy chair at the University of Padua and who now occupied that same professorship at Pisa. Colombo arrived in Rome about 1547, expressly to persuade Michelangelo to illustrate an ambitious anatomy treatise he was writing. He won the artist's confidence and became his personal physician. A letter from Colombo to his mentor, Duke Cosimo I of Florence, still survives in which Colombo begs leave from Pisa to stay in Rome where "the leading painter in the world is helping me," and that the "supply of bodies is plentiful here," by which he meant the cadavers of criminals, since Rome boasted one of the highest crime — and therefore execution — rates of any city in sixteenth-century Europe.¹⁶ Unfortunately, Michelangelo declined the commission, which would certainly have resulted in one of the most magnificently illustrated books of all time. It is generally assumed that the artist was just too old and busy to take on the new project, but I would also suggest that Michelangelo, increasingly conservative in his religious views, began to disapprove of the dissection of criminals' bodies, and that he expressed this sentiment to some degree in his *Pietà*, where the old sculptor likens himself to a *fratello* tending the forlorn body of Jesus. In any case, Colombo's book did finally go to press in 1559 without any illustrations at all save a frontispiece, a handsome Venetian-style woodcut in which we see Colombo in the center, standing imperiously before a great classical niche and surrounded by admiring colleagues as he anatomizes a corpse of a young man posed quite remarkably like the popular image of Christ taken down from the Cross; that is, with right arm hanging limp and head leaning on its shoulder just as one sees in so many Renaissance depictions including of course, Michelangelo's *Pietà*. I should like to believe that Colombo deliberately intended such a pictorial association between the well-known pose of dead Christ, and the anatomist's cadaver on the dissecting table, and that this association was part of his argument to Michelangelo as to why the artist should help him with his project. This argument in effect wanted the anatomist to be accepted as a kind of priest, offering the corpse of the condemned criminal just as Christ sacrificed His body to save Mankind. By dissecting the criminal's body, the anatomist saves mankind by advancing the science of healing medicine. By having his body anatomized for such a noble purpose, the criminal does penance for the sins of his evil life, and therefore helps his soul win redemption at the Last Judgment. That this rationale for dissecting the human body was prevalent in Colombo's circle can be further supported by examining the popular anatomy treatise published by his student, Juan de Valverde, first in the Spanish language in 1556 and then translated into Italian in 1560. The first edition was printed in Rome, the second in Venice, and both were lavishly illustrated by Gaspar Becerra, a minor assistant of Giorgio Vasari and therefore by extension a follower of Michelangelo.[17] Valverde too was an admirer of Michelangelo whom he singled out for special praise as anatomist and artist in his text. On the title page of his Spanish edition, he had his artist borrow the two heraldic figures, holding up the coat-of-arms, directly from Michelangelo's *Last Judgment*. Significantly, these figures in Michelangelo's fresco represent saved souls ascending to heaven. Valverde must also have instructed Becerra concerning this unique illustration, since nearly all the others in his book are straight plagiarisms from Vesalius. This is an *écorché*, or *flayed-man* showing off his muscles, a standard figure in all sixteenth-century illustrated anatomy books, but Becerra has drawn his version in the extraordinary pose of displaying its own just-removed skin. Valverde undoubtedly had his artist adapt Michelangelo's recent flayed-skin iconography from the *Last Judgment* to this figure, and the reason would seem to be that he wished this image not only to demonstrate anatomical facts, but also to preach the message of spiritual redemption.[18] By removing the skin of the executed criminal on the dissecting table, the anatomist not only discovers new medical truths, but he figuratively removes the criminal's sinful humors according to the old Christianized allegory of Cambyses in the *Gesta romanorum*.

William Heckscher has already documented this same religious-scientific

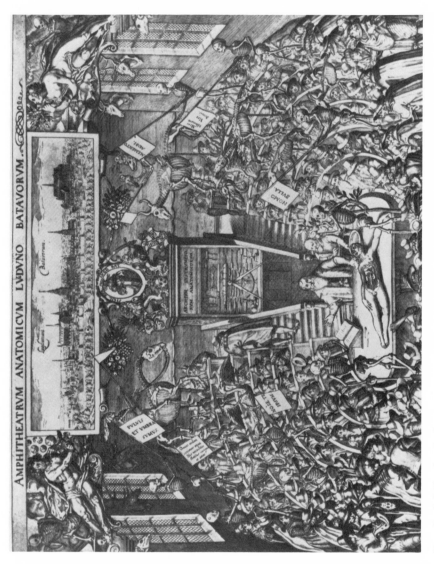

Fig. 7.   F. de Wit after J. C. van't Woudt, Anatomy Lesson of Doctor Paaw of Leiden, engraving, ca. 1650.

rationale in seventeenth-century Protestant Holland, especially as it concerned Rembrandt's famous painting, *The Anatomy Lesson of Dr. Tulp*. The artist has imputed priestly powers to the real-life professor of surgery as he performs his medical dissection of Aris Kindt, just-hanged murderer.[19] How interesting indeed that the Renaissance physician, in order to legitimate a controversial aspect of his professional practice, began also to see himself, like the medieval judge, posed in a setting remindful of the Last Judgment! The medical faculties of the sixteenth and seventeenth centuries in Europe even created special architectural "theaters" for the performance of dissection, as we see in a popular Dutch engraving, ca. 1650, showing *The Anatomy Lesson of Dr. Paaw of Leiden* (figure 7).[20] Here in the midst of traditional Christian props warning of mortality and the wages of sin, presides the professor, the archetypal judge and saviour. It is noteworthy that in the far left corner of the print, or to the right of Dr. Paaw's raised right hand, two men can be seen discoursing over a flayed human skin, once more the overt symbol of an executed criminal's redemption through medical anatomization of his body. Such traditional Christian symbols commonly made up the "decor" of anatomy theaters everywhere in Europe by the seventeenth century, thus presenting to the public a "safe" image of the medical profession's research needs, no longer perceived as devilish and blasphemous acts carried on in secret, but as highly moral, Christian performances for the public benefit. In this service it can be said that the old *Last Judgment* iconography repeated for the science of medicine on the eve of the scientific revolution just what it did for communal law and order on the eve of the European urban revolution, four centuries before.

Notes

* This essay is a short review of the first and last chapters of my forthcoming book, *Pictures and Punishment: Art in the Service of Criminal Prosecution During the Florentine Renaissance*, Ithaca: Cornell University Press.

1. *Praxis criminis persequendi, elegantibus aliquot figuris illustrata, Ionne Millaeo Boio Sylvigniaco...authore*, Paris, 1541. This famous legal treatise, published in several subsequent editions in Lyon and Paris, contains thirteen woodcut illustrations by an unknown artist. They refer to the progression of a hypothetical case, from the commission of a crime to the apprehension of the culprits, their eventual indictment, torture, trial, and execution.

2. See St. Antonine's *Summa theologica* republished in facsimile from a 1740 printed edition, Graz, 1959, Volume 2, tit. 4, cap. 5, cols. 590 ff. under *De praesumptione....*

3. This fresco, however, was described by Vasari (*Le vite de'più eccellenti pittori scultori ed architettori*, ed. Gaetano Milanesi, Florence, 1878, Vol. 1, p. 400:

> *E nella sala grande del podesta di Firenze dipinse* (Giotto) *il Comune rubato da molti: dove, in forma di giudice conlo scettro in mano, lo figurò a sedere, e sopra la testa gli pose le bilance pari per le giuste ragioni ministrate da esse; aiutato da quattro virtù, che sono la Fortezza con l'animo, la Prudenza con le leggi, la Giustizia con l'armi, e la Temperanza con la parole....*

For an interpretation and reconstruction of this lost fresco, see Salomone Morpurgo, "Bruto, 'il buon Giudico,' nell 'Udienza dell'Arte della Lana in Firenze," in *Miscellanea di storia dell'arte in onore di I.B. Supino*, Florence, 1930, pp. 141–63.

4. Nicolai Rubinstein, "Political Ideas in Sienese Art: The Frescoes of Ambrogio Lorenzetti and Taddeo di Bartolo in the Palazzo Pubblico," *Journal of the Warburg and Courtauld Institutes*, 21, 1958, pp. 179–207; see also Edna Carter Southard, *The Frescoes in Siena's Palazzo Pubblico, 1289–1539; Studies in Imagery and Relations to Other Communal Palaces in Tuscany*, New York, 1979.

5. Rafael Lainez Alcala, *Pedro Berruguete, Pintor de Castilla*, Madrid, 1935, pp. 97–100.

6. For histories of the Bargello regarding both form and function, see G. B. Uccelli, *Il Palazzo del Podestà*, Florence, 1865; Luigi Passerini, *Curiosità storico-artistiche fiorentine*, Florence, 1866; Janet Ross, *Florentine Palaces and Their Stories*, London, 1905, pp. 208–34; Walter Paatz, "Zur Baugeschichte der Palazzo del Podestà in Firenze," *Mitteilungen des Kunsthistorischen Institutes in Florenz*, 3, 1931, pp. 287–321; and Wolgang Braunfels, *Mittelalterliche Stadtbaukunst in der Toskana*, Berlin, 1953, pp. 189–93.

7. Gherardo Ortalli, *La pittura infamante; "...pingatur in Palatio'*, Rome, 1979.

8. Concerning the Rinaldeschi case, see Luca Landucci (Alice de Rosen Jarvis, ed. and trans.), *A Florentine Diary from 1450 to 1516; Continued by an Anonymous Writer till 1542*, New York, 1927, pp. 187–88.

9. See Leo Steinberg, "Michelangelo's 'Last Judgment' as Merciful Heresy," *Art in America*, 63, 1975 (Nov./Dec.), pp. 49–63; and Marcia B. Hall, "Michelangelo's 'Last Judgment': Resurrection of the Body and Predestination," *The Art Bulletin*, 58, 1976, pp. 85–92.

10. *Christus non tantum pellem in sede crucis pro nobis dedit sed etiam vitam* (*Gesta romanorum*, Louvain, 1494, chapter 29).

11. See the famous fresco from the Via Latina catacomb, discovered in 1956, dated in the fourth century; illustrated in William Heckscher, *Rembrandt's 'Anatomy of Dr. Nicolaas Tulp;' An Iconological Study*, New York, 1958, plate 12–15.

12. While the unknown artist of this woodcut image surely intended to impute such prestige to the seated figure, it has recently been argued that the chief surgeon in the picture is not the seated young man, but the older-looking person standing below who actually performs the dissection. In fact, the young man at the lectern was only a junior assistant appointed for the occasion to accompany the anatomy lesson by reading from Mundinus. See Jerome J. Bylebyl, "The School of Padua: Humanistic Medicine in the Sixteenth Century," in Charles Webster, ed., *Health, Medicine, and Mortality in the Sixteenth Century*, Cambridge, Eng., 1979, pp. 335–71.

13. Heinrich Schmidt and Hans Schadewaldt, *Michelangelo und die Medizin seiner Zeit*, Stuttgart, 1965.

14. In my forthcoming book, *Pictures and Punishment: Art in the Service of Criminal Prosecution During the Florentine Renaissance*, Cornell University Press, Ithaca, New York, I will be publishing documents indicating how Michelangelo's follower Vincenzo Danti, and Bronzino's successor Alessandro Allori, both received a number of bodies of just-executed criminals from the Tempio Brotherhood during the 1560s.

15. Concerning Michelangelo's *Pietà*, see Wolfgang Stechow, "Joseph of Arimathea or Nicodemus ?," in Wofgang Lotz, ed., *Studien zur toskanischen Kunst: Festschrift für Ludwig Heinrich Heidenreich*, Munich, 1963, pp. 289-302.

16. Concerning Realdo Colombo's relationship with Michelangelo, see Edward D. Coppola, "The Discovery of the Pulmonary Circulation: A New Approach," *Bulletin of the History of Medicine*, 31, 1957, pp. 44-77.

17. On the life and work of Valverde, see Francisco Guerra, "Juan de Valverde de Amusco," *Clio Medica*, 2, 1967, pp. 339-62; also R. Herrlinger, *History of Medical Illustration*, op. cit., pp. 123-27. Apparently, there was some entrepreneurial relationship between the publication of Colombo's *De re anatomica* in 1559 and the Italian version of Valverde's treatise published a year later. Even though Valverde's title page states that it was published in Rome by Antonio Salamanca (the same printer who did the 1556 Spanish edition), the colophon at the end of the book gives the printer as Nicolai Bevilacqua of Venice, the same who published Colombo's treatise in 1559. Moreover, the typographical style of Valverde's Italian edition is identical with that of Colombo, and many of the same decorated initials were used in both. Otherwise, Colombo's *De re anatomica* was not illustrated. As far as I know, no one has ever pointed out this similarity between the two books before, and I have no further evidence as to why the same publisher, Bevilacqua, was so involved with Valverde. I can only hazard a guess that Bevilacqua, disappointed that Michelangelo had failed to contribute to Colombo's treatise (thereby diminishing its sale), then approached Valverde's Roman publisher with a deal, that they jointly put out an Italian edition with all the original engravings. The Roman publisher who owned the originals would then take title-page credit, the Venetian translator and typographer would receive his credit in the colophon. Vesalius, after all, had proven that an illustrated anatomy treatise was profitable to the book trade, and Bevilacqua may have wished to return some of that business to Venice.

18. While the similarity of Valverde's skin-holding figure to Michelangelo's St. Bartholomew would be obvious to any art historian, historians of medicine seem not to have been aware of this until recently. Mortimer Frank in his translation of Ludwig Choulant's *History and Bibliography of Anatomical Illustration*, Chicago, 1920, p. 59, believed Valverde's idea was "undoubtedly" inspired by a fourteenth-century French miniature. Only in the publication of Harvey Cushing's *A Bio-Bibliography of Andreas Vesalius*, New York, 1953, p. 146, was the relationship with Michelangelo first noticed. In the next year, Lola Szladits, in her "The Influence of Michelangelo on Some Anatomical Illustrations," *Journal of the History of Medicine and Allied Sciences*, 4, 1954, pp. 420-27, rounded out the idea. In spite of the obviousness of the case, subsequent historians of medicine have taken issue with this Michelangelo connection. For instance, Loris Premuda in his *Storia dell'iconografia anatomica*, Milan, 1957, p. 143, stated, *La figura non ha in effetti nulla di particolarmente michelangiolesco, mentre arieggia molto da vicino esemplari di scultura classica.* L. H. Wells, in "A Note on the Valverde Muscle-man," *Medical History*, 3, 1959, p. 213, similarly opined that Valverde's figure was not derived from Michelangelo but from the *Apollo Belvedere*. Unfortunately, Lawrence Amerson, in his excellent doctoral thesis, "Problem

of the Écorché: A Catalogue Raisonne of Models and Statuettes from the Sixteenth Century and Later Periods," Doctoral Dissertation, Pennsylvania State University, 1975 (University Microfilm Service, Ann Arbor, Mich.), pp. 138–39, note 11., has seen fit, even though he is an art historian, to join in with these denials. However, even for a medical historian to observe the similarity of Valverde's muscleman to the classical statue of *Apollo Belvedere* is only to acknowledge that all Cinquecento artists borrowed the pose of this ubiquitous prototype at one time or other including Michelangelo, who, incidentally, derived his own *Last Judgment* St. Bartholomew from the equally inspirational antique sculpture, the *Belvedere Torso*. We are now left with the following bare facts: Valverde's artist was a fellow Spaniard living in Rome named Gaspar Becerra, a minor imitator of Raphael and Michelangelo (see Ulrich Thieme and Felix Becker, eds., *Allgemeines Lexikon der bildenden Künstler*, Leipzig, 1909, vol. 3, pp. 131–32.). Nearly all of the hundred plus engraved illustrations for Valverde's *Historia* are straight copies after Vesalius, whose artists in turn derived their figures from classical and High Renaissance sources. Since Becerra's *écorché* figure holding its own skin is one of his few without a Vesalian antetype, it should have to be judged as a work of uncharacteristic genius if no other immediate model could be found for it. Furthermore, Valverde himself was familiar with Michelangelo. His own teacher, Realdo Colombo, was Michelangelo's personal physician and *quondam* partner in the enterprise to publish an illustrated anatomy treatise. Valverde specifically acknowledged Michelangelo in the text of his *Historia* as "having given himself to Anatomy along with Painting and has come to be a most excellent and famous painter" (see the text page following Figure III, Book II in all editions). At the beginning of Chapter V, Book III, Valverde's artist decorated the first initial "L" with a miniature of Michelangelo's *Leda and the Swan*. We can only conclude that Valverde's artist was as aware as everyone else in mid-Cinquecento Rome that Michelangelo had created a unique interpretation of St. Bartholomew (this is attested to by Pietro Aretino who accused the painter of having depicted a *Marsia senza pelle* instead of a Christian saint; see Edgar Wind, *Pagan Mysteries of the Renaissance*, New York, 1958 and 1968, p. 188.) which he then borrowed precisely because it was so sensational. In typical Mannerist fashion, he grafted this detail on to an otherwise conventional High Renaissance classical form in order to give his illustration special *invenzione*.

19. W. Heckscher, *Rembrandt's Anatomy of Dr. Tulp*, op. cit.

20. Engraved by F. de Wit after J. C. Woudanus (van't Wouldt) (1570–1615).

The Spectacles of State

STEPHEN ORGEL

My title comes from Ben Jonson's poem *An Expostulation with Inigo Jones*, a long and vitriolic attack on his old collaborator by whom Jonson felt betrayed. Neutral enough out of context, the phrase is in Jonson's verse bitterly ironic:

> O shows, shows, mighty shows!
> The eloquence of masques! what need of prose,
> Or verse, or sense t'express immortal you!
> You are the spectacles of state!   (39–41)

The intensity of Jonson's outrage at what he sees as the soulless spectacle of the Caroline masque is a measure also of the real depth of his commitment to the masque as a form. Jonson's profound ambivalence, the deep ambiguities of that neutral-sounding phrase The Spectacles of State, may serve us as a cultural touchstone for his age.

I begin with a well-known painting of a group of people performing in a spectacle of state. Figure 1 shows Queen Elizabeth, in the last year or two of her reign, transported in triumph through an imaginary landscape combining both urban and rural visions, city palaces and country castles, surrounded by her courtiers and watched by her subjects. The picture is attributed to Robert Peake, and is usually called *Queen Elizabeth Going in Procession to Blackfriars in 1600*. It is traditionally said to commemorate the Queen's attendance at the marriage at Blackfriars of one of her maids of honor, Lady Anne Russell, granddaughter of the Earl of Bedford, to Henry Somerset, Lord Herbert, son of the Earl of Worcester, and ultimately the inheritor of the title. But recently Roy Strong has argued persuasively that

Fig. 1. Robert Peake (?), Elizabeth and the Earl of Worcester in Procession, c. 1601. (By courtesy of Mr. Simon Wingfield Digby, Sherborne Castle.)

this identification must be wrong.[1] To begin with, the setting can hardly represent Blackfriars. Secondly, the only woman who could be the bride, in white in the right middle-ground, is not dressed for a wedding: Elizabethan brides wore their hair down, in token of their virginity. Through a complex and fascinating analysis of the iconography, history and provenance of the painting, Strong arrives at a quite different interpretation.

Many of the male figures in the procession are identifiable, through personal iconography and other portraits. They include the most powerful aristocrats in the realm. In a group of Garter Knights in the left foreground we can recognize the Lord Admiral, Lord Howard of Effingham; the Earl of Cumberland; the Lord Chamberlain, Lord Hunsdon, among others. Most important of all, we recognize the central figure just below the Queen: Edward Somerset, Earl of Worcester, Elizabeth's last Master of the Horse, who succeeded the Earl of Essex in that crucial ceremonial office after his disgrace and execution in 1601. Worcester is the father of the young man in white behind him: this is Henry Somerset, Lord Herbert. The woman in white is Lady Anne Russell, now Lady Herbert, Worcester's daughter-in-law — not a fiancée going to her marriage, but a wife of a year or more. The landscape probably depicts his two castles of Chepstow and Raglan, and the town house may be his mansion in the Strand. What the picture commemorates, in this analysis, is the triumph not of Elizabeth but of Worcester, and it must have been he who commissioned it. In the drama presented here, the Queen, though a central figure, plays a distinctly secondary role. She is the background, the necessary context, the crucial prop; but the protagonist is Worcester. The painting celebrates his elevation to the position of Master of Ceremonies for this most ceremonial of courts. He continued in this office long after Elizabeth's time, serving as Earl Marshal for James's coronation and again for his entry into London in 1604, and as late as 1610 overseeing the solemnities at the creation of James's son Henry as Prince of Wales.

In the performance embodied in this painting, the central actor is also the primary spectator. The picture records not a moment of history but an assertion of status and power, the creation of a public self. This is the way the Earl of Worcester presents himself, the way he wants to be seen — above all, the way he wants to see himself. In such a performance, any distinction between actors and audience will be misleading. The protagonist *is* the audience, and other spectators, to view the spectacle correctly, must see it through his eyes. The persona he adopts, his mask, is not intended as a disguise but as a revelation: of the truest, essential, Platonic self.

Let us now consider one example of the public self in the process of creation. Henry Prince of Wales is an excellent test case for our purposes because the iconographic documentation is so thorough and the time span so brief. Henry was born in 1594. He became Prince of Wales in 1610 at the age

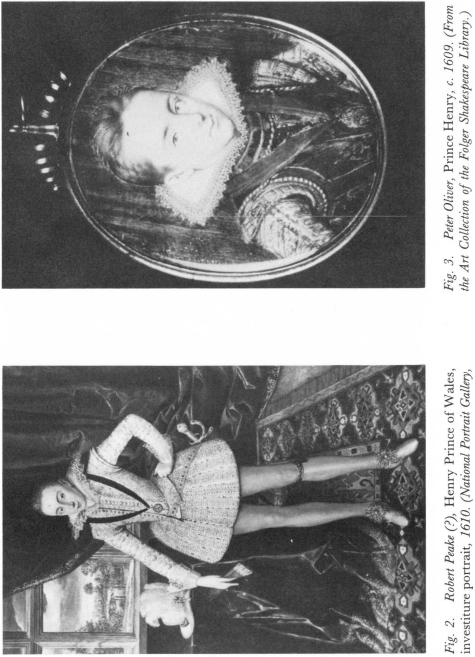

Fig. 2. Robert Peake (?), Henry Prince of Wales, investiture portrait, 1610. (National Portrait Gallery, London.)

Fig. 3. Peter Oliver, Prince Henry, c. 1609. (From the Art Collection of the Folger Shakespeare Library.)

Fig. 5. Isaac Oliver, Prince Henry, c. 1611. (Permission of Her Majesty the Queen.)

Fig. 4. Isaac Oliver, Prince Henry, 1610–11. (Fitzwilliam Museum, Cambridge.)

Fig. 6. William Hole, Prince Henry at the Lance, frontispiece to Michael Drayton's Poly-Olbion, 1613.

Fig. 7. Inigo Jones, costume for Prince Henry in Ben Jonson's Oberon, 1611. (Devonshire Collection Chatsworth. Reproduced by Permission of the Chatsworth Settlement Trustees.)

of 16, and died two years later, in 1612. He embodied, for that brief two years, all the militant idealism of Protestant England chafing under a pacifist king who was increasingly pro-Catholic. All the portraits I have included were done during that two-year period.

Figure 2 is the standard official portrait, with the subject aged about sixteen. The picture can be dated by the ostrich feathers on his hat: these are the emblem of the Prince of Wales, hence the date must be after his investiture. He is presented as a slim, boyish, splendidly appointed young man. Figure 3, from about the same period, is a Peter Oliver miniature: a lovely portrait of a rather delicate looking boy. Figure 4 is by Isaac Oliver, painted only a year or so later: this is basically the cameo portrait of a Roman emperor. Figure 5 is another Isaac Oliver portrait: the face has become forceful and manly, and the iconography is explicitly military, with the armor, and the tents in the right background. Figure 6 shows the Prince practicing at the lance, a very popular engraving that appeared as the frontispiece to Drayton's *Polyolbion*. The military idealization appears here, too; and we note the imperial Roman profile again. And figure 7, finally, shows how Inigo Jones presented him in Jonson's masque *Oberon* at New Year's, 1611, when the Prince was sixteen — this drawing was done less than a year after the first portrait, of the slim youth. It hardly needs to be emphasized that the idealization here — the classic musculature, the commanding stance — is the work of the artist: this young man has not been lifting weights for the last six months, and the process of heroic definition is not a function only of court masques. Jones's way of presenting Prince Henry is fully consistent with that of other artists, and most to the point, fully consistent with the role that he clearly imagined for himself. Had he lived, his plan was to follow his sister Elizabeth to Bohemia after her marriage to the Elector Palatine, and to lead the Protestant armies there.

What I have been suggesting is that the theatrical and ceremonial were crucial aspects of political life for the Elizabethan and Stuart crown. Such a claim will come as no surprise, and will scarely distinguish the English monarchy from any other, in almost any historical era whatever. But theatre and ceremony as employed by Elizabeth, James, and their courts, are double-edged, and have dimensions that are ambiguous, ironic, and often subversive. It is this special quality that I want to identify and consider.

A logical place to begin is with the literally theatrical, the Elizabethan public theatre. Figure 8 shows the closest thing we have to an eyewitness sketch, an early copy of the Dutch traveler Johannes de Witt's drawing of the Swan Playhouse in London in 1595. It shows an arena with a simple platform stage and an architectural back façade containing two doors and a gallery above. The apparent simplicity of the sketch, however, is belied by de Witt's accompanying description, which reports that the pillars were painted to look like marble and the roof over the stage was richly decorated.

*Fig. 8.   Arend van Buchel after Johannes de Witt, the Swan Playhouse, London,
c. 1595. (University Library Utrecht, Ms., 842, fol. 132r.)*

Other accounts of Elizabethan playhouses bear out de Witt's impression
of visual splendor. The splendor was conveyed through costumes and symbolic properties — robes, crowns and thrones, badges of office, heraldic ban-
ners, shields and the like: the splendor, that is, was an aspect less of the
setting than of the persons and their roles, and the theatre itself constituted
an appropriately lavish context for the action.

One of the chief attractions of the Elizabethan popular theatre was clearly
this kind of pageantry, and it provided a ceremonial dimension that could
be conceived in the broadest sense. Through it the stage was able to mime
the spectacle of courts and aristocratic enterprises to an urban, predominant-
ly middle-class audience, in a society that had grown relatively mobile —
and that contemporary critics said had grown *dangerously* mobile.[2] Ironically, the attraction was especially powerful when the pageantry was presented

in the service of a nostalgic medievalism, expressing the traditional values of an established hierarchy and a chivalric code, since that was precisely the mythology of the Elizabethan court. The symbolism was evident, for example, in Elizabeth's coronation procession in 1558, a spectacle of knights, feudal trappings, heraldic paraphernalia. Tudor chivalry was a mythology consciously designed to validate and legitimate an authority that must have seemed, to what was left of the old aristocracy, dangerously *arriviste*. Indeed, it must have seemed so to Elizabeth herself, the granddaughter of a prosperous London merchant, faced with continual questions about the sources of her authority and the very legitimacy of her birth.

Both Elizabeth and her half-sister Mary Tudor were legally illegitimate. They were declared so on the birth of their father's male heir, the future Edward VI. Even without a formal declaration of bastardy, the dubious validity of Henry's first two marriages would have rendered the status of his daughters doubtful enough to leave their place in the line of succession open to challenge; and Elizabeth had the additional problem of her mother's conviction and execution on a charge of adultery. Mary herself maintained, at least in moments of anger, that Elizabeth was not the daughter of Henry VIII at all, but of Anne Boleyn's lutenist Mark Smeaton, who confessed to the adultery, pleaded guilty at the trial, and was executed as the Queen's lover (along with four other men who did not confess). Henry confused the issue even further by maintaining both his daughters' illegitimacy to the end, but at the same time including them in the line of succession, next after Edward, in his will. This legacy was the sole source of Elizabeth's claim to the throne. Her chivalric ceremonials have been described as a gradually developing Elizabethan phenomenon, but they are no such thing. They are present from the moment of her accession, and they are a conscious assertion of her rightful lineage through a powerful allusion to her father's and her grandfather's personal mythology.

The chivalric code, with its attendant social forms and public displays, had been a crucial element in Tudor policy from the beginning; and it always had to do with questions of legitimacy and authority. Gordon Kipling has shown how consciously Henry VII imported Burgundian chivalric models as the basis of a broad cultural program to project the image of a noble and honorable court.[3] The image, for this monarch, was everything, since Henry reigned without even a doubtful claim to the English throne. Chivalry here was a mask for the inelegant realities of military power on the one hand, and the mundane details of administrative efficiency on the other. For his son Henry VIII, as quickly became apparent, chivalry served as a mask for the lack of either. The splendid fantasies of the Field of the Cloth of Gold were universally admired, but nobody, least of all the French king whom they were designed to impress, was deceived into thinking they represented real power.

What happened under Elizabeth was that Tudor chivalry was increasingly codified into a mode of ceremonial assertion and official behavior. Every year from about 1572 onward the anniversary of the Queen's accession was celebrated with a tilting. Elizabeth redefined Tudor chivalry to make of the family mythology a drama that was peculiarly her own. In it, the essence of knighthood was service to a lady, and when the lady was a version of the Queen, frustration was indissoluble from heroic achievement. The chivalric under Elizabeth thus merges with the Petrarchan; Spenser's epic, *The Fairy Queen*, sums up and embodies decades of royal image-making, accurately expressing not only the ideal but its powerful ambivalence — for example, in the endlessly delayed or aborted marriages (think of the Redcross Knight and Una, Scudamore and Amoret), and summed up in the narcissistic paradox of the lady knight Britomart, trapped in her own chivalric disguise.

Chivalric ideals and their expression in courtly spectacle, in Accession Day tilts, royal entertainments and court protocol generally, constitute a good instance of the utility of ceremonial fictions — of pageantry and poetry in the largest sense — within a society. It is clear that Spenser grew increasingly dubious about the values inherent in his chivalric metaphor, and that Elizabethan society did so too. Recent criticism has tried to see in Elizabethan chivalry an effective cultural mediator, a social trope that allowed for the channelling and sublimation of potentially dangerous energies. Ceremonials and their attendant fictions certainly *can* function in this way, as the work of Clifford Geertz amply demonstrates, and Elizabeth clearly had something of the sort in mind; but it is also clear that, by the last two decades of the reign at least, a strong sense of impatience and disillusion with the royal mythology was being felt. The mythology had become increasingly private, a way for Elizabeth to see herself, and its rhetoric was adopted only by those who had a vested interest in mirroring her self-image. People whose livelihood did not depend on court patronage adopted quite a different tone in addressing her.

Consider, for example, the case of John Stubbs. Stubbs was a Puritan barrister who, in 1579, appalled by Elizabeth's apparent intention of marrying the Duc d'Alençon, published a pamphlet entitled *The Discovery of a Gaping Gulf Wherein England is Like to be Swallowed...*, which energetically argued against the match. The pamphlet included nothing that wasn't a popular commonplace, but it became notorious because of Elizabeth's explosive (and uncharacteristic) reaction to it, which was outraged, panicky and vindictive. The Queen wanted Stubbs and the publisher charged with seditious libel and hanged. This turned out to be legally impossible, but they were imprisoned (ironically, charged under a statute of Mary Tudor's providing penalties for those who libelled her husband Philip II of Spain) and their right hands were cut off by the public executioner. A reading of the pamphlet reveals no intention of either sedition or libel, but it does tell a good deal about Elizabeth's pathology on the subject of marriage — or perhaps simply on the subject of conducting her own affairs without interference. Stubbs is undeniably rude about Alençon, whom he despises as an adventurer and a Papist, but his attitude toward Elizabeth, while not exactly reverent, is unquestionably loyal and loving. The tone he takes might best be described as fraternal: scolding and impatient, but also affectionate and indulgent; above all, straightforward and commonsensical — about matters like Elizabeth's advanced age, for example. Stubb's model for his relation to the sovereign is not the chivalric court, but the family. We surely err in taking the Queen's version of herself as a working model for the life of the commonwealth. King James's son Prince Henry, in 1610, saw himself as the center of a chivalric revival: chivalry had to be *revived* in 1610, having been dead, in Henry's mind, not for the seven years since Elizabeth's time, but since the Middle Ages.

Let us look at Prince Henry again, in figure 5: those are tents and soldiers, an army camp in the background. He is surrounded by the trappings not of ceremonial tilts but of war. The program that Henry proposed, militaristic and aggressively Protestant, involved a very different notion of chivalry from that of Elizabeth. It is the same notion that thirty years earlier had informed Sir Philip Sidney's pleas for royal employment, and that was responsible for his aborted career. The cause was a Protestant crusade against the Catholic powers of Europe, something Elizabeth did not at all want to be involved in. Sidney's version of chivalry was antithetical to the Queen's, and dangerous to it. Henry's, in the same way, was energetically resisted by a powerful court faction, including both his father the King and his poet Ben Jonson.

Such reactions are not merely political or narrowly pragmatic. The age's complex attitude toward chivalry is exemplified in Book VI of *The Fairy Queen*, in which chivalric courtesy turns out to be the most dubious of moral principles. The age's attitude toward chivalry is part of a larger attitude toward poetry as a whole, toward the relation of symbolic fictions to effective action — that is, to real life. There is a remarkable touchstone for this in Book V of Spenser's epic, the Book of Justice, in the trial of Mary Queen of Scots, who is represented here as the beautiful and treacherous Duessa. After a prosecution by Zeal seconded by Artegall, the Knight of Justice, Duessa is declared guilty by the court, and Elizabeth, called here Mercilla, is appealed to for judgment. Here is Spenser's account of what happened:

> But she, whose princely breast was touchèd near
> With piteous ruth of her so wretched plight,
> Though plain she saw by all that she did hear
> That she of death was guilty found by right,

Fig. 10. Nicholas Hilliard, George Clifford, 3rd Earl of Cumberland. (National Maritime Museum, London.)

Fig. 9. George Gascoigne, Self-Portrait before Queen Elizabeth, 1575. (British Library.)

Yet would not let just vengeance on her light;
But rather let instead thereof to fall
Few purling drops from her fair lamps of light,
The which she covering with her purple pall
Would have the passion hid, and up arose
withall.

(V.9.50)

Allegorized as Mercilla, what else can Elizabeth do? Four stanzas into the next canto, after lavish praise of the Queen's incomparable mercy, Spenser does face up to the facts: Mary was, after all, executed — though even here he cannot quite bring himself to say so. The death is referred to as Duessa's "willful fall," thereby effectively exonerating Elizabeth from making the decision. This was a clear mirror not of events but of the Queen's mind. Elizabeth had devised a similar fiction for her own conscience, by signing Mary's death warrant but declining to send it. It was sent by her Privy Councillors — on her tacit instructions, of course — and they thereby bore the direct responsibility for Mary's execution. A less shrewd poet would have undertaken to *justify* Elizabeth's actions, and would have offended her as deeply as Spenser's account of Duessa's fall offended King James, who on the publication of *The Fairy Queen* demanded that Elizabeth arrest the poet and punish him for the insult this episode clearly offered to James's mother. (Elizabeth instead granted Spenser a pension.) As for the poet's own attitudes here, they remain utterly obscure: the poem is an expression not of the poet's mind, but of his patron's.[4] The moment, however, is a dangerous one — this is not merely flattery, and Spenser is not playing it safe. Obviously the Queen cannot be criticised in an epic celebrating her greatness, especially in a section of the poem devoted to the theme of Justice; but why does Spenser want to include such an ambiguous episode at all? This is not an isolated example. In the latter books of *The Fairy Queen* Spenser repeatedly confronts the realities of his society with his poetic mythology, and keeps making the same point: it doesn't work.

The choice of this particular myth, and its extraordinary elaboration under Elizabeth, are not difficult to understand. The idea that knighthood consists of service to a lady is surely the most *disarming* of fictions, and we find it asserted again and again in the official iconography of the age. Figure 9, for example, shows the soldier-poet George Gascoigne offering his works to the Queen. His motto declares him "Tam Marti quam Mercurio," devoted as much to Mars as to Mercury, but the image represents him as a suitor offering a love token. And in figure 10, even more strikingly disarmed, is the Queen's Champion George Clifford, Earl of Cumberland, soldier and privateer. He is dressed for a tilt as the Arthurian Knight of Pendragon Castle, but his shield, helmet and gauntlets are laid aside, he wears a richly decorated coat and skirt, and he carries his lady's favor in his hat, Elizabeth's jeweled glove.

Spenser himself testifies to the ineffectiveness of this disarming mythology, even as an image of order, even within the courtly circle mirrored in the sixth book of the *Fairy Queen* with its quintessentially courtly hero Calidore, the Knight of Courtesy, or in that more personal and profoundly ambivalent image of the court, *Colin Clout's Come Home Again*. Needless to say, it expressed even less the realities of Elizabethan society. And for Elizabeth's successor James I, chivalry was a *dangerous* myth. The King's favored personae were instead biblical or classical: Solomon, Aeneas, Neptune. When his son undertook to revive the chivalric mythology in the interest of his own military ambitions, he was firmly put down — disarmed — as much because he had got the point of the myth wrong as because, in the King's terms, it was the wrong myth.

II

Perhaps the richest example the English Renaissance affords of persons in groups participating in ceremonial fictions is provided by the Elizabethan theatre. Expressions of communal fantasies, stage plays are consistently described, from the opening of the first public playhouse in 1576 till the closing of all the theatres in 1642, in violently antithetical terms. Educative and subversive, moral and licentious, theatres are seen — sometimes simultaneously — as a way for princes to maintain order and a continual threat to the stability of the commonwealth.

The ambiguities of chivalry, too, are insistently present. On Shakespeare's stage, we find it throughout the Lancastrian tetralogy, for example, epitomized most clearly, perhaps, in the character of Hotspur; or in the account of the Field of the Cloth of Gold that opens *Henry VIII*, which provides an enormously admiring description of the festivities, but then concludes that they weren't worth the expense; or in Hamlet's yearning for a time when kings settled their differences heroically, in single combat, and honored their compacts; or in the fairy-tale first scene of *King Lear*, with its lucid vision of the darkest sides of hyperbolic rhetoric and feudal relationships; or in the subversive career of the ill-made knight Bertram, the anti-hero of *All's Well that Ends Well*; or in that most profoundly anti-chivalric drama of love and war, *Troilus and Cressida*.

If the mythology is evident, the realities of courtly spectacle are insistently present too, whether chivalric, Roman, or simply opulent. The richness of the costumes surprised and impressed foreign visitors, and in 1599 an inquisitive Swiss traveller named Thomas Platter investigated and found that they were real court clothes, the slightly used suits and dresses of genuine aristocrats. At a theatre like the Blackfriars, where one could, for a relatively high price, buy a seat on the stage, the distinction between spectacle and spectator would have all but disappeared. At court masques, those quintessential instances of Renaissance pageantry, the audience was as much on display as the performers, and contemporary accounts tend to dwell at greatest length on the spectators, not on the players or the drama. This was, of course, entirely appropriate, since the center of the spectacle was not the entertainment but the entertained, the monarch.

The interchangeability of spectacle and spectator does not end here. Upon his accession in 1603, one of King James's first acts was to bring all the theatrical companies under royal patronage. Shakespeare's company, the Lord Chamberlain's Men, became The King's Men, and thereby took a giant step up in social status. The actors, traditionally on the fringes of society, and still, in Puritan rhetoric at least, stigmatized as mountebanks, vagabonds, even male whores, were suddenly Gentlemen, the King's Servants, technically members of the royal household, and entitled to wear the royal livery. Thus clothed, they were in fact part of the pageantry of Jacobean royal power, outward and visible signs of James's sense of his office. Shakespeare himself registers the same ambitions as his upwardly mobile audience by reviving his father's application for a coat of arms. To do this was not simply to move up into — or in this case back into — the gentry. It was to become a part of that same courtly mythology of romantic medievalism, whereby the mark of a gentleman was a heraldic shield. And — fortuitously no doubt, but the fact must have pleased the Shakespeares — the shield designed by the College of Heralds bore a recognizably chivalric symbol, a lance, the spear of the family name, but one that looks, in the extant drawing, more ceremonial than serviceable. The motto, which would have been devised by Shakespeare, not by the heralds, asserted his right to the honor he claimed in an appropriately antique French: *non sanz droict*.

The spectacle of the Elizabethan stage went deeper than displays of courtly magnificence. At the beginning of the reign, two aristocratic political playwrights, Thomas Sackville, Lord Buckhurst, and Thomas Norton, the famous parliamentarian, entertained the queen with a historical drama that spoke directly to her own situation, the neo-Senecan tragedy *Gorboduc*. This was an exemplum designed specifically for Elizabeth. The play recounts how, in his old age, an ancient British king divided his kingdom between his two sons, and thereby plunged the realm into civil war and anarchy. The resemblance to the plot of *King Lear* is not accidental: Gorboduc was Lear's grandson. What the play expressed through its historical example was the urgent necessity for a clearly defined and legitimate succession.

For Elizabeth in 1561, the example of Gorboduc would have been doubly powerful, Janus-faced, looking both forward and back. The queen's claim to the throne, like that of the half-sister she succeeded, was profoundly

Fig. 11. Hans Eworth (?), Queen Elizabeth and the Judgment of Paris, 1569. (Hampton Court. Permission of Her Majesty the Queen.)

ambiguous. Both Henry's daughters were legally illegitimate, and their place in the line of succession derived exclusively from their designation in their father's will. Such a proceeding was dubiously valid to begin with; but in any case, their half-brother Edward's will designated his cousin Lady Jane Grey as his successor, and if Henry VIII's will was valid on the question of the royal succession, so must Edward VI's have been. The two sisters' path to the throne, therefore, offered the commonwealth, not for the first time, a dangerous precedent. Like Henry IV and Henry VII, Mary and Elizabeth succeeded to their brother's throne only after the deposition and execution of a reigning claimant whose pedigree was, unlike theirs, impeccable—Lady Jane Grey. When Mary died in 1558, Elizabeth succeeded without difficulty because she was popular and Protestant, and perhaps most important, because there were no longer any other serious claimants; but she still embodied enough dangerous potential for Sackville and Norton to see in her accession the material for a classical tragedy. In her presence at the performance, the essential meaning of the play was made manifest, and the other spectators must have made the connection.

Like the monarch at a court masque, Elizabeth was not merely an audience for this spectacle, but the crucial element in it; and *Gorboduc* may be taken as a prototypical instance of royal theatre. During the course of Elizabeth's reign, the association between the crown and the stage developed into a complex symbiosis. At Oxford in 1565, the scholars of Christchurch made the Queen the visible center of their drama by placing her on the stage for the production of Plautus' *Aulularia* they had devised to entertain her. Twenty-five years later, at the climax of George Peele's *Arraignment of Paris*, she received from the Trojan prince the golden apple that mythology had intended for Venus. The conceit had already been used of her in a painting, dated 1569, perhaps by Hans Eworth (figure 11). By 1590 she had a drama that was truly her own.

The relationships I have been describing sound fairly cosy, but in fact they are distinctly uneasy and involve a good deal of tension. Theatrical pageantry, the miming of greatness, is highly charged because it employs precisely the same methods the crown was using to assert and validate its own authority. To mime the monarch was a potentially revolutionary act—as both the aging Elizabeth and the rebellious Earl of Essex were well aware.

In February, 1601, Essex undertook his final, desperate adventure, to lead an uprising and seize the throne. In order to marshal public opinion in his favor, he commissioned Shakespeare's company to revive the old tragedy of *Richard II*, a play about the overthrow of a vain, weak and histrionic monarch. On the day after the performance he marched with his men through the streets of London, but the popular support never materialized, and he was arrested, tried and executed in short order.

In August of the same year, Elizabeth had an interview with her archivist William Lambarde, who presented her with a summary of all the royal documents he had catalogued. She paused at length over the reign of Richard II, and when Lambarde expressed his surprise, she explained, "I am Richard II, know ye not that?" Lambarde acknowledged that he understood this to be an allusion to the drama of the late Earl of Essex, and the Queen continued, "He that will forget God will also forget his benefactors; this tragedy was played forty times in open streets and houses."[5]

The point here is not merely that Elizabeth understood how Essex was attempting to use the play; it is that she and Essex shared the same assumptions about it. In her moving and baffling expostulation to Lambarde, she transformed the drama of *Richard II* into a piece of very dangerous civic pageantry, an allegory of her own reign performed, as she put it, "forty times in open streets and houses." Forty times is doubtless an accurate enough, if somewhat hyperbolic, assessment of the old play's popularity, and the houses may reasonably be assumed to include theatres as well as Essex's palace in the Strand. But the "open streets" must be the Queen's invention, a fantasy whereby the whole city became a stage for a continual performance in which, in the person of her ancestor, she was mimed and deposed.

In 1599, Ben Jonson mimed the Queen openly in *Every Man Out of His Humor*. The play presents a complex debate which only the Queen's presence can resolve; and in the first performance, at court, the dénouement constituted an elegant compliment to the royal spectator. But on the public stage, the Queen's presence had to be counterfeited, and here, understandably, the theatre was considered to have overstepped its bounds, making the monarch subject to the whim of the playwright, a prop for his drama. Jonson alone among dramatists would have presumed so far, using — like the Earl of Worcester in the Procession painting — the power of royalty to establish the authority of his fiction; but the case is exceptional only because Jonson's ego is involved. Other plays — for example Jonson's tragedy *Sejanus*, and *Eastward Ho*, of which Jonson was a part-author — were *presumed* to be miming, and thereby undermining, the royal authority, even though Jonson protested (from prison in the latter case) that this time he had no such intention. Examples like these place that famous fraud, Richard Venner's *England's Joy*, in a rather different light from the one we are accustomed to. *England's Joy* was a pageant play about Elizabeth, and it was to be performed (or so the advertisements asserted) not by professional actors but "only by certain Gentlemen and Gentlewomen of account." The prospect of seeing the gentry on stage attracted a very large audience; but at the last moment Venner was found to have decamped with the receipts, and there was no play — and probably never had been one. Venner's genius lay in claiming to have created a theatre that would at last present not impressions of courtly life, but the real thing. The conception actualizes one of the deepest corporate fantasies of the Elizabethan stage and its audience.

In fact, in the period the alliance between court and theatre works both ways. King James wanted the theatrical companies under royal patronage because he believed in the efficacy of theatre as an attribute of royal authority; and no doubt when the actors, poets, designers and musicians provided court masques celebrating his wisdom and glory, the investment looked like a good one. But the theatre is too anarchic to be so confined, and often enough the protection of the crown was interpreted by the actors to be protection *from* the crown. Take, for example, the strange case of the Children of the Revels producing plays satirizing the King, his favorites, and his new Scottish knights. One particularly offensive production not only had a go at the knights, but depicted James himself, as the French ambassador put it, "ivre pour le moins une fois le jour" — drunk at least once a day. This play so enraged the King — not surprisingly — that he swore he would never have the company play before him again and would make them "beg their bread."[6] In fact, the players were back at court within the year: the incident reveals how little we really understand what must have been a very complicated and ambivalent relationship.

Why did the company produce such plays to begin with? They pitted the prejudices of the Blackfriars audience, or at least of some segment of it, against the wishes and authority of their own patron: how was this in their interest? Why did they not anticipate the king's displeasure, or if they did, why were they willing to risk it — what was in it for them? Where was the censor: why did the Lord Chamberlain allow such a production? And surely most baffling of all, why did the King cool down? Consider a few dates: the play depicting the King drunk was produced in March, 1608 — the French ambassador's letter about the King's fury is dated March 25. The boys next played at court on January 1 and 4, 1609, the Christmas season of the same year. But their *last previous* appearance at court had been in the season of 1604/5: they were not a company that regularly played before the King. The invitation to perform at New Year's 1609 was therefore extraordinary, a mark of special favor. The troupe's insolence had greatly advanced their standing.

What are we to make of all this? James was used to being attacked and insulted to his face by ministers preaching in his chapel, but surely neither he nor the players could have believed that theatrical companies, like preachers, served a higher law. Ben Jonson, characteristically, regretted the fact. He told his friend William Drummond that "he hath a mind to be a churchman, and so he might have favor to make one sermon to the King, he careth not what thereafter should befall him, for he would not flatter though he saw Death."[7] Like the Children of the Revels Jonson dreamt of attacking with impunity; and the target of the attack in both

cases is not the playhouse audience but the King. The relationship between
the Renaissance stage and the crown was a complex mixture of intimacy
and danger. Given this context, Queen Elizabeth's statement to William
Lambarde sounds less like a paranoid fantasy.

Sir Henry Wotten's remarks on the first performance of Shakespeare's
Henry VIII, that celebration of kingship all of which, as the contemporary
subtitle assures us, is true, may be taken as paradigmatic. The play was,
he wrote, "sufficient in truth within a while to make greatness very familiar,
if not ridiculous."[8] For this spectator, to mime nobility on the stage was
to diminish it. And yet Elizabeth and James could not remain aloof, for
this was precisely how they saw themselves: both regularly employed the
metaphor of the player-monarch. "We princes," Elizabeth told the Lords
and Commons in 1586, "are set on stages, in the sight and view of all the
world duly observed."[9] Surely the Queen imagined the threatening tragedy
of *Richard II* being performed not at the Globe but in the public streets
because she herself repeatedly took to the public streets, in splendid pageantry, to assert and confirm her authority. King James avoided the streets,
but he fully concurred with Elizabeth's view of the royal situation. "A king,"
he told his son, "is as one set on a stage, whose smallest actions and gestures
all the people gazingly do behold."[10] This is a central precept of the
Basilicon Doron, James's treatise on kingship. "A king is as one set on a stage":
a king is like an actor. But the passage as I have cited it comes from a second edition of the treatise, published after James ascended the English
throne. In the first edition, the sentence reads, "A king is as one set upon
a *scaffold*. . . ." The King's emendation of the ambiguous word surely reveals
something of the danger James must have felt to be inherent in the royal
drama. It was a danger that, needless to say, was not merely linguistic;
and it could not be eliminated through judicious emendation. As Charles
I learned, a king *is* as one set upon a scaffold. Elizabeth was undoubtedly
a better performer than either of her successors; but whether the pageant
constituted celebration or satire lay ultimately not in the power of the actor or the intentions of the inventor, but in the eye and mind of the beholder.

Notes

*Some of the material in this paper has previously appeared in "Making Greatness Familiar," in *Genre* 15, 1 / 2 (1982).

1. Roy Strong, *The Cult of Elizabeth* (London, 1977), pp. 17–55.

2. For a general discussion, see Stephen Orgel, *The Illusion of Power* (Berkeley, 1973).

3. See *The Triumph of Honour* (Leiden, 1977), and "Henry VII and the Origins of Tudor Patronage," in *Patronage in the Renaissance*, ed. Guy Fitch Lytle and Stephen Orgel (Princeton, 1982), Chapter 5.

4. The best account of the politics of the incident is by Jonathan Goldberg in *James I and the Politics of Literature* (Baltimore, 1983), Chapter 1.

5. See the summary in the Arden edition of *Richard II*, ed. Peter Ure (London, 1956), p. lix.

6. E. K. Chambers, *The Elizabethan Stage* (Oxford, 1923), 4: 500.

7. Conversations with Drummond, in *Ben Jonson*, ed. C. H. Herford and Percy Simpson (Oxford, 1925), 1: 141, lines 330ff.

8. Chambers, *Elizabethan Stage*, 2: 419.

9. J. E. Neale, *Elizabeth I and Her Parliaments* (New York, 1958), 2: 119.

10. C. H. McIlwain, ed., *Political Works of James I* (Cambridge, Mass., 1918), p. 43.

Ritual Behavior and Political Solidarity: Radical Groups in Revolutionary England

ROBERT B. SEABERG

I n the social confusion and general breakdown of authority during the late 1640s in England, numerous groups proliferated whose existence reflected that breakdown and whose behavior questioned the validity of remaining and reestablished order. Indeed, one can almost chart the progress of events by an examination of that behavior, which culminated in the wearing of special colors and standards, attempts to establish primitive Christian communities and increased incidents of public "indecency." The anthropologist Abner Cohen reminds us that "we 'see' groups through their symbols"; and, though people engage in ritual for a variety of personal purposes, these patterns of behavior "affect and are affected by relations of power between individuals and groups." This paper will focus on the ritual behavior of three groups, Levellers, Diggers and Ranters, in an attempt to offer some suggestions about the relationship between symbolic forms of action and political cohesion.[1]

In 1647, during the interim between the two civil wars, the Levellers advanced their proposals for a settlement of the national disputes. Recognizing the important role played by the new model army and the power base it offered, the leaders of the group attempted to gain army support for their ideas, presented in a document called the *Agreement of the People*, at a general meeting of the army. This meeting, known as the Putney debates, did not result in adoption of the Leveller program, but it won converts to the cause.

One of those apparent converts, Thomas Rainsborough, presented a copy of the *Agreement* to the army commander, Fairfax, at a rendezvous two weeks later, as agents distributed copies to soldiers and two officers exhorted them to subscribe to it. Soldiers in one regiment did in fact wear copies of the

Agreement, inscribed with the words ENGLAND'S FREEDOM, SOLDIER'S RIGHTS, stuck in their hats. Later, various companies of another regiment arrived at the rendezvous, having refused to obey marching orders. These men "stood with white papers in their hats, as if they were going to engage with an enemy." The mutinous action failed, however. Soldiers in the first regiment were ordered to tear out the papers and did so. Men of the second regiment were ordered likewise to remove copies of the *Agreement* from their hats. Upon the refusal of a number of them, "some officers rode in amongst them and plucked out the papers of some that were most insolent." But if the action failed, the event itself was significant. The Levellers had utilized traditional army custom to signify their influence and their main idea. The use of field-signs, such as sprigs of oak or pieces of paper stuck in hats, was an accepted military custom, employed to identify troops of one side on occasions when uniforms may have been lacking or when both sides wore similar colors. On this occasion, the field-sign had become more than mere identification; the pamphlet had become symbol. For whatever the Levellers would do, the *Agreement of the People* symbolized their group and their aims.[2]

Rainsborough's death in November 1648 provided the Levellers with a unique opportunity. Several newspapers, one of them the pro-Leveller *Moderate*, invited sympathisers to follow Rainsborough's corpse in a five-mile funeral procession. All accounts of the event noted that the mourners wore ribbons of Rainsborough's sea-green colors. And indeed from this first appearance in the London streets of the Levellers as a recognizable group, the colors were identified with Levellers and the *Agreement*.[3]

The display of Rainsborough's colors entailed the conscious adoption by the Leveller leaders of a visual symbol which would easily identify the group; that would both set the group apart as an exclusive entity and broaden the group's appeal and base. Specifically, use of a military color furthered the Levellers' attempt to include elements of the army among their backers. And it could appeal to civilians as a visible alternative. Certainly the leaders understood the import of such display. John Lilburne stated that, given the social confusion and tumult, the people would be safer adhering to the *Agreement* than wearing a "blue ribband," Col. Fairfax's color (and thus one associated with the army grandees).[4]

When the army officers adopted an emasculated version of the *Agreement*, engineered the purging of Parliament and participated in the execution of Charles I early in 1649, the Levellers felt betrayed. Again they appealed to the army rank-and-file for support. After the mutiny of one troop in April 1649, one soldier was executed as an example. The funeral for Robert Lockyer became the occasion of another large Leveller demonstration. Again thousands of mourners wore the familiar sea-green colors. That the Levellers meant the display as a symbol of army-civilian solidarity is clear: they had preceded the funeral with the distribution of a broadsheet addressed to the soldiers, urging an assembly of elected representatives and adoption of the full *Agreement of the People*.[5]

In a series of mutinous actions the next month, the Leveller symbols figured prominently. In Oxfordshire, one troop refused marching orders (to Ireland) and displayed a copy of the *Agreement* in their hats. Their actions sparked panic in London. When Fairfax and Cromwell called a troop review in Hyde Park, preliminary to quelling the mutinies, many of their own soldiers appeared wearing sea-green ribbons in their hats. But the soldiers readily submitted to Cromwell's offer of pardon. At Burford, the army surprised the mutineers and took many prisoners. Of those who escaped, William Thompson and a group headed to Northampton with the *Agreement of the People* inscribed on their standard. Thompson soon was killed and the mutinies put down. A general wave of relief greeted news of the restoration of order.[6]

The civilian Levellers, minus four imprisoned leaders, awaited news of events in a London tavern. No Leveller had urged armed revolt; none had been involved directly in the mutinous actions. But the Levellers had pitched many recent pamphlets to the soldiers. And the defeats were crushing to the movement in general. Lilburne, soon to be tried for treason, wrote that he never had incited anyone to declare anything but the *Agreement*. But, in effect, that is what the mutineers had done, by virtue of their symbols. And the Levellers certainly took the opportunity to denounce the perfidy of the generals in an account of events appropriately entitled *Sea-Green and Blue, See which Speaks True*.[7]

Not only by pamphlets but by the use of visual symbols, the Levellers set out a program and a group identity that spoke to and brought together army and civilian dissident elements. In an important sense, as the events indicated, the symbols succeeded. The *Agreement of the People* in soldiers' hats and the sea-green ribbons came to stand for opposition to the established government, as well as a range of grievances. Their use provides evidence of the existence of a political group and is graphic testimony for the reality of a Leveller movement or party, albeit amorphous in character.[8]

In early spring 1649, a group calling itself "True Levellers" began to work land in common on St. George's Hill in Surrey. Sometime between October 1648 and January 1649, Gerrard Winstanley, the leader of the group, had a vision in which God commanded him to "make the earth a common treasury." By the end of the first two weeks, about twenty people were involved in the collective venture, fulfilling the divine mandate to "work together; eat bread together."[9]

On one level, the digging of the "True Levellers" was an act of survival. Civil war had disrupted agriculture, intensifying a series of bad harvests which began in 1645. By 1649, the price of bread had doubled. But it was also a ritual symbol and a ritual drama. The events on the Surrey hillside represented a "transformative performance": "True religion and undefiled," Winstanley wrote, was to "make restitution of the earth" to all people.[10]

As political drama, the digging represented the free enjoyment of the earth, "true commonwealths freedom." As religious drama, it symbolized and effected the restoration of prelapsarian innocence. Adam's fall resulted from the accession to temptation, that is, the division of the land into the curse of property. When presented before Col. Fairfax to explain the digging, Winstanley and William Everard professed their intent to "restore the creation to its former condition," on the basis of God's promise "to make the barren land fruitful."[11]

Private property had split creation, torn Christ's garment. And the digging in common, symbolizing the "true ancient law of God," made "Christ's garment whole again." Like the soldier who cut the robe into pieces, the law of property moved people "to fight one against another, for those pieces, viz. for the several enclosures of the earth, who shall possess the earth, and who shall rule over others." Communal digging prevented and transcended possession in the name of and by means of an ancient power. It symbolized the seamless robe, the union of nature and grace, flesh and spirit, the Earth and the Sun.[12]

According to T. Wilson Hayes, Winstanley's words recalled the ancient alchemical tradition, in which the father, "the *petra genetrix* or master alchemist, unites with the *terra mater*, the Mother Earth, which ... is a kind of purifying furnace" or womb. As symbols have an orectic or sensory role, involving natural processes, so the use of fire (alchemy) and seed (farming) had an "immediate sensuous appeal to Winstanley's audience because fire and seed (were) essential parts of their daily lives." But this is only one level of representation. The sensual also had a political referent. It is no coincidence that the first formal complaint against the Diggers, lodged with the Council of State April 17, complained of their sowing the ground and firing of the heath.[13]

Neighbors, in fact, became obsessed with the Diggers. They harassed the colony physically and legally. One particularly violent encounter had unusual characteristics. According to Winstanley, four Diggers were viciously attacked and beaten senseless by a group of men dressed in women's clothes and led by two freeholders who wore male outfits. Why the women's apparel? On one level, the female clothes provided a disguise which may have enabled the attackers to get close enough to overpower the four men. On another level, the clothing reflected an attack on the equality, within the Digger community, between men and women. The husbandmen stood in relation to the freeholders as women were to stand in relation to men. It was a hierarchic, structural response to a commonality without degrees.

In addition, the female dress may also have been prompted by rumors of sexual licence in the colony (following from the arrival of several Ranters in the colony), thus reflecting a defense of the traditional honor of women.[14]

Ultimately, the harassment forced the abandonment of the colony. In late 1649, the small band moved near Cobham Manor and began again to build and plant. But again local antagonism quickly surfaced. Landowners and others ran cattle into the grain, destroyed the houses, and forced the men, women, and children out into the surrounding heath. At the same time, a true bill for trespass was found against Winstanley and fourteen others in the Surrey assizes. Winstanley's *Humble Request* of April 1650 was an admission of defeat. In place of the actual drama, he had only a millenial hope: "When the lamb turns into the lion, they will remember what they have done and mourn."[15]

In the course of the experiment, the Diggers had been joined by some persons whose beliefs and practices threatened to undermine the colony from within and fan the flames of local enmity. In February 1650, Winstanley protested in writing against the "Ranting Practice," a "Kingdome that lies in objects; As in the outward enjoyment of meat, drinke, pleasures, and women." This "practice" burst into prominence in 1649–1650, a product of social upheaval and poverty, of the alehouse society and the tendency to antinomianism in the Puritan doctrine of Christian liberty. To some, they were the logical end of a progression that began with the Levellers and passed to the Diggers. In fact, Ranters often saw themselves in just that light. "All things are reconciled to me, the Eternall God (in me)," wrote Abiezer Coppe, "yet sword levelling, or digging levelling are neither of them his privileges." Coppe asserted that the Ranters "had as live be dead drunk every day of the weeke, and lye with whores in the market place; and account these as good actions." Coppe was as good as his word.[16]

Ranter spiritual liberty *cum* libertinism encouraged exaggerated stories about them and their influence. Norman Cohn concluded that the persistent accounts of "communal 'adamitic' orgies" lacked any confirmation. But I believe that a close reading and comparison of the discrediting accounts with Ranter tracts does produce a residue of evidence for Ranter practices and for the participants' belief in the ritual character of their behavior.[17]

Ranter behavior included long bouts of swearing, smoking tobacco, communal drinking and eating, fornication and adultery, nudity and nude dancing. The credal basis for such behavior lay in a mystical pantheism which identified God with men and tended to dissolve into a "virtual materialism" which dispensed with God altogether; and a virulent antinomianism which affirmed that "there was no sin, but as man esteemed it sin." In fact, Ranters believed not simply in the absence of sin, but in the necessity to sin to prove its absence. Relying on a passage from Paul (that there was nothing unclean but what man esteemed unclean), Laurence Clarkson said that the saint meant "all acts, as well as meats and drinks, and therefore till you lie with all women as one woman, and not judge it sin, you can do nothing but sin." And quoting Isaiah ("I will make darkness light"), he said of swearing, drunkenness, adultery and theft that: "these acts simply, yea *nakedly*, as acts are nothing distinct from the Act of prayer and Prayses ... they are all one in themselves." In fact, the real whores, Abiezer Coppe protested, were formal prayer, gospel ordinances and conventional morality, practised at the expense of justice and mercy.[18]

The Ranters practised what they preached. Clarkson told of one meeting after which a woman (whom he named) invited him to "make tryall" of what he expressed. She took him to a private home where there were "one or two more like herself," and they all slept together that night. Clarkson proclaimed himself "Captain of the Rant" and admitted to having "most of the principle women" over his lodging.[19] It is not surprising that many anti-Ranter tracts abhorred such sexual promiscuity. *The Ranters Last Sermon* recorded an interesting scenario at a Ranter meeting:

> Mistris E. B. striking fire at a Tinder-Box lights up a candle, seeks under the Bed, Tables, and Stooles, and at last coming to one of the men, she offers to unbutton his cod-piece; who demanding of her what she sought for? She answereth, for sin: whereupon he blows out her candle, leads her to Bed, where in the sight of all the rest, they commit fornication.[20]

At least three pamphlets described another Ranter meeting, basing the accounts on evidence presented at the trial of seven who attended. During this alehouse meeting, the participants sang blasphemous songs to the tune of certain psalms, swore violently and addressed each other as "fellow-creature." One man supposedly displayed himself indecently, and another took beef, tore it apart and said, "This is the flesh of Christ, take and eat." A third took a cup of ale, threw it into the chimney corner and proclaimed, "There is the blood of Christ." Yet another was quoted as saying "that he could go into the House of Office and make a God every morning, by easing his body." If profane to most contemporaries, the actions were no less a religious ritual for those who engaged in them. This was no simple antinomianism, but a belief that indulgence in common and base acts — such as those "base impudent kisses" of which Coppe was so fond — was itself a sign of holiness, indeed of the individual divinity of the actors.[21]

There were other accounts of communion feasts with prodigious eating and drinking, lots of tobacco and pronounced swearing, of open sexual indulgence and nudity. Some are no doubt apocryphal. But well-intentioned men who had dealings with them, such as George Fox and Gerrard Winstanley, accused them of the same activities. And the Ranters' own testimonies support the accusations. Among other things, for example, Clarkson's autobiography, *The Lost Sheep Found*, verifies the practice of ritual nudism as a "symbol of their liberation from the bondage of the moral law." In that same work, he called a tavern the house of God.[22]

On the orectic level, Ranter ritual behavior centered on the "enjoyments of the flesh" and typical pastimes of the lower classes in the alehouse society. In making such behavior ritual, they justified ordinary lives and the pleasures that made them bearable. But that justification had an important political dimension. The behavior had a shock value which confounded the high and the mighty and openly defied dominant social and religious conventions. The Ranters realized the land of Cockayne, if only fleetingly. Norms and values intermingled with emotion in the drama of Ranter meetings. The transformative performance, though crude, represented an attempt by the actors to seize and exercise power over their own lives.[23]

Nevertheless, Ranter ritual included elements which diminished its communal impetus and loosened any political cohesion. The reliance on apparent stimulants to heighten effects, while itself a political act of defiance, eroded any sustained *communitas*. Even the indefatigable Clarkson admitted to being worn down by his activities, and Coppe clearly suffered from alcohol-induced dementia. But more important, the *space* in which these activities took place—homes or alehouses—was private, certainly more private than common lands or public streets and parade grounds. The alehouse, itself often set up in homes, functioned as an alternative heir to the medieval community; but it was less socially comprehensive and more fragmented, its clientele heterogeneous and transient. In comparison with the rituals and symbols of the Levellers and Diggers, Ranter ritual drama seemed more to engage the body than the body politic.[24]

The "Rant," to be sure, caused great alarm and prompted passage of the Blasphemy Act of 1650. But the real horror concerned Ranter perversion of individuals. The ritual meetings never presented much of a group political threat. Oppression of the Diggers, however, was directed to the group as a group and occasioned group responses (like that of the refusal of fifty Diggers to disperse upon orders of the justices of the peace, for which they were subsequently indicted). The ritual digging reflected more a totality of experience within public space and resulted in a far greater solidarity.

Persecution of the Levellers included both individual and group attacks. The use of emblems (identifying symbols) by soldiers in mutinous activities sparked group reprisals; but the combined effect of that and the use of symbols in public funerals by soldiers and civilians produced attacks on the recognized leaders. Of the three groups, the Levellers were most formally organized as a group (with leadership, set meetings and a network of agents who ran petition drives and collected subscriptions to defray costs), reaching out to include a larger constituency. While the Diggers also hoped to attract greater numbers, they believed the increase would result solely by the force of the ritual behavior itself. For them the behavior clearly was not only the means but the end.

In a sense, however, what the Diggers understood about their ritual drama inheres in the very nature of ritual and symbol. That is, once created and employed, symbols and rituals take on a life of their own and a multiplicity of meanings. They are themselves historical facts. Thus, in an important sense, Leveller symbols helped provoke the mutinies and the relief at their failure. But they also obscured real problems and differences among the users. The product of a small group of London civilians, the Leveller program never had any consistent mass appeal, nor had the leaders any real alternative to army discipline or way of capturing the hearts of a majority of soldiers, whose real grievance concerned arrears of pay. More important, the emblems produced conflicting perceptions of how the leaders viewed themselves and their aims (as traditionalists, their goal was restoration of a version of the ancient constitution) and how they were seen by many contemporaries (as revolutionaries, their aim the overthrow of existing political and social order).[25]

The example of the Ranters supports the notion of the independent force of rituals and symbols. Although their activities did not result in any conscious political solidarity on the level of that achieved by the Levellers and Diggers, they too created fear and engendered reprisals. Significantly, the written words produced by the groups would not in and of themselves have produced the vehement and violent reactions, though certainly they informed (and inform) the meaning of the various rituals and symbols. In the world as stage, the actors may shape their drama, but they are in turn shaped by the play; and the audience is affected by that creative interplay, the total — and transformative — performance.

Notes

1. Abner Cohen, *Two-Dimensional Man: An Essay on the Anthropology of Power and Symbolism in Complex Society* (Berkeley: University of California Press, 1974), pp. 30, 136–37.

2. William Clarke, "A Full Relation of the proceedings at the Rendezvous," *Select Tracts relating to the Civil Wars in England*, ed. F. Maseres (London: 1815), 1: lviii. William Bray, *The Army Vindicated*, B.L.E558. / 14. See also S. R. Gardiner, *History*

of the Great Civil War, 1642-1649, (London: 1898), IV: 22-23. (In a recent essay, Mark Kishlansky has debunked the long-standing myth of Cromwell's fiery charge amongst the mutinous soldiers, to tear out the offending papers and personally restore discipline. But he does support the presence of soldiers with copies of the *Agreement* in their hats and even refers to that as "outward symbols of their mutiny." "What Happened at Ware?", *Historical Journal* 25, 4 (1982): 835-36.) Peter Young, *Edgehill 1642* (Kineton: The Roundwood Press, 1967), p. 30.

3. H. N. Brailsford, *The Levellers and the English Revolution*, ed. Christopher Hill (London: The Cresset Press, 1961), pp. 360-61. See also *The Levellers Institutions for a good People and a good Parliament* (London, 1648. McAlpin Collection, Union Theological Seminary Library).

4. John Lilburne, *The Legall Fundamentall Liberties of the People of England* (London, 1649. British Library E.560.14). On the meanings of various military colors, see Gervase Markham, *Souldiers Accidence* (London, 1625. British Library 1398 d.), p. 31.

5. For accounts of Lockyer's funeral, see the following newspapers: *Mercurius Pragmaticus* (24 April-1 May); *The Moderate* (24 April-1 May); *A True Narrative of the late mutiny* (1 May 1649).

6. Various contemporary accounts of the mutinies can be found in: *A Full Narrative of the Proceedings between Lord Fairfax and the Mutineers* (London, 10 May 1649 E.555.27); Major Francis White, *A True Relation of the Proceedings in the businesse of Burford* (London, 17 September 1649. E.574.26); *Sea-Green and Blue, See which Speaks True* (London, 6 June 1649. E.559.1).

7. Richard Overton, *The Baiting of the Great Bull of Bashan Unfolded* (London, 1649. E.565.2). Lilburne, *Legall Fundamentall Liberties*.

8. For a definition of ritual symbol (and the difference between symbol and sign), see Victor and Edith Turner, *Image and Pilgrimage in Christian Culture* (New York: Columbia University Press, 1978), pp. 244-45.

9. Gerrard Winstanley, "A Watchword to the City of London," *The Law of Freedom and Other Writings*, ed. Christopher Hill (England: Penguin Books Ltd., 1973), p. 127. Idem, "The True Levellers' Standard Advanced," ibid., pp. 88-89.

10. On transformative performance, see V. and E. Turner, *Image and Pilgrimage*, n. 8. Winstanley, "A New-Year's Gift for the Parliament and Army," *Law of Freedom*, p. 185.

11. Winstanley, "The Law of Freedom in a Platform," *Law of Freedom*, pp. 289-93. "Fire in the Bush," ibid., pp. 253-56, 264, 272.

12. Winstanley, "The Law of Freedom," p. 377.

13. T. Wilson Hayes, *Winstanley the Digger* (Cambridge: Harvard University Press, 1979), pp. 104-5. *Clarke Papers*, ed. Charles H. Firth (London: Camden Society, 1891-1901), 2: 209.

14. Winstanley's account is in "A Declaration of the Bloudie and Unchristian Acting," *The Writings of Gerrard Winstanley*, ed. G. H. Sabine (Ithaca, N.Y.: Cornell University Press, 1941), pp. 295-98. Hayes' argument, that the attackers could not have worn male clothing since that would have been an admission of their fear and Digger equality, I find too fanciful for the evidence. For a more reliable interpretation, see Stephen Greenblatt, "Filthy Rites," *Daedulus*, vol. iii, no. 3, p. 14. He reminds us that cross-dressing was a "familiar and traditional emblem of the carnivalesque," and that it was calculated to deride the Diggers. On the relation between structure and *communitas*, see V. and E. Turner, *Image and Pilgrimage*, p. 252, and V. Turner, *The Ritual Process* (Chicago: Aldine, 1969), p. 111 f.

15. G. H. Sabine, "Introduction," *The Writings of Gerrard Winstanley*, pp. 17–18. Winstanley, "An Humble Request," *The Writings*, pp. 436–37.

16. Winstanley, "A Vindication," *The Writings*, p. 399. Abiezer Coppe, *A Fiery Flying Roll* (London, 1649. E.587.13), 1: 2, 5.

17. Norman Cohn, *Pursuit of the Millenium* (Fairlawn, N.J.: Essential Books, 1957), p. 328. On the function of promiscuity and sexual release in millenarian cults see also Peter Worsley, *The Trumpet Shall Sound. A Study of "Cargo" Cults in Melanesia* (New York, 1968), *passim*; and R. Knox, *Enthusiasm*, (Oxford, 1950), 566–77.

18. A. L. Morton, *The World of the Ranters: Religious Radicalism in the English Revolution* (London: Lawrence and Wishart, 1970), p. 74. Laurence Clarkson, "The Lost Sheep Found," *Pursuit of the Millenium*, appendix, pp. 345–46, 351. Coppe, *A Fiery Flying Rolle*, 1: 5.

Power, Commitment, and the Right to a Name in Beowulf

EUGENE GREEN

Almost all the personal names in *Beowulf* have an affinity, according to linguistic analysis, with forms of power. That brute strength, for example, is a quality highly prized among members of the *comitatus* surely accounts for names of such Geatish warriors as Wulf "wolf," Eofor "boar," and Beowulf "bear."[1] That powers of mind should also affect the choices of name is evident in Hygd "thought," in Freawaru "lordly awareness," and also in Hygelac "instability of mind," as well as Unferth "nonsense, folly."[2] For kings, especially, the significance of power emerges directly in their names: Eormenric "immense ruler" and the first element of Hrethel and Hrothgar — *hroð* and *hreð* — signifying "glory" or "triumph."[3] The monster Grendel also has in his name suggestions of power, albeit destructive or alien; proposed etymologies include the glosses "destroyer," "storm," and "the bottom of a body of water."[4] In all these analyses and others the process inevitably is to explain the particular name by means of generic nouns (Daeghrefn as "day raven") or through the use of predicates (Wonred as "wanting reason").[5] The effect, then, is that each name and its etymology constitute, as it were, an argument and a predicate, together expressing a form of power. And as Fred C. Robinson says, "the etymological significance of names" may often suggest the narrative function that a character has in the poem.[6] The meaning of a name is the force that seemingly dictates one's actions and one's relations to others.

The emphasis on aspects of power in the poem's roster of personal names is, moreover, very largely a matter of Germanic tradition. From generation to generation, the royal lines of different peoples announce their continuity in part through the consonantal or vocalic alliteration of their names: among the Geats Hrethel gives to his sons the names Herebeald, Haethcyn, and Hygelac (who in turn has a boy Heardred); among the Swedes Ongentheow uses vocalic alliteration in his son's name Ohthere, who preserves the same practice for his children Eanmund and Eadgils. This use of alliteration thus supports the idea that in one's name lies the source of one's identity, an identity largely shaped by what parents, kin, and community expect. The act of naming in the medieval Germanic world is consequently a token of what a person's life might well be. As Colin Morris says, one's role in such a world was normally "dictated by the group within which he was born; his ideals and standards would be those of his class, his loyalties those of his lord and his family, and he would have little choice but to follow the calling in life to which his birth appointed him."[7]

The ethos that Morris describes, its validity supported by the analyses of names in *Beowulf*, assigns to all groups their characteristic functions. Within the episodes of the poem the gatherings of servants, scops, warriors, counselors, and the royal family exemplify no instance of a concern for one's individuality but rather a continued attention to matters of communal responsibility and power, to the possibilities of mutual assistance as well as to those of threat and challenge, whether from Grendel or Hrothulf. Yet despite the activities within Hrothgar's hall—the prayer to the pagan gods, the arrival of Beowulf and his men, the defeat of Grendel, the rounds of tale-telling and banqueting—the poet names very few of the participants. In the second half of the poem, the number of those identified in the battle against the dragon is just two. Compared to the plenitude of names from all backgrounds in the *Forsyte Saga* or from scenes related to the trench warfare of *In Parenthesis*, the incidence of names in *Beowulf* is limited indeed. This limitation, furthermore, does not depend merely on a distinction between major and minor figures: the poet has no name for Grendel's dam, for the dragon, for the coast guard who greets Beowulf and his men, nor for the woman who mourns him at his funeral, yet he does mention such figures as Handscio and Guthlaf, who appear briefly in a recollection or in an episode recited by a scop. What instead may help to explain the poet's choices of names are the very same assumptions that are at work in determining the forms of the names themselves. Just as analyses of these forms reveal a concern for manifestations of power and its uses within a community, so a like concern may govern the actual appearance of personal names. The discussion that follows centers first on the ways that power and commitment influence the naming of participants in *Beowulf* and then considers some reasons for the absence of a name.

The relations between power and the naming of royalty, already mentioned as an aspect of alliteration, contribute to a complex history of hope and strife. The poem opens with a genealogical sequence, a recounting of royalty whose names in the first generations are mythical or fictional (Scyld and Beowulf) and, then, in historic time are linked mostly by alliteration: from Healfdene to Hrothgar, his brothers Heorogar and Halga, and sister (Yrse?) married to Onela, a king of Sweden.[8] Only later in the poem, however, do Hrothgar's sons Hrethic and Hrothmund appear; his daughter's name Freawaru (possibly in vocalic alliteration with that of her mother Wealhtheow) occurs in a prediction of Beowulf's that her marriage will not prevent turmoil. Hrothgar's nephew Hrothulf (his brother's son) also enters later in the poem, not to solidify royal power, but as a cause of anxiety, as a possible threat to the throne. Thus the names of royalty in the poem function as centers of solidarity and continuity or else as indicators of tension.

Within the context of royal kinship, the poet especially associates the names of nephews and maternal uncles. As Ellen Spolsky argues, the royal kinship between Beowulf and Hygelac, Sigemund and Fitela, Swerting and Hygelac, Heardred and Hereric, as well as Hnaef and Hildeburh's son is noteworthy, because these men are generally "near enough in age to make good fighting pairs"; they are committed to the defense or to the avenging of the same families.[9] What Spolsky could have added is that particular pairs of names appear close to each other in episodes concerned with risk and battle: Beowulf announces himself as "Higelāces / māēg" (407b-08a) shortly before his encounter with Grendel; Swerting's name immediately precedes the report of Hygelac's defeat by the Frisians; Heardred's name, in the passage noting his death, appears shortly before his uncle's; the scop sings of Fitela's loyalty to Sigemund during many a fight.[10] Only Hildeburh's son remains nameless—the last in his line, dead upon a pyre together with his uncle after the strife in his father Finn's house. The closeness of the bonds in this kinship of uncle and nephew and the closeness of names in context may also help to explain the poet's subtle inclusion of Wael's name; for Waels (related etymologically to Gothic *walis* 'legitimate') is the father of Sigemund, in turn the father (according to a legend not in the poem) as well as the uncle of Fitela.

In addition to close relatives, retainers near to a king or leader are among those the poet is likely to name. These retainers, as Stanley B. Greenfield shows, appear in contexts associated with the person of the leader, as if they had functions marked by a "significant resonance for the body politic."[11] To have an association with the person of the leader is to appear almost physically attached to him. The coast guard is the first to welcome Beowulf, yet he remains anonymously on duty some distance from Heorot. The counselor, however, who places himself before the shoulders, "for eaxlum" (358b), of Hrothgar to announce the presence of Beowulf, is identified as Wulfgar. To lose a trusted counsellor, as Hrothgar does after the attack of Grendel's dam, is an occasion for lament and eulogy; and Aeschere is lamented as an intimate of the king's, a shoulder companion in battle, an "eaxlgestealla" (1326a). That the poet mentions Aeschere's younger brother Yrmenlaf—from *eormen* 'immense' + *lāf* 'remnant' = "immense remnant"—suggests all the more how valuable Hrothgar's body companion was. Wiglaf, who stands against the dragon shoulder to shoulder with Beowulf, his "frēan eaxlum neah" (2853b), also has a name that in its meaning—'remnant of battle'—is indicative of loss. Of all the Geatish warriors, Wiglaf's name alone is recalled in the fatal battle against the dragon. In the earlier battles at Heorot, the poet identifies but one of Beowulf's fifteen companions—the dead Handscio. And the meaning of his name, 'handshoe' or 'glove,' suggests an attachment to Beowulf's body, to the strength in his grasp that enables the wresting from Grendel of his monstrous limb. Unferth, too, is a retainer identified by name, not attached like the others to the king's upper limbs, but to his feet. Introduced as sitting "aet fōtum ... frēan Scyldinga" (500), he has an honorary position, yet it is, as Greenfield says, "perhaps, dubiously so."[12]

The three criteria so far listed—membership in a royal family, a royal uncle and nephew, a retainer linked to a king's body—subsume beneath them a very large majority of the personal names in *Beowulf*. The power lodged in these relationships is extensive enough to include within its scope Ecglaf, the father of Unferth, and Hemming, possibly an affinal relative to a Mercian king, either Offa or Garmund.[13] In fact the only king in the poem who appears deliberately alone is Heremod. Afflicted with "sorhwylmas" (904b), he is the one king to turn on his own people, to cause them and his nobles great care.[14] The hellish passion that possessed him—"hine fyren onwōd" (915b)—likens him to Grendel, introduced as an outlaw who commits crimes, "fyrene" (101a).

Of the remaining personal names that the poet includes, all are involved in intertribal conflict. The names of representative victims as well as vanquishers serve as mnemonics in recollected warfare, feuds, thefts, and treacheries.[15] Thus Beowulf recalls the conflict of the Geats and the Hugas, in which he seized the enemy's standard bearer, the "cumbles hyrde" (2505b) Daeghryfn, and killed him with his hands. The fomenting of a feud, the slaying of Heatholaf the Wylfing by Beowulf's father Ecgtheow is an intertribal event, requiring negotiations by Hrothgar and the payment of wergild. Nor do negotiated settlements always ensure peace, for as the poem notes, the marriage of Freawaru to Ingeld cannot erase the bitterly remembered slaying of the Heathobard Withergyld by the Danes. Moreover, folk memory retains examples of extraordinary theft and plunder—the daring of Hama, who risked Eormenric's treacherous hatred, his "searonīðas" (1220b), to steal off with the precious necklace of the Brosnings. But maybe the treachery that most sharply depicts distrust among Germanic tribes is the carnage at Freslond. The names of the War Scyldings slain—Hnaef and Hunlaf—together with that of the surviving leader Hengest, form an alliterative bond that emphasizes the continued loyalty of the living to the dead and the inadequacy of wergild as a stay against vengeance. To achieve a heightened sense of the lust for revenge, the poet introduces Guthlaf and Oslaf as representative warriors, who speak of their sorrows, their inability to restrain their "wæfre mōd" (1150b), their restless spirit in their breasts. Soon after, the War Scyldings renew hostilities against Finn, and victorious, return home with booty in their ships.

Yet if the poet sees fit to include the names of representative warriors — the Eofors, the Wulfs, and the Wonreds — names, furthermore, that are not necessarily historical, his reliance on circumlocution to refer to Grendel's dam and on epithets such as *eorðraca*, *hordweard*, and *fyrdraca* for the dragon needs explanation.[16] So, too, does his practice of omitting some royal names like that of Hildeburh's son and those of royal daughters, Hygelac's, for example, who marries Eofor, and Hrethel's, who marries Ecgtheow. Other figures appear who have more to say than Oslaf and Guthlaf — the prophet of Geatish decline, the speaker at the dragon's barrow — yet neither has a name. The absence of a name, in fact, has led to speculation on the identity of the mourner at Beowulf's pyre as probably Hygd.[17] Clearly the urge to identify significant figures in the poem is an aspect of modern sensibility. That the poet resists such naming, however, is due to a sense of propriety, a sense of representative figures who are to have names and those who are not.

Thus in the immediate families of kings, the genealogies within the poem exclude women of the past. The poet identifies Hrethel as Hygelac's father; he does not allude to his mother. As for ascending generations, we have the names of royal daughters who themselves marry kings — Yrse (?), Hildeburh, Freawaru — but not of those who marry anyone lower in station. So we do not have the name of Beowulf's mother, Eegtheow's wife whom Hrothgar recalls as receiving the kindness of God in child bearing, "þaet hyre Ealdmetod ēste wære / bearngebyrdo" (945-46a). Nor do we know the name of Hygelac's daughter, wed to Eofor as a reward for his taking the Swedish king Ongentheow's life.

Of royal sons in the poem, Hildeburh's alone has no name, both because he dies uncrowned and because his death deprives Folcwalda and Finn's line of a successor. Other young men who are not yet kings — Hrethric and Hrothmund — are under threat but still possible inheritors of the throne. Heardred dies in battle, but not before he becomes king. More broadly, the death of a king and the demise of a people result in anonymity. Unnamed speakers appear who mourn the death of leaders and companions, who prophesy the end of a tribe. Thus the account of the dragon's barrow begins with an anonymous mourner's lament for his companions, his "duguð" (2254b), and for his war chief, his "wigfruman" (2261a), none of them named, not the companions, the war chief, nor the people. At the conclusion of the poem, likewise, the anticipated decline and exile of the Geats appear in an anonymously delivered prophecy, and the lament for Beowulf is that of a woman's who also remains nameless. In sum, the loss of power and the severance of commitment by death deny soon enough to a people and their leaders a recollection of personal identity.

If mourners and prophets are unidentified, so are scops and the lusty coast guard. Neither the scops nor the coast guard is a body companion of a king or a leader such as Beowulf. None of them has a rôle comparable to Volker in the *Nibelungenlied*, whom Hagen in Hungary, after he looked over his shoulder, "dô blicht über ahsel," chose as his comrade-in-arms.[18] The scops in *Beowulf* recite but enter none of the poem's battles. The coast guard is a warrior, yet in place of a gift for song, he displays a ready gusto in welcoming Beowulf, a boisterousness in addressing Beowulf's companions as a band of spies, as "lēasscēaweras" (253a).[19] Committed to the defense of his fellow Danes, the coast guard possesses none of the power reposed in the royal family or in the king's body companions. And so he, too, is nameless.

That almost all the criteria for according a name apply to Beowulf is perhaps no surprise: he is a king's nephew, a king himself, a victor in single combat. What is indeed surprising is that two of his formidable antagonists—Grendel's dam and the dragon—should have no names of their own. Of Grendel, the poet says that he is a fiend or monster, that he held sway, "rīxode" (144a), for twelve winters over Heorot, and that he is a descendant of Cain. As a usurper, a mock king, Grendel has enough human contact to refuse counsel and terms of peace, to reject all those commitments that characterize a human society. His name, then, is an emblem of the outlaw. But Grendel's dam and the dragon live beyond the reach of law. The poet describes them also as fiends and monsters, as denizens outside the districts of human habitation (the dam has her den beneath the waters of a mere, the dragon lies inside a barrow of treasure). Grendel's dam emerges from the mere for the sole purpose of seeking vengeance for her son's death; in fact most instances in the poem of *wrecan* 'to avenge' and its variants are predicates attributable to her. The dragon's actions resemble yet differ from human purpose; he responds to impulse, not to thought. The poet's account of him is that of a creature driven by fury; his is the joy of war, "wīges gefeh" (2298b); his aim is to redeem his precious drinking-cup with fire, "wolde ... līge forgyldan / drincfaet dȳre" (2305–06a). As Edward B. Irving says, the dragon's nature is "Alien even to such humanoid monsters as Grendel and his mother."[20] His reasons for action, if there are any, are inexplicable. Thus of Beowulf's three monstrous opponents, Grendel alone has a sufficient presence among men to be named. Grendel's dam and the dragon, however, are agents of the alien, one identified as "āglǣcwīf," 'monster wife,' the other as "fȳrdraca," but neither by a personal name.

Personal names, finally, are denied to the thief who steals from the dragon's barrow and to his master. The poet readily explains the governing motives, the sore distress, "þreānēdla" (2223a), that the thief has, who is already accused of wrong doing, "synbysig" (2226a). His hope is for a compact of peace, a "frioðowǣr" (2282b). Though risky, the theft is not an act of will, "nealles mid gewealdum" (2221a); it scarcely resembles Hama's purposeful audacity in snatching Eormenric's splendid necklace. If anything, the sheer anonymity of the thief and his master contributes to the stark ironies with which *Beowulf* concludes. The thief's effort to gain a grant of peace initiates the fall of his king and of the Geatish people. The same theft has the unanticipated effect of exposing in Beowulf's chosen retainers a lack of valor, an unwillingness to join Wiglaf in battling the dragon. Retreating to the woods, these men reveal, in effect, what it is to suffer a loss of courage and power, a loss that opens the Geats to the incursions of other tribes, to events that will rob them of a continuing identity.

Like the etymological analysis of names, then, the distribution of names in the poem suggests a consciousness of power and commitment. The criteria used for distinguishing the named from the anonymous are inclusive enough to account for all the participants. That the criteria should have such generality contributes, too, to the idea that the poet, no matter how much distinction and virtue he accords to the heroic Beowulf, the wise Hrothgar, and the loyal Wiglaf, defines them primarily as significant members of their society. Their aim is to fulfill the expectations of their culture, not to establish themselves as individuals concerned with the promises of life or with the state of their souls. In short, no one in the poem has a name because he is an individual in his own right. The right to a personal name, instead, comes from the power one has to realize his commitments to his society.

Notes

1. These etymologies appear in Fred C. Robinson, "Personal Names in Medieval Narrative and the Name of Unferth in *Beowulf*," in *Essays in Honor of Richebourg Gaillard McWilliams*, ed. Howard Creed. *Birmingham-Southern College Bulletin* 63, no. 2. (Birmingham, Ala.: Birmingham-Southern College, 1970), 43–48. A review of etymologies for the name "Beowulf" appears in Fr. Klaeber, ed., *Beowulf And The Fight At Finnsburg*, 3rd ed. (Boston: D.C. Heath, 1951), xxviii. See, also, Erik Björkman, *Studien über die Eigenname × im Beowulf*. Studien zur englischen Philologie 58 (Halle, 1920), and Henry Bosley Woolf, *The Old Germanic Principles of Name-Giving* (Baltimore, 1935).

2. The etymology of Hygd appears in Klaeber, *Beowulf*, p. 438; of Freawaru in Kemp Malone, "Ingeld," *Modern Philology* 27 (1930): 258; of Hygelac and Unferth in Robinson, *op. cit.*, 43–48. The name Unferth has also had the gloss "mar-peace"; see Morton W. Bloomfield, "*Beowulf* and Christian Allegory: An Interpretation of Unferth," *Traditio* 7 (1949–1951): 412. Even if Bloomfield were correct, his gloss

would simply provide another perspective on power, germane to the argument of the essay.

3. Klaeber, *Beowulf*, xxxii n. 1. and p. 434.

4. Ibid., xxviii–xxix.

5. Ibid., p. 432 and p. 441.

6. Fred C. Robinson, "The Significance of Names in Old English Literature," *Anglia* 86 (1968): 15.

7. *The Discovery of the Individual 1050–1200* (New York: Harper & Row, 1972), p. 32.

8. The genealogy of the Danish royal line is fully discussed by Klaeber, *op. cit.*, xxx–xxxvi. On the questionable reference to Yrse as Onela's queen and on the appearance of these two names in line 62 of the poem, see Norman E. Eliason, "Healfdene's Daughter," in *Anglo-Saxon Poetry: Essays in Appreciation for John C. McGalliard*, ed. Lewis E. Nicholson and Dolores Warwick Frese (Notre Dame, Ind.: University of Notre Dame Press, 1975), pp. 3–13. Eliason's essay also notes, pages 9 and 10, the infrequent use of women's names in the poem, an issue that is part of the argument presented here. More generally, the poet uses alliteration for other royal lines: Hygelac's, Finn's, Hoc's, Breca's, but not of Froda's and Garmund's, and Waels's.

9. "Old English Kinship Terms And *Beowulf*," *Neuphilologische Mitteilungen* 78 (1977): 233. The relation of Swerting to Hygelac is not altogether defined; see Klaeber, *op. cit.*, p. 440. Norman E. Eliason, "Beowulf, Wiglaf and the Waegmundings," *Anglo-Saxon England* 7 (1978): 101, n. 1 argues that Hereic may be a descriptive epithet, not a name. Even if correct his argument does not affect the thesis of this essay.

10. All quotations from the poem, including this first one, refer to lines in Klaeber's edition, cited above.

11. "The extremities of the *Beowulf*ian body politic," in *Saints Scholars And Heroes*, Vol. 1, ed. Margot H. King and Wesley M. Stevens (Collegeville, Minn.: St. John's Abby and College; distributed by University Microfilms International, Ann Arbor, 1979), p. 7.

12. Greenfield, ibid., p. 7.

13. This extension of power applies to the inclusion also of Wiglaf's father Wihstan and to his kinsman Aelfhere.

14. Heremod also fits among those cited for treachery, for his attack on the sons of Egwela, a king of the Danes. See the paragraph below.

15. The category of representative antagonists might well include the competition of Breca and Beowulf, especially since it is first presented by Unferth in an inhospitable manner.

16. On the questionable historicity of Eofor, see R. W. Chambers, *Beowulf*, 3rd ed. (Cambridge: The University Press, 1963), pp. 411–12, n. 2.

17. John C. Pope, "*Beowulf* 3150–3151: Queen Hygd and the Word 'Geomeowle'," *Modern Language Notes* 70 (1955): 84, suggests that Hygd "cannot with any certainty be denied the position of Beowulf's chief mourner." Tauno F. Mustanoja, "The Unnamed Woman's Song of Mourning over Beowulf and the Tradition of Ritual Lamentation," *Neuphilologische Mitteilungen* 68 (1967): 27, concludes that the poet may have "had a professional mourner in mind ..., [that] he had no reason to be interested in the woman's identity."

18. Ursula Hennig, ed., *Das Nibelungenlied* (Tübingen: Max Niemayer, 1977), 277, line 1801a.

19. Margaret W. Pepperdene, "Beowulf and the Coastguard," *English Studies* 47 (1966): 413–18 discusses the coast guard's diction convincingly.

20. *Introduction to "Beowulf"* (Englewood Cliffs, N.J.: Prentice-Hall, 1969), p. 82.

La femme et le lignage florentin
(xive–xvie siècles)

CHRISTIANE KLAPISCH–ZUBER

e fut une vertueuse, chère et bonne dame; elle vint chez son mari en l'année du Christ 1349, le 1er octobre 1349, de sorte qu'elle est venue habiter dans notre maison 67 ans deux mois et vingt-six jours."[1] Dans la brève oraison funèbre de sa mère, "Madame Bartolomea fille de feu Filippo Bagnesi et veuve de Giovanni di Lapo Niccolini, notre père," Lapo Niccolini insiste d'emblée, en 1416, sur les traits qui dessinent le mieux l'individualité d'une Florentine: elle s'est mariée, elle est venue chez son époux, elle a vécu là longtemps, dans cette maison qui n'était pas vraiment la sienne, mais "la nôtre" selon son fils. Une double référence à un père, mort depuis longtemps, et à un mari disparu trente-cinq ans plus tôt la désigne encore près de sept décennies après cette installation. Ni Bartolomea Bagnesi, ni Bartolomea Niccolini, elle reste la fille de Giovanni, la veuve de Filippo, celle qui s'était installée là soixante-sept ans avant....

Des textes aussi éloquents, on en trouve à foison dans les archives toscanes. Ils posent un problème: comment définit-on, à quoi réduit-on l'identité féminine dans une société où le lignage—la *casa*—privilégie fortement la filiation en ligne masculine et installe systématiquement l'épouse dans la famille du mari? Cet essai propose sinon des réponses, du moins des approches successives fondées sur l'observation des Florentins en diverses circonstances de leur vie d'époux et de pères: à la naissance ou à la mort de leurs enfants et de leurs proches, à leur mariage, bref en toutes ces occasions où se rédéfinissent, par des décisions concrètes ou des comportements rituels, les rapports entre l'individu et le groupe.

Nomination et filiation

Commençons à nouveau par une citation révélatrice, tirée d'un autre livre de famille. "Comme ce nom (Cilia) ne nous plaisait plus, nous l'avons appelée Vaggia, puisque son aînée ainsi nommée était morte." C'est ainsi qu'un Florentin, Uguccione Capponi, décide de changer le prénom de l'une de ses filles, plusieurs années après sa naissance.[2] Lorsque, en revanche, quelque quarante années plus tard, Filippo Strozzi meurt, sa veuve rebaptise leur fils de trois ans, Giovanbattista, du prénom paternel, "pour renouveler la mémoire de son défunt mari."[3]

Les renominations d'enfants florentins ne sont pas tout à fait rares dans la Florence des XIVe–XVIe siècles.[4] Ces deux exemples, cependant, révèlent une différence fondamentale, sensible à bien d'autres indices, dans le comportement des parents. Rebaptiser un enfant mâle, c'est toujours assurer la circulation des noms d'ancêtres, insérer davantage l'enfant dans la longue série des hommes de son sang. Renommer une fille peut répondre, au premier chef, au caprice des parents, parce que tout simplement le prénom d'abord choisi "ne plait plus."

L'identité anthroponymique des Florentines apparait en effet beaucoup plus flottante que celle de leurs frères. Si je prends pour point de départ de cette réflexion sur l'identité des femmes au sein des lignages urbains de la Renaissance leur désignation personnelle, c'est que l'une des fonctions de la dénomination est de classer l'individu. Ainsi, le prénom donné à la naissance doit classer l'enfant par rapport aux lignées de ses parents, dans sa généalogie et à l'intérieur même de la fratrie, surtout si des enjeux matériels ou symboliques lui sont attachés.[5] C'est pourquoi on le répète d'une génération et d'un individu à l'autre. A Florence, il est de règle de donner aux nouveau-nés les noms portés par des aïeux ou par des parents morts, passés au rang d'ancêtres, en privilégiant la lignée paternelle. Si un enfant aîné disparait, on réaffecte à un puîné le prénom laissé vacant. Il importe peu que, dans une fratrie décimée par la mort, l'ordre initial soit finalement bouleversé et que, par exemple, le grand-père paternel se retrouve dans un cadet et non pas dans le fils aîné, car l'hêritage paternel est également divisible entre les fils survivants. En revanche, il importe que ceux-ci portent des noms tirés du stock familial, marquant ainsi leur appartenance au groupe lignager et leur droit à participer de son héritage matériel et spirituel.

Pour les filles, cette fonction qu'a le nom de classer dans une parenté s'efface derrière la fonction de signification. Le prénom, ici, veut surtout induire le destin souhaité par les parents. Alors qu'au XVe siècle, les prénoms auguratifs—du type Benvenuto, Bonavere, Buonmercante—ou les prénoms descriptifs qui attribuent une qualité morale ou physique à l'enfant hors de tout contexte chrétien—tels Buono, Morello ou Biondo—ont presque disparu parmi les baptisés florentins de sexe masculin, ils sont encore très fréquents chez les filles. La fantaisie des parents se déploie plus librement à leur endroit qu'autour de leurs frères, elle néglige les noms de grands saints chrétiens pour des prénoms flatteurs, elle ne s'interdit pas d'écorcher les noms des saints patrons ou de les abréger si les consonnances en sont ainsi rendues plus plaisantes. Le prénom qu'une fille reçoit au baptême classe peu, il signifie plus. Dès sa venue au monde, la Florentine se trouve ainsi moins profondément insérée dans le groupe des vivants et des morts qui forme le lignage. Mais l'exemple cité plus haut montre en outre que la personnalité qui lui est attribuée par son nom de baptême est fragile. Qualifiée, plutôt que classée par rapport à sa généalogie, souvent considérée comme interchangeable avec ses soeurs aînées,[6] reflétant dans ses variantes anthroponymiques les préférences personnelles et les revirements de ses parents, la Florentine parait dotée par son nom personnel d'une identité, lignagère autant qu'individuelle, beaucoup plus floue que ses frères.

Si l'on considère maintenant l'ensemble des noms qui, derrière le nom de baptême, désignent l'individu à Florence, au moins dans les classes supérieures, on peut y reconnaître la même variabilité tout au long de la vie d'une femme. Le système anthroponymique toscan fait suivre le nom personnel de ceux des ascendants paternels directs—père, grand-père, parfois aïeuls plus lointains encore—et du nom de famille paternel. Comme son frère, la fille est donc désignée par la série des noms d'ancêtres paternels et par le nom du lignage de son père aussi longtemps qu'elle demeure sous son toit. Mais quand elle sort de cette maison pour se marier, son appellation change. Son propre prénom est désormais suivi par le prénom de son mari, ceux des ascendants de celui-ci et leur nom de lignage. Ainsi, dans son appellation, la femme voit substituer à sa filiation paternelle une sorte de "filiation maritale," celle-là même qui caractérisera les enfants du couple. "La Giovanna (fille) di Lapo di Giovanni Niccolini" devient "Mª Giovanna (femme) di Giovanni di Gentile Albizzi" dans l'usage courant. Veuve, enfin, si elle retourne chez son père ou ses frères, elle a toutes chances de retrouver ses désignations originelles, accompagnées parfois de la mention de son défunt mari. Mais il n'est pas toujours facile de distinguer au travers de leurs appellations familières le véritable état-civil des femmes, tant les références aux hommes dont on fait suivre leur prénom personnel emmêlent filiation et alliance.

Ces variations anthroponymiques, que ne subissent pas les hommes, révèlent l'incertitude du rattachement des femmes aux lignages dont elles sortent et où elles entrent. Certes, comme ailleurs en Europe, le système de désignation "permet de récupérer la bilatéralité caractéristique des systèmes de parenté européens et d'atténuer l'accentuation patrilinéaire du nom de famille qui identifie l'individu à une seule lignée."[7] Cette remarque s'applique sans doute à la Toscane de la fin du Moyen-Age. Mais, ici, l'accentuation patrilinéaire est particulièrement forte. Aussi les rappels de la lignée maternelle sont-ils moins fréquents dans les noms masculins qu'ailleurs; quant à la prénomination des filles, elle échappe plus souvent aux règles gouvernant celle des garçons, tandis que l'ensemble de leurs références anthroponymiques marque l'indécision et le caractère provisoire de leur classement familial.

Il importe peu, en effet, que les femmes qui sortent avec leur dot de leur famille et sont exclues de l'héritage soient reconnues à travers leur prénom comme membres d'un groupe de filiation, possesseurs potentiels d'un patrimoine transmissible en ligne masculine. Les femmes ne produisent pas d'ancêtres mémorables comme les hommes; elles ne perpétuent pas d'identité féminine au bénéfice d'un groupe unique, le lignage patrilinéaire. Alors même que la parenté reconnue et contrôlée par l'Eglise dans les échanges matrimoniaux est officiellement bilatérale, la pratique des lignages florentins démontre clairement que jusque vers 1450 au moins, on fait peu de cas de la parenté par les femmes. Les généalogies établies par les contemporains ne conservent pas de souvenir étendu des lignées maternelles, et l'exogamie lignagère, empêchant d'épouser une parente paternelle du même nom, même située à un degré de parenté permis par l'Eglise, parait beaucoup plus forte et spontanément observée que ne le sont les empêchements théoriques de parenté dans la ligne maternelle, mal mémorisée et tôt oubliée.

Dot et remariage

Parallèlement à l'accentuation patrilinéaire de la parenté, s'est accomplie depuis le XIIe siècle une lente révolution affectant la transmission des biens.[8] Dans les classes urbaines de la fin du Moyen-Age, l'héritage reste divisible en parts égales entre les fils, mais les soeurs, "convenablement" dotées, en sont désormais exclues. Le patrimoine foncier, en particulier, est réservé aux mâles: à Florence, les femmes n'emportent en dot que des biens mobiliers. L'exclusion de l'héritage paternel s'aggrave pour elles d'une réduction de leur autonomie économique et de leur capacité juridique. Ce sont leurs maris qui prennent le contrôle et la gestion des biens dotaux. Dans ce contexte, la Florentine garde, attachée à elle, sa dot jusqu'à sa mort. Mais le veuvage, l'éventuel remariage qui marquent couramment sa vie de femme adulte, remettent en question la situation sociale des hommes qui gèrent ses biens dotaux. Ils suscitent de nouvelles incertitudes, des tensions parfois violentes dans la définition de ses relations avec son entourage, dans son identité même.

Si la future veuve est assez jeune et si le couple a été fécond, le mari, par son testament, s'efforce de conserver leur mère, avec sa dot, aux enfants qu'elle lui a donnés et qui doivent rester dans le lignage paternel, en porter le nom, y tenir leur place d'héritiers s'ils sont mâles, y puiser leur future dot s'ils sont du sexe féminin. Mais la jeunesse de la veuve ranime aussi les prétentions de la famille où elle est née sur les biens qu'elle a emportés en dot et sur son corps, sur sa fécondité. En la remariant, en faisant passer la dot récupérée à une nouvelle famille alliée, les consanguins de la veuve montrent bien que le mariage n'abolit jamais, à Florence, les liens qu'ils entretiennent avec une femme de leur sang et les droits qu'ils continuent de faire prévaloir sur la dot qu'ils lui ont jadis donnée. Leurs interventions révèlent aussi que l'alliance est fragile, car le couple passe après les intérêts du lignage. Le maintien de la veuve sous l'autorité des parents de son mari aussi bien que sa sortie de leur maison manifestent symétriquement la puissance des lignages par rapport à l'individu et au couple ou à sa descendance. C'est une relation ambigue — de défiance réciproque, tempérée d'entr'aide et sourcilleusement contrôlée — qui caractérise à Florence les rapports entre alliés; elle se trouve ainsi fragilisée par la promptitude mise par les parents de la veuve à la reprendre et à la relancer sur le marché matrimonial.

Comment les Florentins concilient-ils cette attitude avec l'éloge de l'alliance dont ils pimentent si souvent leurs considérations théoriques sur l'économie domestique? *Imparentarsi* forme, aux XIVe–XVIe siècles, l'un de leurs thèmes de réflexion préférés et les traités abondent en recommandations sur le choix de l'épouse et de sa parenté. Pour eux, toutefois, l'alliance offre moins un moyen de s'enrichir que d'assurer sa situation sociale en acquérant des "amis" qui sachent vous défendre dans la jungle de la vie publique.[9] Il est donc tentant, pour un homme qui voit mourir son beau-frère, de vouloir récupérer sa soeur afin de constituer, en la remariant, un nouveau réseau d'amis centré autour d'un homme vivant et actif.

De fait, les Florentins résolvent les contradictions naissant de la prédominance des intérêts lignagers, malheureusement contrastés, en reportant sur la femme, ballottée d'une famille à l'autre, la responsabilité d'une position aussi instable. C'est à sa nature, faible et inconstante, qu'ils en assignent tout à la fois les causes (la nécessité d'assurer sa protection et de la gouverner)[10] et les suites (son incapacité à s'attacher durablement à une seule famille). Constamment réaffirmée dans les faits et dans les écrits des hommes de ce temps, l'idéologie du lignage traîne comme son ombre une image dévalorisée de la femme; non pas certes de l'épouse en titre, installée dans les rassurantes perspectives d'une union que tous souhaitent durable, féconde et utile, mais de la femme qui, au moment de son veuvage, cède aux exigences du lignage opposé. Qu'elle reste dans la famille de son mari ou qu'elle soit reprise par sa famille d'origine pour être remariée, la veuve offre une cible de choix. Sa nouvelle union implique qu'elle laisse derrière elle les enfants de son premier lit et qu'elle les dépouille, du moins jusqu'à sa mort, de l'usage de sa dot.[11] Si elle préfère, à l'inverse, rester chastement veuve, ou si ses parents par alliance l'y contraignent en retenant sa dot, on va lire dans son attitude un refus de reconnaître à sa propre parenté un droit que celle-ci juge lui appartenir encore. D'une manière ou de l'autre, les Florentins ne se font pas faute de l'accuser de trahir les intérêts de la famille. Et quand elle reçoit un nouvel époux, ils corsent l'accusation en lui déniant sa "nature" maternelle: la femme perd alors jusqu'à son identité de mère. Incapable d'aimer assez ses enfants pour les préférer à une nouvelle union, elle est taxée non seulement de légèreté, mais d'inhumanité. Elle représente le désordre dans l'ordre du lignage. Le féminin est ici comme le versant négatif du bel édifice construit par l'homme.

Maternité et fécondité

Cependant, au sein de ces groupes lignagers et parmi leurs porte-parole, règne l'idée que le destin de la femme est de donner des enfants aux familles où le mariage les a fait entrer. Peu de fils, à vrai dire, atteignant l'âge de prendre femme, se voient autorisés par leur père à le faire sans tarder[12]; beaucoup de familles, qui ont contrôlé trop sévèrement la nuptialité de leurs garçons pour éviter une fragmentation rapide du patrimoine, paient aux XIVe–XVIe siècles leur rigidité d'une pure et simple extinction.[13] Aussi est-il urgent que ceux que l'on marie procrèent rapidement et abondamment.

Ce que les Florentins prisent donc chez leurs épouses, c'est, outre leur vertu, la fécondité qu'elles montreront, accroissant de la sorte l'honneur de la *casa*. Quand Alberti, pour ne citer que le plus célèbre des penseurs de la famille, évalue les caractères à préférer dans la future épouse, il met en vedette la beauté, reflet des qualités morales et mélange de grâce, de propreté et de robustesse. La jeunesse de la fille surtout va compter: le Florentin veut une adolescente de moins de dix-huit ans, encore innocente, et qu'il pourra, lui l'adulte averti, modeler et morigéner efficacement.[14] Toutes ces qualités lui promettent beaucoup de fils, dont on croit alors que la maturation demande dans le sein maternel plus de soin, de temps et de force que celle des filles.

Les données d'observation confirment que les Florentines ont répondu à l'attente de leurs maris, lorsque la mort ne les fauche pas prématurément. En moins de vingt ans de vie commune, elles mettent au monde plus de dix enfants en moyenne; si l'on prend aussi en considération les unions où le décès de l'un des époux vient interrompre la vie du couple encore fécond, c'est, malgré tout, plus de sept enfants en moyenne qui voient le jour dans les familles de la bourgeoisie florentine. Ces femmes se montrent aussi obéissantes qu'on le leur prêche de tous côtés: à l'évidence, elles ne pratiquent pas d'autre contrôle des naissances que celui, tout naturel, lié aux absences de leurs époux, occupés à leurs affaires. Les enfants se suivent à moins de vingt et un mois d'écart et cette succession de grossesses rapprochées explique que la vie féconde de ces femmes s'arrête relativement tôt. Mariées vers 17 ou 18 ans, elles portent leur dernier enfant vers 37–38 ans. En contrepartie de l'honneur qu'elles accroissent dans la famille de leur époux en se montrant fécondes et du respect que leur vaut leur aptitude à procréer, elles doivent connaître une usure physique précoce, à supposer qu'elles survivent jusqu'à l'âge d'un légitime et canonique repos.... A quarante ans, une Florentine des milieux de la bourgeoisie marchande ne procrée plus, on ne la remariera donc pas si elle devient veuve.[15]

Un fait explique sans doute la fréquence des grossesses. Dès la seconde moitié du XIVe siècle, quand on peut l'étudier dans les livres de famille, on constate que l'allaitement mercenaire est tout à fait général dans la bourgeoisie urbaine. Au lendemain de leur naissance, en tout cas dans les semaines qui suivent celle-ci, les nourrissons nés dans ces familles partent chez une nourrice, dans une ferme, souvent lointaine, de le campagne toscane. Un sur cinq seulement de ces bébés reste chez ses parents pour se voir confié à une nourrice salariée installée là ou à une esclave domestique. Ceux qui ont été envoyés au dehors ne reviendront dans la maison paternelle qu'après vingt mois d'absence. Dans l'intervalle, la plupart seront passés entre les mains de plusieurs nourrices; une infime minorité aura tété le lait maternel, tout à fait au début de sa vie, dans quelque période de soudure entre deux nourrices, ou en raison d'une situation exceptionnelle, guerre, épidémie.[16]

La généralité de la pratique pose deux ordres de questions. D'abord, les Florentins sont-ils conscients des risques et des avantages de la mise en nourrice de leurs enfants? Ensuite, s'ils jugent les seconds supérieurs aux premiers, comment résolvent-ils la contradiction entre le fait de détacher les enfants de leur mère pendant près de deux ans et les conceptions en vigueur sur l'allaitement?

Il faut rappeler que tous les bons auteurs, Anciens ou Modernes, qu'ils peuvent lire et les prédicateurs qu'ils entendent ressassent les bienfaits de l'allaitement maternel.[17] La nourrice est un moindre mal, qu'on devrait réserver aux cas où la mère ne peut nourrir, et il faut alors la choisir d'une complexion aussi proche que possible de celle de la mère. L'alchimie qui s'est poursuivie dans la matrice maternelle se prolonge en effet quand l'enfant tête le lait, dérivé direct du sang menstruel. La nourrice risque de pourrir le fruit qui lui est confié en le nourrissant d'un lait malsain, grossier, animal.

Ainsi mis en garde, les Florentins observent en outre les dangers encourus par leurs nourrissons placés dans une campagne reculée. Ils savent qu'il est difficile d'y surveiller la santé de l'enfant et le comportement de la nourrice. Les médecins sont loin. L'enfant sera-t-il bien couché dans son berceau et non pas aux côtés des nourriciers, dans le lit conjugal? Ne risque-t-il pas davantage là-bas d'être étouffé dans leur sommeil? Plus d'un nourrisson sur six meurt avant l'âge d'un an en nourrice et, dans 15% de ces décès, la responsabilité incombe aux nourriciers qui ont "suffoqué" l'enfant. Cependant, la lente prise de conscience des parents, à qui l'Eglise répète que dormir avec un bébé est un crime, ne se traduit pas encore au XVe siècle par le refus de l'allaitement salarié, bien au contraire. Vers 1500, les nourrices extérieures, recrutées toujours plus loin de Florence, sont attestées jusque chez des artisans et des citadins aux revenus fort modestes.

De fait, c'est d'un autre danger, la grossesse de la nourrice, que les Florentins se méfient surtout. Le lait d'une femme enceinte est redouté de tous les parents soucieux de la survie de leur progéniture. Ils le considèrent non seulement comme moins riche et plus grossier, mais aussi comme véritablement pollué (*sozzo*). Les arguments savants n'ont pas grand chose à voir avec cette crainte; des lettrés, tels Alberti, peuvent même soutenir que la grossesse augmente le lait.[18] La peur des parents les incite à suivre avec suspicion la santé de la nourrice et entraîne de fréquents changements dans le placement de l'enfant; elle ne ralentit pas pour autant la recherche de la parfaite nourrisseuse, cet oiseau rare qui a perdu son propre enfant et peut réserver un lait frais au petit Florentin.

Alberti rappelle aussi des autorités antiques selon lesquelles l'allaitement affaiblit et rend parfois stérile la mère. Dans sa conviction que le couple doit procréer au maximum, ce serait la seule raison de recourir à une nourrice mercenaire. Des Florentins aussi éduqués que lui pouvaient donc mettre en balance l'avantage de hâter les grossesses maternelles en recourant à des nourrices salariées et le risque de retrouver des enfants moins vigoureux au retour de chez celles-ci que si le mère les avait nourris.[19] Mais ces calculs ne paraissent pas avoir marqué le comportement courant des citadins. En revanche, le risque, bien réel celui-là, que la nourrice extérieure, enceinte ou peu soigneuse, fait courir au nourrisson est, répétons-le, pratiquement accepté de tous.

Certains moralistes contemporains préviennent aussi les parents contre le nourrissage mercenaire parce qu'il interdit à l'enfant et à sa mère de développer ce rapport intime qui seul peut tisser entre eux des liens affectifs indestructibles.[20] C'est là qu'est la clé de la réponse à notre seconde question. Et cette réponse est brutale. Par leur comportement, les Florentins montrent qu'ils se soucient peu, en fin de compte, de l'apport de la mère à l'enfant. Il leur suffit que leurs épouses soient fécondes et vertueuses et que les nourrices soient saines et aussi continentes que possible. On peut s'interroger, de fait, sur l'influence réelle des conceptions médicales concernant les deux semences, masculine et féminine, les qualités physiques et morales transmises par le mère — et, au delà, par sa lignée — ou par le lait de la nourrice. Tout se passe en réalité comme si comptaient seulement les patrimoines matériel, symbolique et, pour oser un anachronisme, génétique de la lignée paternelle ainsi que les rapports affectifs développés là, entre hommes du même sang. Les règles sociales de la filiation en arrivent à nier la part physique de la mère dans la transmission de tout caractère. Comment s'étonner, dès lors, que l'identité maternelle concédée à la Florentine repose, dans la pratique, sur sa fécondité beaucoup plus que sur son rôle d'éducatrice, quoi qu'en disent les théoriciens? Le lignage, encore une fois, prévaut sur le ménage.

Identités rituelles

Les comportements rituels ont pour but de dépasser ces conflits latents, au moins temporairement. Je prendrai l'exemple de certains rites de mariage, inscrits dans cette période où l'alliance est proclamée et la femme glorifiée par le mariage.[21] Les rites dont j'analyserai ici seulement quelques aspects se déroulent tous dans un cadre domestique: au jour dit "de l'anneau," parce que la femme est remise à son époux, sous le toit de son père, et qu'elle reçoit du mari un anneau après l'échange des consentements; et quand elle est introduite dans la famille de son époux, le jour des noces, parfois longtemps après la première cérémonie.

Ces deux journées solennelles comportent des échanges de cadeaux entre le mari ou sa famille et l'épouse ou la sienne. Par leur réciprocité, ces cadeaux expriment l'échange que l'alliance instaure entre deux lignages et qui ne doit pas s'arrêter aux seules festivités des noces. L'examen plus minutieux de la nature de ces présents, de la qualité de leurs donateurs, du moment et du lieu où ils prennent place, révèle les limites de l'association entre les deux familles. A Florence, il est frappant de voir que les deux parentés ne se mêlent vraiment que dans la grande cérémonie préliminaire, célébrée dans une église, au cours de laquelle se conclut l'accord entre le père de la fille et celui de son futur gendre. Ensuite, les parentés interviennent par leur présence et leurs dons dans la partie surtout de ces rites de passage qui les implique plus directement: au rite de séparation, pour la parenté de la femme, qui est conviée au "jour de l'anneau" mais ne prend qu'une faible part au rite des noces; au rite d'agrégation pour la parenté de l'homme, dont quelques membres masculins accompagent le mari le "jour de l'anneau," mais qui est tout entière présente le jour des noces. Les rites nuptiaux florentins semblent vouloir clarifier la nouvelle appartenance de l'épouse, faciliter ou expliciter son agrément par le lignage marital. Ils insistent sur le passage d'une femme d'un groupe à l'autre beaucoup plus que sur la formation du couple, l'instauration d'un nouveau "ménage" ou même l'association durable des deux familles alliées.

Un rite qui se déroule à l'arrivée de la femme chez son mari, le jour des *nozze*, prend tout son sens si l'on se souvient de la fragilité de l'insertion des femmes dans le lignage de leur mari, démontrée par l'attitude à l'égard de la veuve. Ce rite du "jour où l'on donne les anneaux" voit le mari offrir à sa femme de nouvelles bagues, ornées de pierres précieuses, qui viennent s'ajouter à celles qu'il lui a déjà offertes au moment où on la lui a promise, puis quand il l'a "épousée." Après lui, ses propres parents réitèrent son geste; ils sont suivis enfin par les femmes de sa parenté, soeurs et belles-soeurs, femmes d'oncles, de cousins plus lointains. Ces épousailles collectives insèrent donc la nouvelle venue dans des cercles de parenté de plus en plus larges. En même temps, les donatrices parentes de l'époux signifient clairement à la mariée son statut de femme à l'intérieur de son nouveau lignage, une femme soumise à une hiérarchie d'autorités masculines: mari, beau-père, beau-frères, voire cousins....

Les anneaux ne sont pourtant donnés à la jeune femme que pour un temps limité. Les parentes de son mari qui offrent une bague se défont d'un présent qui leur avait été fait dans les mêmes circonstances. Les anneaux sont donc pour la plupart offerts à la nouvelle mariée par des épouses déjà "initiées"; mais leurs maris restent maîtres du jeu. Tenant compte de leurs obligations envers ceux qui avaient jadis "donné" à leur propre femme, ils décident des destinataires des anneaux qu'elle avait reçus. Dans leurs livres personnels, ils tiennent le compte difficile de ces échanges; un magnifique exemple en est conservé dans le livre d'un Médicis, Giovenco di Giuliano, conservé dans la Selfridge Collection de la Baker Library à Harvard. Entre 1448, date où il se marie, et 1490, date à laquelle il marie son troisième fils, ce Florentin ne mentionne pas moins d'une trentaine de ces échanges de bagues qui mettent en jeu sa parenté.[22] Ainsi est réaffirmée la solidarité des parents et même des générations, puisque la bru peut recevoir un anneau que sa belle-mère avait naguère rendu à la femme du frère de son mari, lequel frère le lui avait initialement "donné." J'ajouterai que, lorsqu'il n'est plus de mariage à sanctionner par la restitution d'un anneau, les naissances d'enfants prennent le relais et l'on offre à la mère accouchée un hanap orné des armes des deux familles alliées qui suivra les mêmes règles de circulation que les anneaux. Ainsi, la circulation des bagues comme celle des coupes de baptême exprime et reserre l'alliance entre des lignages qui ont jadis échangé des femmes.

L'effacement de l'épouse en tant qu'individu co-fondateur d'un ménage apparait aussi clairement dans le rite d'habillement de la femme par son mari. Classique rite de passage et d'initiation à son état de femme mariée, la constitution d'un trousseau d'apparat et l'offrande de bijoux par le mari avant les noces et dans les mois qui les suivent, engagent celui-ci à "investir," à "mettre sur le dos," comme on dit alors, de sa femme des sommes considérables, jusqu'aux deux tiers de la dot qu'elle lui apporte. Or, pas plus que les anneaux, ces cadeaux n'entrent dans la possession pleine et entière de leur destinataire. Si, devenue veuve, elle quitte le foyer des héritiers de son mari, elle doit leur laisser toutes ces parures — vêtements ou bijoux — reçus au temps de ses noces, à supposer qu'elle les ait conservées jusque là. Car, dès l'année qui suit le mariage, le mari dispose librement de ses propres présents: il les revend, les prête, les loue. Notre Giovenco Medici éparpille ainsi les plumes de paon d'une *ghirlanda* offerte à sa femme quatre ans après les noces, mais auparavant, il l'a prêtée à diverses reprises contre une juste rétribution.[23]

La vêture rituelle de la Florentine facilite symboliquement son entrée dans la maison de l'époux et dans son état de femme mariée. Mais cette identité nouvelle n'est rendue apparente par les vêtements d'apparat que pendant une courte période, du reste autorisée par les règlements somptuaires communaux. Quand, par la suite, le mari reprend ses cadeaux pour en tirer profit, quand ses héritiers retiennent ce qu'il en reste à sa mort, tout se passe comme si, en dépouillant la femme installée dans le mariage ou la veuve, on voulait proclamer que sa famille d'accueil a digéré la présence de l'intruse et n'a rien perdu de ses droits et de ses avoirs.

Tentons quelques conclusions.

En premier lieu, il me semble que ces rites démontrent qu'aux yeux des Florentins, l'union d'un couple particulier compte moins que toutes les alliances conclues par la famille du mari lorsqu'elles jouent encore un rôle important et qu'il convient de les préserver. A toute entrée d'une femme dans l'un ou l'autre de deux lignages alliés, le "don" d'un anneau offert par une femme, mais décidé par son mari, réaffirme que les alliances passées tiennent bon, même si la nouvelle venue a été prise ailleurs. Manière de proclamer que les liens créés par d'anciennes unions résistent à l'extension des parentés dans de nouvelles directions, qu'ils s'accommodent de l'exogamie lignagère et de l'échange des femmes.

En second lieu, la femme nouvelle mariée se trouve ainsi assimilée à toutes les femmes mariées, "entrées" dans le lignage du mari. Cette identité, soulignée avec force par le rite, reflète le désir d'intégrer la femme au lignage marital beaucoup plus que le souci d'affirmer la personnalité d'une nouvelle cellule conjugale. En mettant l'accent sur la nouvelle appartenance de la femme, les rites de noces expriment donc en termes positifs ce qui fait en réalité si cruellement défaut aux alliances florentine, à savoir la certitude que la femme est définitivement transférée par son mariage dans une autre famille et que, même si son mari disparait, elle lui restera solidement attachée. Toutefois, en autorisant les donateurs à récupérer leurs "dons," les rites nous disent aussi que la femme mariée n'a pas d'identité permanente.

Enfin, il me semble qu'un aspect important de ces rituels est la manipulation des épouses par leurs maris pour construire et resserrer les liens d'alliances passées. Ainsi, les Florentins utilisent leurs femmes comme des agents rituels nécessaires à la consolidation du tissu social, alors même — répètent-ils à l'envi — qu'elles constituent un danger pour la cohésion du lignage. Danger dont il leur faut bien s'accommoder, puisque la survie de la famille dépend de leur fécondité.

Les contradictions repérées dans la pratique de la vie familiale affleurent donc jusque dans les rituels, qui affichent pourtant le souci de les résorber ou de les dépasser symboliquement. De fait, le système dotal florentin, qui repose sur le seul apport féminin, soumet la femme à la loi du lignage le plus fort. Sans nom, sans enfants, sans cadeaux et vêtements de noces bien à elle, la Florentine n'a guère d'identité précise. Elle reste une figure incertaine, dont la silhouette est tôt oubliée par les généalogies dressées par les hommes. Les femmes de la Renaissance n'ont pas vraiment trouvé leur place ni leur identité propre dans ces "maisons" édifiées par les hommes qui en jugent les fondations perpétuellement menacées par leur inconstance.

Notes

1. *Il libro degli affari proprii di Lapo di Giovanni Niccolini de' Sirigatti*, éd. par C. Bec (Paris, SEVPEN, 1969): 134.

2. Archivio di Stato di Firenze (ASF), *Conventi soppressi, S. Piero Monticelli*, 153, f. 4 rv. L'épisode se situe entre 1438 et 1444.

3. Lorenzo di Filippo Strozzi, *Vite di uomini illustri di Casa Strozzi* (Florence, 1892): 85–86.

4. Cf. C. Klapisch-Zuber, "Le 'nom refait.' La transmission des prénoms à Florence (XIVe–XVIe siècles)," *L'Homme. Revue française d'anthropologie*, 20 (1980): 77–104.

5. F. Zonabend, "Le nom de personne," ibidem: 7–23.

6. 32 % des prénoms féminins dans les familles connues par leurs livres privés, contre 13 % de ceux des garçons, reprennent le nom d'un aîné prédécédé du même sexe.

7. Zonabend, *art. cit.*,: 12.

8. Cf. G. Duby, *Le chevalier, la femme et le prêtre. Le mariage dans la France féodale* (Paris, Hachette, 1981). D. O. Hughes, "From brideprice to dowry in Mediterranean Europe," *Journal of Family History*, 3 (1978): 262–296. C. Klapisch-Zuber, "Le complexe de Griselda. Dot et dons de mariage au Quattrocento," *Mélanges de l'Ecole Française de Rome. Moyen-Age — Temps Modernes*, 94 (1982): 45–83.

9. Cf. L. Martines, *The Social World of the Florentine Humanists. 1390–1460* (Princeton, 1963): 18–84. Herlihy et Klapisch-Zuber, *Les Toscans* (cf. n. 12): 543–551.

10. Cf. la récente étude de Th. Kuehn, " 'Cum consensu mundualdi': Legal Guardianship of Women in Quattrocento Florence," *Viator. Medieval and Renaissance Studies*, 13 (1982): 309–333.

11. C. Klapisch-Zuber, "La mère cruelle. Maternité, veuvage et dot dans la Florence des XIVe–XVe siècles," *Annales, E.S.C.*, 38 (1983): 1101–03.

12. D. Herlihy et C. Klapisch-Zuber, *Les Toscans et leurs familles. Une étude du catasto florentin de 1427* (Paris, 1978): 204–209, 393–419, 583–584.

13. Cf. I. Chabot-Pirillo, *Les Ciurianni, une famille et un patrimoine de la fin du XIIe au début du XVe siècle* (mémoire de maîtrise, Aix-en-Provence, 1981). R. Bizzocchi, "La dissoluzione di un clan familiare: i Buondelmonti di Firenze nei secoli XV e XVI," *Archivio storico italiano*, cxl, 1 (1982): 3–46.

14. L. B. Alberti, *I Libri della Famiglia*, éd. par R. Romano et A. Tenenti (Turin, Einaudi, 1969): 133–137.

15. Si deux tiers au moins des veuves de moins de vingt ans ont chances de se remarier et le tiers entre 20 et 29 ans, ce sont seulement 11 % entre 30 et 39 ans qui reprennent un mari; la proportion est quasi nulle après 40 ans.

16. Cf. C. Klapisch-Zuber, "Parents de sang, parents de lait. La mise en nour-rice à Florence (1300–1530)," *Annales de Démographie Historique* (1983): 33–64.

17. J. B. Ross, "The Middle-Class Child in Urban Italy, 14th to early 16th cent.," *The History of Childhood*, Ll. DeMause ed. (New York, 1975): 183–228; Herlihy et Klapisch-Zuber, *Les Toscans...*: 555.

18. Alberti, *I Libri della famiglia*: 44.

19. Ibidem: 44.

20. Herlihy et Klapisch-Zuber, *Les Toscans*: 555–556.

21. Ch. Klapisch-Zuber, "Zacharie ou le père évincé. Les rites nuptiaux toscans entre Giotto et le Concile de Trente," *Annales, E.S.C.*, 34 (1979): 1216–1243.

22. Baker Library (Harvard Business School), *Selfridge Collection of Medici Papers*, Ms. 500: f. 4r, 6v.

23. Ibidem: f. 6r.

Earrings for Circumcision: Distinction and Purification in the Italian Renaissance City

DIANE OWEN HUGHES

I

Although the Italian city provides the geographical center of this study, it will begin and end in another city — in Jerusalem, at the temple, where, in compliance with the Law of Moses, Mary and Joseph went after the birth of their son Jesus. That law allowed parents to redeem their firstborn son, whom God claimed as his own. The child's presentation took place thirty days after his birth when his father offered him to the priest and redeemed him for five shekels.[1] Jewish law excluded mothers from the temple until, forty days after they had given birth, they underwent the rite of purification, sacrificing on that occasion a pair of turtle doves or pigeons — or, if they were rich, a lamb.[2] By uniting Jesus' presentation and Mary's purification in one ceremony that took place forty days after the birth, Luke found a way for the Virgin to witness the first public recognition of her son's divinity, a divinity that prevented the customary redemption. Jesus was merely presented to the Lord, who was, of course, his true father. If this was the occasion on which Christ's divinity was revealed, so too was his superiority to the terms of the old covenant foretold: Simeon recognized him as the Messiah, and the prophetess Anna saw that he would be not only a glory to his people Israel but also a light to lighten the Gentiles.[3]

While Jesus' presentation at the temple points to a new law, Mary's purification places her firmly within the requirements of the old, a position that Christians pondered as her place in the Christian drama became more central. How could Mary, whose intercessory role placed increasing stress on her purity, have needed purification? This was a question that Jacopo da Voragine posed at the end of the thirteenth century in his immensely popular

Golden Legend, where, as an answer, he transformed the rite into a symbolic act. Just as Christ could not be redeemed because he was God's son, so Mary did not need to be purified

> since her childbearing was not due to human contact but to the overshadowing of the Holy Spirit. Nonetheless she was minded to submit to this law for four reasons: namely, to give an example of humility; to do homage to the Law...; to put a term to the Jewish purification, and to mark the beginning of the Christian purification...; and to teach us to purify ourselves throughout our whole life.... Candlemas was established to show forth the purity of the Virgin Mary. To impress her purity upon the minds of all, the Church ordered that we should carry lighted candles, as if to say, "Most blessed Virgin, thou hast no need of purification; on the contrary, thou are all light and all purity."[4]

Candles seldom shone in Italian presentation scenes, as they did in those painted by Northern artists, to transform the purification rite into an incarnation of purity.[5] Instead, pigeons, usually carried by Joseph, whose role in the presentation had been usurped by his wife, served as a brutally explicit sign of Mary's need for purification.[6] Yet the rite itself received little direct attention until the Sienese artist Ambrogio Lorenzetti painted in 1342 an altarpiece for the Duomo of his native city that exploited the dramatic possibilities inherent in the dual presentation and purification (fig. 1).[7] In Lorenzetti's hands, Mary's purification stands as a sign of the old law, as her son's presentation foretells the triumph of the new. The centrality of the richly garbed high priest, who is about to sacrifice her pigeons on the altar fire, reminds us of the simultaneity of the two rituals, which are explained by the messages on the scrolls that Moses and Malachi hold over the temple. On the right, Malachi proclaims Christ's messianic role: "The Lord whom you seek shall suddenly come to his temple, even the messenger of the covenant whom you delight in" (Mal. 3:1). To the left, on Mary's side of the scene, Moses establishes the appropriate purification offering: "And if she be not able to bring a lamb, then she shall bring two turtles or two young pigeons" (Lev. 12:18). Smaller details make explicit the contrast between Mary's entrapment in the old law and Christ's power to free mankind from its demands. The statuette of Moses holding the tables of the law is, for example, positioned above Mary and her companions, while above Christ stands the figure of Joshua, the deliverer of the Jews.[8] And although Christ, as a baby, is without distinguishing social marks, Lorenzetti deliberately assigns Mary a Jewish identity. Her silken clothing with its elaborately woven gold border may adhere more closely to Byzantine traditions than to current Sienese taste, whether Jewish or Christian, but Mary's earrings—and those of her companion—would have signaled to any contemporary that she was a Jew (fig. 2).

By placing earrings on his madonnas, Lorenzetti took Mary out of the Christian society of the northern commune, where earrings were practically unknown and were certainly unworn. This had not been true in the precommunal period when German empresses like Agnes, wife of Henry III, were portrayed with earrings just as their Byzantine models had been.[9] Nor is this simply artistic convention, for archaeological finds have provided us with earrings that date to the end of the tenth or the beginning of the eleventh century.[10] We do not have to assume that they were imperial. In Rome, saints are regularly portrayed wearing earrings in the ninth-century mosaics that adorn some of the city's churches; and a fresco executed in San Clemente at the end of the eleventh century shows a lay donor with earrings in her ears.[11] By the following century, however, both saints and donors had cast them off. Only in the South, where closer contact with Eastern traditions may have helped to keep them in fashion, did earrings survive during the period of social upheaval that threw up the commune.[12] Their absence from urban documents, such as notarial records, suggests that citizens neither bought earrings, nor pledged them, nor passed them on to others at their death. From about the middle of the thirteenth century, the popular governments of most medieval cities issued extensive sumptuary regulations, designed to curb not only expenses but also aristocratic pretensions; and to this end, they oulawed crowns and trains, cloth of gold, and various kinds of jewels and buttons. But earrings form no part of these lists of forbidden pleasures.[13] When Ambrogio Lorenzetti himself portrayed the life of his city in the frescoes of Good and Bad Government that still adorn Siena's Palazzo Pubblico, he put no earrings in the women's ears.

An earring might occasionally serve as the sign of a woman's exotic background, as it was clearly meant to in Pietro Lorenzetti's rendering of St. Margaret of Antioch in the lower church of San Francesco at Assisi, or as it had earlier in a twelfth-century mosaic in the basilica on the island of Torcello in the Venetian lagoon, which portrays earringed heathen in Hell.[14] But only one group of women regularly encountered on the streets of northern Italian cities adorned their ears with rings. These were Jews, who by Lorenzetti's day were establishing and strengthening their communities in the Italian cities of the North.

II

Their success was built on the chronic financial need of urban governments, which encouraged cities to ignore ecclesiastical hostility to the Jews and their usury. They were welcome both for the forced loans extracted as the price of their admission and for the good of the urban poor, who could often find no other creditors. Orvieto extended a charter of privileges (*condotta*) to Jewish money lenders as early as 1287, but most cities waited until the bank failures of the mid-fourteenth century and until a shrinking tax base caused by the plagues after 1348 produced an economic crisis.[15]

The decades following the Black Death saw the formation and growth throughout northern Italy of Jewish communities around a nucleus of banking families who signed *condotte* with the communes. Often, as in Siena, the immigrant bankers swelled an older, occupationally more diverse Jewish community.[16] But sometimes, as in Gubbio and Perugia, they were the community's founders, and their *condotte* the acts of settlement. By the beginning of the fifteenth century, northern Italy had more than two hundred Jewish communities, about twenty times the twelfth-century figure.[17]

Such an influx of Jews, many of whom traveled north from Rome and the Angevin South or south from the even more distant world of Germany, undoubtedly created social tension; but it should not be exaggerated. The Jewish community, which had always insisted on its right to stand apart, had always been visible and vulnerable. Yet Jews often became full members of Italian cities, which not only recognized their rights to citizenship but also occasionally appointed them to public office.[18] Almost everywhere their houses were scattered throughout the city, side by side with those of Christian citizens. In 1348, the year of the great plague, feelings against the Jews were running high enough in Siena that the government tried to clear the Campo and the principal streets of Jewish houses, but we know that decades later Jews still held property there.[19] In spite of occasional harrassment, Jews managed, furthermore, to enter into urban life and to mingle in Christian society.

Indeed by the fifteenth century, it had become extremely difficult to distinguish Jews from Christians. They spoke the same language, lived in similar houses, and dressed with an eye to the same fashion. Jews who settled in Italy from German cities were indeed shocked by the extent of assimilation among their Italian co-religionists, who thought nothing of buying their wine from "the uncircumcised."[20] Social assimilation without religious conversion troubled the church, which had advocated at the Fourth Lateran Council in 1215 that the Jews be marked with a special sign.[21] Yet the sign made little progress in Italian cities. While Frederick II forced the Jews of Sicily to attach a distinguishing mark to their clothes in 1221,[22] no urban government seems to have made its Jews conform to the conciliar legislation. When the requirement was restated in 1311 by the Council of Ravenna,[23] a few cities heeded the call for distinction: Pisa placed on its Jews an O of red cloth in 1322; and Rome insisted by 1360 that male Jews wear a red tabard and females a red overskirt.[24] But such civic initiative was unusual, and some cities actively opposed ecclesiastical imposition of the sign. The governors of Siena tried in 1373, for example, to persuade their bishop to protect a Jew who was being prosecuted by church authorities for neglecting to wear the required sign.[25]

The marking and eventual segregation of Italian Jews was a direct product of the preaching of San Bernardino and his Observant followers, who
accomplished in a few decades of the fifteenth century through their
preaching what church councils had tried to effect for centuries by legal
means. Their role in creating in Italy a climate of hatred and fear of the
Jew is well known and does not need to be retold.[26] What does need stress-
ing here is their fanatical commitment to policies of segregation and the
outward signs that made it possible. For the Jewish sign, which came to
mark Jews throughout the Italian peninsula in the fifteenth century, can
almost everywhere be traced to Franciscan preaching. Ancona's Jewish sign
of 1427 was a direct response to the sermons of the Franciscan Observant
Giacomo della Marca; Assisi's of 1452, to those of the friar Cherubino da
Spoleto.[27] Even when a direct connection cannot be found, Franciscan sermons had usually prepared the ground. San Bernardino's insistence on the
separation of Christians and Jews, expressed for more than a decade in
sermons in their squares and churches, provides a necessary background
to Padua's institution of the Jewish sign in 1430, Perugia's in 1432, and
Florence's and Siena's in 1439.[28]

When the Observant friars persuaded cities to distinguish Jews with a
sign, they had recourse almost everywhere to the infamous circle cut out
of red, or more commonly in northern cities, yellow cloth, which was
displayed prominently on the chest.[29] In Rome and further south,
legislators always felt obliged to insist on signs for both male and female
Jews. Hence in the papal city both sexes had to put on red overclothes,
men the tabard and women an overskirt. In Sicily, where Jews had been
assigned distinguishing marks as early as 1221, both men and women were
required to attach a red wheel to their garments, men to the outer clothing
of the chest, women to the long mantles they traditionally wore over their
heads. These were the signs still required of both sexes at the time of their
expulsion from Sicily in 1492.[30]

However, in spite of such southern example and in the face of a long
history of ecclesiastical prescription of distinguishing headgear for Jewish
women, the Italian cities north of Rome were inclined to ignore women
when they arranged to mark their Jewish populations. It might be argued
that Pisa's early insistence that its Jews attach a red O to their clothing
was intended to apply to both men and women, but unlike Sicilian legislators,
who always specified that the sign was to be worn by both sexes, *lu iudeu
oy iudea*, those of the Tuscan city spoke only of *iudei*. When, moreover, northern cities bowed to Franciscan pressure and regularly began to mark their
Jews in the early fifteenth century, the circle of cloth they required was
not specifically assigned to Jewish women, who only toward the end of the
century found in the yellow veil an equivalent sartorial mark.[31]

The veil probably appeared only when a more "natural" sign, the earring, had been cast off. Perugian Jews had certainly taken off their earrings by 1432. When in the spring of that year, after almost a decade of intense Franciscan propaganda, the Council of Perugia unanimously decided to place a sign on the city's Jews, it required of every male over the age of eight the round yellow circle. All Jewish women, however, were obliged to step into the past, to put on once more the long mantles they used to wear when they went out of the house and — except for the widows among them — to put back in their ears the earrings they had obviously begun to remove as they adopted the fashions of Christian society.[32] South of Rome, and particularly in Sicily, where we know Christian women delighted in their earrings, neither those jewels nor the holes that contained them could be seen as Jewish signs, and other marks had to be appliquéd on women as they were on men, whose authoritative physical mark — that of circumcision — was ineffective as a social sign.[33]

In the north where Christians abstained from the jewel, Perugia had not been the first city to restore earrings as the sign of the Jewish woman. When in the spring of 1427 Ancona bowed to the pressure of Giacomo della Marca and required of Jewish men a yellow sign, women were assigned rings in their ears. Although the Jewish community protested to the pope, who condemned the measure as an offense against Christian charity, Ancona persisted, and the signs remained. Only in an hour of extreme need when the government was near bankruptcy in 1497, did it turn once more to the Jewish bankers, whom the Franciscans denounced: in return for their loans, it agreed to let their wives remove their earrings.[34]

As a traditional sign of the Jewish woman, the earring may have been seen as necessary by more cities than existing legislation would suggest. In some northern cities it may precede both chronologically and existentially the clothing appliqué assigned to men. We have no evidence that the zealous inquisitor Giovanni de Piziqotis da Bologna succeeded in attaching O's to many Ferrarese Jews in the early fourteenth century. Indeed, there seems good negative evidence that Ferrara left its Jews unmarked until Ercole d'Este required in 1496 that Jews and Marranos apply a yellow O to their clothing.[35] Yet on the streets of that city in July, 1419, Allegra, wife of Joseph, was apprehended by the authorities and fined ten ducats because she had left her earrings and her Jewish identity at home.[36]

At the very time that Jewish women sought to renounce the earring for the jewels and fashions more acceptable to a Christian society, they were becoming ever more closely identified with it through the sermons of Giacomo della Marca. From the time he first put on his Franciscan robes in 1416 until his death in 1476, he preached extensively in Umbria, the Marches, Lombardy, and the Veneto, combating domestic extravagance, calling for civil peace, prescribing Christian charity, and demanding the segregation of the Jews. In an Advent sermon which formed part of his Sunday sermon book and which he must have preached from many pulpits and on city squares when churches could not contain the crowds, the friar lingered for a moment over earrings — almost in passing, for they clearly did not form part of the jewel cases of the Christian women whose extravagance the sermon condemned. Earrings, said Giacomo, are jewels "that Jewish women wear in place of circumcision, so that they can be distinguished from other women."[37] Can we doubt that this signaled an appropriate way for cities to mark their Jewish women — women who so recently, by removing those earrings, had sought to escape their distinguishing mark?

III

By forcing earrings back into Jewish ears, cities strengthened a Jewish identification with vainglory and concupiscence, vices which Franciscan rhetoric clothed in full infernal splendor and linked in a creative way with women's dress. The bonfires of the vanities that San Bernardino and his followers lit in Italian cities as rites of spiritual purification were fueled with women's finery and with the gambling boards at which Jews were considered particularly adept.[38] During those sermons that closed down towns as the mountain of vanities to be burned rose ever higher in the city square, Jews must have felt especially vulnerable. For Franciscan sermon cycles linked the impoverishing extravagances of gaming and fashion with the usury of the Jews, which threatened even more dramatically to erode the cities and to destroy Christendom itself.[39] The laws enacted in many towns in the wake of purification testify to this association. Their program of reform concentrated on banning or controlling in the future the vanities that a visiting friar had just burned and in marking or segregating the Jews, whom he had just castigated.

Hence the same legislation that put a red O on the Jews of Recanati in 1427 also banned cards, dice, and gaming boards and condemned the high-heeled shoes, false hair, and other deceitful finery of women; the governmental action at Terni that in 1444, at the urging of Giacomo della Marca, limited velvet and silk to the sleeves of women's dresses, restrained the jewels they might wear on their heads, and set the height of their shoes at four inches, also kept Jews from Christian butchers and vintners, from whom until that time they had gone to buy their ritually butchered meat and specially prepared wine.[40] Given this Franciscan pairing of sumptuary and Jewish controls, it is not surprising that when in 1449 the Observant friar Battista da Genova preached in Viterbo such a rousing sermon on the vanities of women that all the city's councilors rushed to repair their sumptuary laws, the first woman arrested under the new dispensation was

Perna di Sabato, a Jew.[41]

According to the friars, women's endless appetite for finery made them partners of the Jew. The demands they made on their families fed and nourished the Jewish usurer, whose gains at Christian expense put those rich clothes on women like Perna. As Giacomo della Marca saw it, female extravagance so impoverished Christians that they were driven "to pawn to the Jews for ten [pounds] a garment that he will sell back for thirty. And so it is never redeemed and the garment is lost. Whence Jews become rich and Christians, paupers."[42] In sermons written to promote the great scheme of the Observants, the *Monte di Pietà*, a charity loan bank designed to replace Jews and their usury, Fortunato Coppoli of Perugia, who established *Monti* throughout Tuscany and Umbria, described the Jews as "truly wild and thirsty dogs, that have sucked and go on sucking our blood," who devour Christians "as rust devours iron."[43] That draining and devouring image linked the Jew with another human parasite against whom the friars railed, the prostitute, who was described from her earliest control as a drain on the city, a creature who contributed nothing to the city's wealth or growth but who, as the reform council of Bologna had noted as early as 1259, voraciously devoured the fragile grain supply on which its well-being depended. And its penalty of the loss of a nose imposed on any resident prostitute who refused to leave Bologna actually forms part of the regulation of the city's grain supply.[44]

A connection between the prostitute and the Jew has often been noticed without ever really being explained.[45] It certainly runs deeper than their supposed parasitical natures; nor is it exclusively the product of the fifteenth-century campaign of the Observant friars. A notary from Viterbo founded in that city as early as 1313, for example, an institution to reclaim penitent prostitutes and another to aid Jewish converts. Pope John XXII blessed them both but recommended separate quarters, which we must imagine were awarded them when the single hospice opened near the city's bordello.[46] Yet the hostility of the Observants to both Jews and prostitutes surely strengthened their popular association. Under the influence of numerous preachers, but especially Bernardino da Feltre, Brescia took up the question of the rights of Jews and prostitutes within the city on a number of occasions during the last quarter of the fifteenth century. At first prostitutes were confined to a bordello and stripped of the mantles and veils that let them resemble other women. Then two years later, in 1478, they were assigned a yellow stripe on the shoulder, a relative of the yellow circle that Jews, after 1474, had to attach to the clothing of their chest. The act that finally expelled the Jews from Brescia in 1494, after the establishment of a *Monte di Pietà* seemed to free the city from dependence on their usury, recognized how closely their position resembled that of the prostitute. Resenting their protection by the papacy and finding themselves unable to confine them to a special quarter, the lawmakers justified the expulsion in these terms:

> While the Christian Church may tolerate the Jews, it has in no way
> decreed that they have to be tolerated in Brescia; they should be treated
> as public prostitutes, who because of their filth are tolerated [only]
> while they live in a bordello, even so should those Jews live their stink-
> ing life in some stinking place, separate from Christians.[47]

If Jews were like prostitutes, were Jewish women whores? The signs in-
vented in some cities for Jewish women said explicitly that they were. In
Rome, for example, Jewish women wore red overskirts, one of the signs
with which prostitutes could be marked.[48] When at the end of the fifteenth
century Recanati decided to change the red circle that had served that city
as a sign of Jewishness for almost two generations, the councilors not only
changed its form and color, they also devised a special sign for Jewish
women. From 1499, Jewish men of Recanati were required to adopt the
yellow hat whose popularity spread quickly through Italy in the wake of
friars' sermons; but their wives and daughters were forced to wind round
their heads, from ear to ear, a band of yellow linen.[49] This was the sign
Pisa in the fourteenth century and Bologna in the sixteenth required of their
prostitutes.[50] That such an association is implicit in these signs is clearly
suggested by a statute of 1450 that established a sign for the Jews of Viterbo.
Men were assigned a circle of red cloth and women a yellow veil that had
to cover the head. If any Jewish woman was discovered on the streets of
Viterbo without her distinguishing veil, she could be stripped by the first
one who apprehended her, the same fate that awaited any prostitute who
dared in fourteenth-century Parma to stray from the main square.[51]

Although it was an older and less obviously degrading sign, the earring
might also convey notions of sexual impurity. It was already available as
a symbol for vainglory in the last quarter of the fourteenth century when
Giovanni del Biondo was commissioned by the Arte della Seta of Florence
to paint a votive panel for its altar in Orsanmichele.[52] The panel shows
John the Evangelist enthroned with cherubs, seraphs and angels, while under
his feet he crushes the vices of pride, avarice, and vainglory. Vainglory
is not a respectable woman as the sumptuary law of Florence and other
cities would have defined her. She is deprived of those rings and brooches
that aristocratic Florentines wore with pride and which, in measure, the
law allowed. Instead she wears a crown with peacock feathers, both items
against which the sumptuary law had waged a long war.[53] In her ears she
wears gold loops which contain a precious stone. One does not need to read
the friars' sermons to recognize on this Vainglory the marks of concupiscence.
With such an association in the air, is it any wonder that Jewish women
wanted to cast off those earrings that were beginning to be signs not only
of a woman's faith but of her moral worth?

Nor were the Jews alone in casting off—or trying to cast off—their earrings. So did the Madonna, who, as emphasis on her purity and intercessory
role grew stronger, could not be associated with jewels that implied impurity. Nor if Jewish women were to be classed with prostitutes could the
Virgin be allowed to wear one of their signs. And so the admittedly eccen-
tric treatment of Mary as a Jew, which we see in Ambrogio Lorenzetti and
his school, must disappear. In 1447–49 another Sienese artist, Giovanni
di Paolo, copied Lorenzetti's Purification scene (fig. 3).[54] A glance at Mary
and her companion, however, shows that in one important detail the work
is different. For Giovanni has removed the earrings from their ears. Although
the temple imagery remains to remind us of a Jewish setting, Mary has
begun to distance herself from a Jewish identity, as by 1449 she would surely
have been forced to as Siena's Jews—under the powerful influence of San
Bernardino's preaching—began to be marked with that yellow sign that
was coming not only to distinguish but to suggest impurity and danger.[55]

By the time that Giovanni di Paolo painted his Purification in Siena,
many Italian towns had begun to treat their Jews as untouchables, as con-
taminators of the larger community from which their signs set them apart.
Most had initially refused to consider the imposition of sanitary laws that
had already been enacted in France in the fourteenth century. In Perugia,
it was not in 1432 when the Jewish sign was first established but seven years
later that the Council enacted sanitary regulations that expressed its fear
of pollution. From 1439, the Jews of Perugia were forced to buy their meat
from separate butcher shops, "to be made in a new place where there has
never been a butcher shop, and set apart from any other butcher shops."
They might not touch any meat from another butcher, nor might other
butchers sell them meat. Jews might not sell pasta, either loose or in boxes;
nor might they touch any vegetable produce unless they had first bought
it or unless, like garlic, onions or nuts, it had a skin or shell. And finally,
Jews might not buy grapes in the city or countryside unless they bought
the whole lot of a vineyard or cellar and kept it all for themselves.[56]

Why was it necessary to see Jews as pollutors? We can approach this
question obliquely by considering the services that Jews rendered the local
Christian community in the fifteenth century. Both city governments and
the city's poor needed the credit that they alone were willing to extend.
In the very period that Jews were being marked and segregated, cities
became ever more dependent on them, to such an extent that they were
often unable to apply to Jewish bankers the regulations established for the
Jewish community at large. When in 1457 Siena drew up a special con-
tract with a Paduan Jew who had agreed to open a loan bank in the city,
it had to exempt both him and his family from the infamous sign, a condition insisted on by most of the Jewish bankers, many of whom supported
their request with papal letters.[57] Neither the urban poor nor urban gov-

ernments were able to survive without a system of credit, which Christians were unable to supply; for, as the friars stressed in their frequent sermons against usury, Christians lent at interest at peril to their souls.[58] The Jew was, therefore, placed in an anomalous position. He offered the community a necessary, though despised, service by engaging in an occupation that was forbidden and dangerous to its other members. As cities became ever more dependent on Jewish loans and, at the same time, increasingly reluctant to accept Jews into the commercial and artisanal occupations of Christian society, ever greater numbers of Jews came, moreover, to specialize in usury.[59] Hence the Jew became identified with an essential service that Christians could only receive from someone who lived outside the bounds of their society.

The connection between Jews and prostitutes now becomes clearer. For these women, whose profession society condemned, were becoming ever more necessary to its health. No one recognized this better than the friars, who regarded sodomy as the ultimate and most pervasive sexual perversion, one intricately tied, as was usury, to the vainglory of women.[60] Those trousseaux that sapped family fortunes and the elaborate jewels and dresses that husbands were expected to award their brides kept people from marrying, driving men to sodomy and women into convents — or, if they were less fortunate or their families less careful, into prostitution. Prostitutes, then, performed a soul-saving sexual service that a father's avarice or a woman's vainglory kept honorable women from undertaking in marriage. Like usury, it was a despised but essential service that could only be undertaken by someone who had put herself outside the bounds of respectable society.

Both Jews and prostitutes expose society's hypocrisy, or, to put it another way, share an ambiguity that arises when social ideology and the common good draw apart from one another. Mary Douglas has placed such ambiguity at the center of pollution concerns.[61] The polluting image of the Jew and the prostitute, which combined, as we have seen, in the Jewish woman, certainly would have served to keep earrings from madonnas, but it must also have made their earthly sisters think twice before rushing off to pierce their ears.

IV

Yet earrings tempted. Galeazzo Maria Sforza, Duke of Milan, had presented his wife Bona of Savoy with a pair of earrings before 1469 when they were enumerated among her jewels; but she did not wear them when she knelt for her portraits before the Virgin.[62] Within half a century, Gian Francesco de' Maineri, in a presentation scene painted at the brilliant court of Mantua or Ferrara, once again allowed the Virgin to display the forbidden jewel in her ears.[63] It did not take long for earrings to move from the court to city streets, where urban governments quickly overcame an initial impulse to ban them and accepted the new fashion. To explain their sixteenth-century rebirth, we must understand the process by which sumptuary display became detached from concupiscence and became again a measure of a woman's worth.

Unlike the royal governments of Spain, France, and England, whose sumptuary controls betray from their origins a strong hierarchical concern, the governments of Italian cities only slowly introduced hierarchical considerations into the laws they wrote to control extravagance. As those governments lost their popular base and became increasingly aristocratic in the course of the fifteenth century, however, hierarchy was legitimized and hierarchical distinction became enshrined in the sumptuary law, as costume became a sign of status. When, for example, the communal government of Bologna issued in 1401 detailed sumptuary controls, women were treated as a sumptuary whole, denied as a group the gold, jewels, silk, and velvets that the lawmakers considered a drain on families and cities.[64] Within two months of the promulgation of those controls, Giovanni I Bentivoglio had been proclaimed lord of the city, a position that his descendants were eventually able to perpetuate.[65] By the time of Cardinal Bessarion's mission to Bologna in 1450 to strengthen the authority of Sante Bentivoglio, decades of lordly rule had changed the relationship between Bolognese women and their clothes, a change that is reflected in the new sumptuary law that Bessarion issued in 1453.[66] Although cloth of gold and silver was denied to all women, other rich clothing had become a legitimate means of social distinction. The wives and daughters of knights might have all their dresses made of that expensive, red-dyed cloth that marked nobility, and they might wear trains a yard long; those of professionals and members of the great gilds were allowed only one garment of red and shorter trains; those, finally, of the minor gilds could wear no scarlet or crimson and were permitted less than a foot of train. Within a generation, to judge from the sumptuary law issued in 1474, gold and silver cloth had become the mark of the urban aristocracy, allowed only on the sleeves of the daughters of the great gildsmen, who dressed in crimson, a color in its turn allowed on the sleeves of the daughters of minor gildsmen, whose dresses were made of less fine cloth dyed to a less noble hue.[67]

These sartorial signs of distinction were refined in the following century when they were also extended to include all classes of the city, even women of the streets, public prostitutes, and Jews. The same law of 1521 that replaced the prostitute's bell with a large yellow scarf put Jewish women in the same visual category as women of the streets (those who sold their sexual services but who were not officially registered as prostitutes). Neither were allowed the dresses of cloth of gold or silver that noble women might wear, nor the dresses of silk that women of the major gilds might wear, nor even the sleeves of crimson that women of the minor gilds might put on. It was no longer concupiscence but virtue and hierarchical distinction that were defined by that rich clothing; stripped of it, loose women and Jews formed a special sumptuary category.[68] Although the law allowed to Jewish women three rings and three gold pins, it denied them any other jewel. If any Jew of Bologna was still putting on earrings, she was now required to cast them off.

As rich clothing and jewelry became everywhere in sixteenth-century Italy the mark of respectability and honor, they were withheld from Jews. In Cremona, for example, not only were the city's Jews denied the swords of aristocrats and the sleeved jackets and plumed black velvet hats of gentlemen, they were also forbidden to be addressed by the title of *messere*, as their wives were by that of *madonna*.[69] That sartorial splendor that had put their honor into question in the days of the friars was denied them when, under the despots, it came to be honor's outward sign.

Clothing forms an obvious semiotic system whose polyvalence challenged social organizers to manipulate its codes.[70] The movement of earrings from a sign of concupiscence and mark of the outsider to a sign of honor and mark of the entrenched testifies to the sixteenth-century victory of aristocratic codification. The aristocratic despotisms of the Renaissance saw virtue in display, nobility in splendor. In spite of the association between trains and loose-living that the bishop of Ferrara had tried to establish in 1434 by assigning trains to prostitutes, the pious but aristocratic Eleanor of Aragon packed in the trousseau she carted to Ferrara in 1473 on her marriage to its ruler Ercole d'Este at least one ball dress made of cloth of gold whose train was over eight yards long.[71] Even at that date in Ferrara the debate was not over: a year later a visiting Franciscan would publicly burn similar vanities offered up by Ferrara's citizens as a visible sign of the city's desire for purification.[72] And the bonfires lit in Florence at the end of the century by a Dominican who hailed from Ferrara — Savonarola — would make a momentary impression not only on Italy's ordinary citizenry but even on the members of its glittering courts.[73] Yet the rhetoric that lit the fires fueled with female vanities was, in a real sense, consumed in the Dominican's fiery and tragic end. Once the last flickers of republicanism were extinguished in Florence in 1530, moreover, the Medici and their aristocratic compatriots set out to build a Golden City, whose gleaming wealth blinded its citizens to that other, egalitarian vision of the New Jerusalem long cherished by republicans and briefly lived by all Florentines in the days of Savonarola.[74]

In those golden cities of the despots, women's trinkets lost their association with concupiscence to become signs of family position and solidarity.

Among aristocrats, jewelry had always served this purpose. Often marked with familial arms, it marked entering women as part of their husband's lineage and might be taken from them when their incorporation was deemed complete.[75] As the aristocratic mode triumphed in Italy's cities in the sixteenth century, jewelry came in a larger sense to mark the family of the women who displayed it as rich and hence aristocratic, aristocratic and therefore virtuous. Earrings were, in this context, an aristocratic jewel, dared originally only by those who had stood outside now-rejected republican constraints.

But the general sixteenth-century triumph of earrings was made possible by the friars' campaign throughout the previous century to mark the Jews with other degrading signs. When earrings really *were* the sign of Jewish women in place of circumcision, Giacomo della Marca and his Observant colleagues might well have hoped through association to keep them out of Christian ears. But when Jewish women, having cast off their earrings, had been marked for decades with yellow veils or circles and when they were deprived by law of the fashionable costumes that had earlier connected them with concupiscence, earrings were freed to form part of new codes.

While the code might change, the power of the sign acting within a code to convey and fix social identity was strong and could even be creative. His sermons, many taken down in the vernacular by devoted listeners, testify to San Bernardino's faith in signs as social markers. He put the matter bluntly to an audience of his native Sienese in the summer of 1427, asking,

> How do you know where to borrow money? By the sign on the awning. How do you know where wine is sold? By the sign. How do we find an inn? By its sign. You go to the taverner for wine because you see his sign. You say to him—Give me some wine—don't you? But tell me what sort of person would approach a woman who puts on clothes or decorates her head with vanities that are the sign of a whore....? You'd ask for her...you know what I mean, as you demand a whore, or, if you will, as you demand wine from a taverner....[76]

Nor did the mendicant attribute to signs a merely reflective power. He reminded his audiences that costume and gesture could actually create identity, as when he exclaimed to the women of Siena, "You are not as you used to be. I see a widow today...with her forehead bare and her cloak drawn back to show her cheek. And how she shapes it over her brow! That is a prostitute's gesture."[77] He argued, as Savonarola would assume later in Florence, that costume both described and developed the social identity of its wearer.[78]

The friars do not seem, however, to have permanently condemned men to the identities in which costume entrapped them. Hence Observants offered to prostitutes who would cast off their baubles or bells a new life of honor. According to his contemporary biographer, Giacoma della Marca,

> preaching one time in Santa Maria Maddalena in Milan, had an ordinance made that all prostitutes had to come that morning to the sermon, and preaching on St. Mary Magdalene so nobly and with such fervor that the prostitutes converted, ... thus he found them dowries of 3000 ducats and married them all and raised them from that sin.[79]

The sermons that Jews were often forced to attend were aimed at a similar conversion, after which Jews might cast off their signs and assume a Christian identity.[80]

Yet signs marked in a more indelible way than the friars were perhaps willing to allow. The houses established in Renaissance cities to help penitent prostitutes develop their new identity responded to the difficulties, not all of them economic, that such women faced when they appeared with new manners and new costume on old, familiar streets.[81] Even more than those Renaissance Magdalenes, Jewish converts to Christianity were to discover even in Italy that rejection of a sign would not fully change social identity. In July of 1492, less than a month after the Spanish king had ordered the expulsion of Jews from Sicily, his viceroy had to remind the island's bishops that Jews who converted to Christianity were to be treated as new social beings, an order eloquently restated in August by Ferdinand himself in a letter sent to all of Sicily's leaders.[82] Although many of these new Christians hid Jewish belief under the outward signs of Christian conformity, it seems unreasonable to believe that they all did. Yet in Ferrara, where many of the expelled found a haven, Ercole d'Este had both Jews and Marranos marked with a yellow circle, a mark which made their natural home in Venice, where many were forced to immigrate when Ferrara turned less hospitable in the sixteenth century, not the open streets of the canals but the enclosed space of the Ghetto. There many of them rediscovered the faith of their ancestors and rebuilt their Jewish identities.[83]

V

The potentially transforming power of signs must certainly have helped in the fifteenth century to keep earrings from the Madonna. But with a partial and remarkable exception to the unadorned madonnas that Franciscan rhetoric demanded and obtained, I will bring this paper to its conclusion. It takes us back to Jerusalem, to a Presentation of Christ in the Temple painted in the middle of the fifteenth century by Mantegna, who would soon become (if he was not already) the court painter of the Estensi at Ferrara (fig. 4).[84] It is a very severe, stripped-down representation: there is neither high priest nor purification symbolism. It looks not to Mary's purification but to Simeon's messianic revelation. Mary's dress is noble, but she is otherwise unadorned. When in about 1470 this painting was copied by Mantegna's brother-in-law, Giovanni Bellini, he enlarged the cast by two; but the Virgin, Christ child, and Simeon remain the central characters, apparently unchanged except for their costume (fig. 5).[85] If, however, we look closely at the Virgin's ear — an unusually elongated ear with a distinctive lobe that both paintings share — we find a significant difference (figs. 6 and 7). Bellini has pierced it.[86]

This hole may give to Bellini's copy a value that it has often been denied.[87] For in the midst of an intense polemic over Jewish signs, the Venetian artist returned an ancient mark of the Jew to the Virgin. We know that Giacomo della Marca preached in the Veneto throughout the 1460's and was actually called to Venice in 1465 to advise the Doge about a projected Crusade. The friar's last recorded visit to the maritime city where Bellini painted took place in 1470, probably around the time that the painter was making this copy.[88] It is unlikely that on these visits he failed to preach on the obsessive subject of women's vanities that sermon in which he labeled earrings the mark of Jewish women in place of circumcision. It would be nice to think that Bellini heard him preach.

By removing her earrings, the painter moves the Virgin to new importance in the presentation drama. For like her son, she also foretells the coming of a new law and a new order. The lack of sacrificial turtle doves and high priest now relays a message; for, as Jesus cannot be redeemed, so she, reborn in Christ, needs no real purification. If Bellini's is the secondhand and arguably inferior piece, Mary's pierced ear infuses it with a spiritual and intellectual force absent from Mantegna's original. That the Virgin, mother of Christ, might, by removing her earrings, attain purification can also be read, in light of Franciscan rhetoric, as a message to the Jews — as a blatant appeal to convert. But her pierced ear may offer a message to Christians, who were letting signs transform their possessors. If Mary could cast off her Jewish identity by removing its outward sign, there could be no indelible mark of the Jew. Circumcised or uncircumcised, pierced ear or whole, there was no distinction in Christ: it was inward belief not outward sign that traced a path to the New Jerusalem.

Notes

1. Exod. 13:12-15; Num. 18:15-16; and see Num. 3:45-51 for redemption money. For a possible connection between the sacrifice (and redemption) of the firstborn and a shift from matrilineality to patrilineality among the Hebrews, see David Bakan, *And They Took Themselves Wives* (San Francisco, 1979), pp. 147-52.
2. Lev. 12:2-8.
3. Luke 2:27-29; 37-38.
4. Jacobus de Voragine, *The Golden Legend*, trans. Granger Ryan and Helmut Ripperber, 2 vols. (London, 1941), 1:150.
5. Dorothy C. Schorr, "The Iconographic Development of the Presentation in the Temple," *Art Bulletin* 28 (1946), 27. Since Schorr is wrong to see a maiden carrying a taper in Giotto's Presentation in Padua, Italian rerpesentations with candles are even rarer than she allows.
6. Pacino di Bonaguida, in a Presentation that appears as a rondelle in his Tree of Life, and Giovanni Baronzio, in an altarpiece in Urbino, exceptionally leave out the pigeons and ignore the aspect of Mary's purification. See Richard Offner, *A Critical and Historical Corpus of Florentine Painting* (New York, 1930), 3, ii / 1:pl. 6ª, and Pietro Toesca, *Il Trecento*, Storia dell'Arte italiana, vol. 2 (Turin, 1971), p. 729. In fact, the mother may have been the dominant figure in contemporary Italian redemptions, which Jewish fathers seem sometimes not to have attended. See Thérèse and Mendel Metzger, *Jewish Life in the Middle Ages* (New York, 1982), pp. 226-27 and fig. 341.
7. Hendrik Willem Van Os, in his *Marias Demut and Verherrlichung in der sienesischen Malerei 1300-1450*, Kunsthistorische Studien van het Nederlands Historisch Instituut te Rome, 1 (The Hague, 1969), p. 3, has shown that contemporaries actually thought of Lorenzetti's work, as they would of Giovanni di Paolo's, who copied him a century later, as a Purification. It was particularly appropriate that the Sienese, who dedicated their city to the Virgin, were among the first to stress her role in the ritual.
8. The detail in George Rowley, *Ambrogio Lorenzetti*, 2 vols. (Princeton, 1958), 2:fig. 17, shows that the figure is clearly marked *Joshua*, not David, as Schorr supposed.
9. See for example contemporary illustrations of Agnes kneeling before the Virgin in *Il Matrimonio nella società altomedievale*, 2 vols. (Spoleto, 1977), II, figs. 45-46.
10. The so-called Gisela jewelry, after the Empress Gisela, wife of Conrad II (crowned 1024), whose jewels they were thought to have been, is now dated to the end of the tenth and beginning of the eleventh century. According to Ingrid Kuntzsch, the Germans had adopted jewelry as a result of Eastern influences after the migrations, *A History of Jewels and Jewelry* (New York, 1981), p. 96. Lombards had sufficient contact with the Byzantine world that earrings formed part of the jewelry with which noble Lombard women were buried, see *Verona e il suo territorio*, vol. 2 (Verona, 1964), pp. 550-52.
11. Many saintly examples exist: St. Cecilia is portrayed in a mosaic at the church of her name in Trastevere in Rome, for example, with elaborate earrings; and Saints Prassede, Agnes, and Pudenziana, in a mosaic in the Church of S. Prassede, all wear round, gold earrings. They are illustrated in Rosita Levi Pizetsky, *Storia del*

costume in Italia, 1 (Milan, 1964), figs. 54, 56, 57.

12. For Neapolitan examples, see Ferdinando Bologna, *I pittori alla corte angioina di Napoli 1266-1421* (Rome, 1969), fig. 69 and pl. XXVIII.

13. They were first controlled by the 1423 sumptuary law of Palermo, which banned all "chirchelli vero, sive ornamenti di li auricchi," ed. Rosarius Gregorio, *Bibliotheca scriptorum qui res in Sicilia gestas sub Aragonum imperio retulere*, 2 vols. (Palermo, 1791-1792), 2:531-35. But in the North, no sumptuary law mentions earrings until the sixteenth century. The *pendicula* which are limited in Bergamo by its sumptuary regulations of 1491 (ch. 3) are not ornaments for the ears, as Pinetti believed, but for the head, as the context makes clear. When earrings were finally outlawed in that city in 1540, they were clearly labelled "gioie nelle oreccie," ed. Angelo Pinetti, *La limitazione del lusso e dei consumi nelle leggi suntuarie bergamasche (sec. XIV-XVI)* (Bergamo, 1917), pp. 59 and 67.

14. This is the only one of Pietro's St. Margarets to be portrayed with earrings. It is significant that she is dressed in a more distinctly Eastern style than the others, wearing, for example, as do Ambrogio's madonnas, silken scarves of Arabic or Byzantine production. See E. T. De Wald, *Pietro Lorenzetti* (Cambridge, Mass., 1930), figs. 23, 24, and 57. The Torcello mosaic is reproduced in André Grabar, *Byzantine Painting*, trans. Stuart Gilbert (Geneva, 1953), p. 120. The earrings are worn by both men and women.

15. Attilio Milano, *Storia degli Ebrei in Italia* (Turin, 1963), pp. 45-108.

16. Nello Pavoncello, "Notizie storiche sulla comunità ebraica di Siena e la sua Sinagoga," *La rassegna mensile di Israel*, 36 (1970), 289-313. Pavoncello's belief that the Sienese Jewish community was always based in moneylending and banking is, however, mere hypothesis. It seems more reasonable to suppose that in Siena, as in other towns where evidence lets us trace their early history, Jews engaged in a variety of occupations. See, for example, Ariel Toaff, *The Jews in Medieval Assisi, 1305-1487*, Biblioteca dell' "Archivum Romanicum," ser. 1, vol. 148 (Florence, 1979), pp. 30-31.

17. Milano, *Storia degli Ebrei*, pp. 109-46.

18. On their frequent holding of citizenship, see Vittore Colorni, *Legge ebraica e leggi locali*, Pubblicazioni dell'Istituto di Diritto romano, dei Diritti dell'Oriente mediterraneo e di Storia del Diritto (R. Università di Roma), 23 (Milan, 1945), pp. 88-94. A Jew was an ambassador for Orvieto in 1313; others were tax collectors there in 1347 and 1350, Giulio Rezasco, "Del segno degli Ebrei," *Giornale ligustico di archaeologia, storia e letteratura* (Genoa), 15 (1888) and 16 (1889), 16:263; but the Church had opposed the practice of appointing Jews to offices that gave them authority over Christians at the IV Lateran Council, D. Mansi, *Sacrorum Conciliorum Amplissima Collectio*, 31 vols. (Florence and Venice, 1759-1789), 22:1058. In Forlì it was a sign of a hardening of Christian attitudes as early as 1359 that Jews were deprived of communal office, E. Rinaldi, "Gli Ebrei in Forlì nei secoli XIV e XV," *Atti e memorie della R. Deputazione di Storia Patria per le Provincie di Romagna*, 4th ser., 10 (1937), 295-323.

19. Pavoncello, "Notizie storiche sulla comunità ebraica di Siena e la sua Sinagoga," p. 292.

20. So, the "Maharam Padova" characterized the Jews of Modena; see Jomtov Ludovico Bato, "L'immigrazione degli Ebrei tedeschi in Italia dal Trecento al Cinquecento," in *Scritti in memoria di Sally Mayer (1875-1953)* (Jerusalem, 1956), p. 25.

21. Mansi, 22: 1055, conveniently reproduced and translated (with commen-

tary) by Solomon Grayzel, *The Church and the Jews in the XIIIth Century*, rev. ed. (New York, 1966), pp. 308–9. The nature of the sign was not specified. On its Islamic background, see Grayzel, p. 61, n. 97.

22. G. Lionti, "La rotella rossa," *Archivio storico siciliano*, n.s., 8 (1883), 15. Its color and dimensions seem not to have been firmly established until the fourteenth century; see Rezasco, "Del segno degli Ebrei," 16:56.

23. Ludovico Muratori, *Antiquitates Italicae Medii Aevi*, 17 vols. (Arezzo, 1773–1780), Dissert. XVI, 1:186.

24. Lonardo, "Gli Ebrei a Pisa sino alla fine del secolo XV," 7:178–79; 204–5. *Statuti della città di Roma del secolo XIV*, ed. Camillo Re, Biblioteca dell' Accademia storico-giuridica, 1 (Rome, 1883), p. 190. Trained Jewish doctors were excepted.

25. G. Mollat, "Deux frères mineurs, Marc de Viterbe et Guillaume de'Guasconi, au service de la papauté," *Archivum Franciscanum Historicum* 48 (1955), 69.

26. The most recent sketch is by Milano, *Storia degli Ebrei in Italia*, pp. 161–66; but it does not replace the more thorough, though unfortunately unannotated, account by Cecil Roth, *The History of the Jews of Italy* (Philadelphia, 1946), pp. 153–76.

27. Rezasco, "Del segno degli Ebrei," 15:323–24; Toaff, *The Jews in Medieval Assisi*, pp. 48–52.

28. For Bernardino's itinerary, see Dionisio Pacetti, "La predicazione di S. Bernardino in Toscana," *Archivum Franciscanum Historicum*, 33 (1940), 283–318. In 1425 after a course of summer and autumn sermons and a burning of the city's vanities, Perugia had issued statutes intended to reform the city's morals, but the Perugians seem to have been unwilling at that point to mark their Jews, of whom the statutes make no mention. They are edited by Antonius Fantozzi, "Documenta perusina de S. Bernardo senensi," *Archivum Franciscanum Historicum*, 15 (1922), 108–29.

29. For a summary of the Italian Jewish sign, which only Lucca seems stubbornly to have refrained from applying to its Jewish population, see Rezasco, "Del segno degli Ebrei."

30. When in 1366, King Frederick IV called on both sexes to attach a red O to their clothing, he claimed merely to be restating the law of his grandfather. However, that law, in its extant version, does not speak of men and women. Bartolomeo and Giuseppe Lagumina, *Codice diplomatico dei Giudei di Sicilia*, 3 vols. (Palermo, 1884–1895), 1:33, 80–82. By the fifteenth century, the shape of the sign is often described as a moon, which suggests it had become a crescent, a shape never found in northern cities, *ibid.*, pp. 229–30. For other late references see *ibid.*, 1:387–89; 2:27; 116–17; 186–87 (when for reasons of their poverty Jewish women of Messina were allowed to go without their sign); 230–31 (when in 1477 and 1478 some men and women of Palermo were excused from wearing the circle).

31. Although some cities had begun to request it in the fifteenth century, it was only in the mid-sixteenth century, at the urging of the papacy, that the Jewish veil became the female equivalent of the yellow circle worn by men. Rezasco, "Del segno degli Ebrei," 15:260.

32. The ordinance is edited by Anodante Fabretti, *Sulla condizione degli Ebrei in Perugia dal XIII al XVI secolo* (Turin, 1891), p. 33. Mantles could be of any color except "nero monachino" and dark green, so that they would not be taken for nuns or women in mourning.

33. Some members of the Jewish community of Trapani were trying, by the beginning of the fifteenth century, to withhold circumcision from their sons yet remain Jews. This outraged the leaders of that community, who successfully peti-

tioned the king for the right to expel them, Lagumina, *Codice diplomatico dei Giudei di Sicilia*, 2:261–63.

34. Rezasco, "Del segno degli Ebrei," 15:323–24.

35. The yellow hat that Venice had begun to insist on, is usually seen as Ferrara's first sign for Jews, imposed by Ercole d'Este on 13 April 1498 (David Kaufman, "Contributions à l'histoire des Juifs en Italie," *Revue des études juives*, 20 (1890), 45). But according to an anonymous diarist, Ercole had first imposed the circle in 1496. *Diario ferrarese dall'anno 1409 sino al 1502*, ed. Giuseppe Pardi, Rerum Italicarum Scriptores, new ed., 24, vii (Bologna, n.d.), p. 174.

36. Andrea Balletti, *Gli Ebrei e gli Estensi* (Reggio-Emilia, 1930), p. 149. Two years earlier Giovanni da Capistrano, "scourge of the Jews," had been commissioned to act as special inquisitor in Mantua; and the position of the Jews in Ferrara and Mantua had become less secure, as was the case throughout Italy. Roth, *The History of the Jews of Italy*, p. 159.

37. S. Jacobus de Marchia, *Sermones Dominicales*, ed. Renato Lioi, 3 vols. (Ancona, 1978), 1:113. It is a comment on the *Decretum*, *De consecr.*, dist. 5, c. 38, *Fucare*, *Corpus juris canonici*, ed. Emilius Friedberg, 2 vols. (Graz, 1959), 1:1422–23. For a summary of his career, see Teodisio Somigli, "Vita di S. Giacomo della Marca scritta da Fra Venanzio da Fabriano, O.M. Obs.," *Archivum Franciscanum Historicum*, 17 (1924), 378–403.

38. See, for example, the later warnings against gambling of Leo of Modena, who was himself an inveterate gambler, *The History of the Present Jews Throughout the World* (London, 1707), pp. 44–45. On his life see Cecil Roth, *Venice* (Philadelphia: Jewish Publication Society of America, 1930), pp. 207–9.

39. See, for example, the Lenten cycle of Giacomo della Marca, Dionisio Pacetti, "I sermoni quaresimali di S. Giacomo della Marca contenuti nel Cod. 187 della Bibl. Angelica," *Archivum Franciscanum Historicum*, 46 (1953), 302–40.

40. The statute is edited by Alberto Ghinato, "Apostolato religioso e sociale di S. Giacomo della Marca in Terni," *Archivum Franciscanum Historicum*, 49 (1956), 373–80.

41. Francesco Cristofori, "San Bernardino da Siena in Viterbo," *Miscellanea Francescana*, 4 (1889), 36.

42. *Sermones Dominicales*, 1:116.

43. Quoted by Toaff, *The Jews in Medieval Assisi*, p. 61.

44. *Statuti del comune di Bologna dall'anno 1245 all'anno 1267*, ed. Luigi Frati, 4 vols. (Bologna, 1869–1884), 1:309–13.

45. See, for example, Maurice Kriegel, "Un trait de psychologie sociale dans les pays méditerranéens du Bas Moyen-Age," *Annales: E–S–C*, 31 (1976), 326–30.

46. Giuseppe Signorelli, *Viterbo nella storia della Chiesa*, 3 vols. in 5 (Viterbo, 1907–1950), 1:394, n. 23.

47. Agostino Zanelli, "Predicatori a Brescia nel Quattrocento," *Archivio storico lombardo*, 3rd ser., 15/16 (1901), 137, 143.

48. As, for example, in sixteenth-century Bologna, *Provissione sopra l'eccesive spese cosi del vivere, come del vestire, & altre pompe, riformata & publicata in Bologna ali XV & reiterata ali XIII di Genaro M.D.LV.* (Bologna: Anselmo Giaccarello [1555]).

49. The governor of the Marches intervened on behalf of the Jewish community, and the government withdrew its requirement of a yellow hat. The woman's sign, however, seems to have remained on the books; Ghetti, "Gli Ebrei ed il Monte di Pietà in Recanati," pp. 25–27.

50. *Statuti inediti della Città di Pisa*, 2:316; *Provisione novissima delle dote et dello ornato delle donne reformata al tempo de reverendiss. sign. M. Bernardo di Rossi governatore pres. et vicer. di Bologna et di tutta Romagna* ([Bologna], 1521).

51. Attilio Milano, "Sugli Ebrei a Viterbo," in *Scritti sull'ebraismo in memoria di Guido Bedarida* (Florence, 1966), p. 143; *Statuta communis Parmae*, ed. A. Ronchini, 4 vols. (Parma, 1855–1859), 3:274. The sanction of such behavior only makes immediate a penalty commonly imposed on prostitutes and other dowryless women — the running of the gauntlet. The Council of Vigevano in the Duchy of Milan extended this shaming to Jewish men, decreeing in the same year that anyone meeting a Jew who was not wearing his badge might strip him of his clothes, *The Jews in the Duchy of Milan*, 1:57–58 (doc. 72).

52. The predella bears the arms of the gild. Offner, *Corpus*, 4, v:67.

53. E. Rodocanachi, *La femme italienne à l'époque de la Renaissance* (Paris, 1907), pp. 123–39.

54. For the details of its commission and a proposed reconstruction of the altarpiece of which it formed the central panel, see H. Wl. van Os. "Giovanni di Paolo's Pizzicaiuolo Altarpiece," *Art Bulletin* 53 (1971), 289–302.

55. The government ordered Jews to place a yellow O on their clothing in 1439 (Pavoncello, "Notizie storiche sulla comunità ebraica di Siena," pp. 293–94).

56. Fabretti, *Sulla condizione degli Ebrei in Perugia*, pp. 38–42.

57. Pavoncello, "Notizie storiche sulla comunità ebraica di Siena," p. 295. Assisi, for example, in 1457 specifically exempted Bonaiuto da Tivoli from the sign required of all other Assisan Jews, something they had not done, however, the year before for Angelo da Ferrara — although both were moneylenders. Toaff, *The Jews in Medieval Assisi*, pp. 154–62.

58. In their repeated sermons on usury, the Observants ignored the scholastic refinements that had, over the centuries, made certain kinds of usury acceptable; see for examples John T. Noonan, Jr., *The Scholastic Analysis of Usury* (Cambridge, Mass., 1957).

59. Jews were aware of the danger. The Rabbi Joseph Colon in a *Responsum* that probably dates from 1470–1480, advised, as Observant demands for *Monti* became more unrelenting, that the risk of opening more loan banks outweighed the gain of profit; for the Observants "have become whips of oppression for Israel. They preach every day, seeking to destroy us. Our bodies and our goods are threatened; and without divine protection, they would have swallowed us alive and their terror would have triumphed. Isn't it then clear to any fair judge that the Jews of this city are right to refuse a newcomer who wants to install himself [as a loan banker] against their wishes if, because of him ..., exile and ruin will follow...?" quoted by Leon Poliakov, *Les banquiers juifs et le Saint-Siège du XIIIe au XVIIe siècle* (Paris, 1965), p. 201. At the same time the cities were excluding Jews from other occupations. In 1453, for example, the city council of Padua lamented a Jewish presence in its gilds, and a century later it petitioned Venice to deny to Jews all occupations except selling at second hand, Ciscaro, *Gli Ebrei in Padova*, pp. 97–98.

60. As Giacomo della Marca, borrowing from San Bernardino of Siena, reckoned, "Youths do not want to take wives because the dowry is not sufficient for the vain and superfluous ornaments of the wife.... And he remains unmarried. The father keeps his daughter beyond marriageable age because there is not sufficient dowry to give a girl enough for useless clothes.... And thus she remains unmarried.... This is the reason that there are many more sodomites in Italy than almost anywhere

else in the world, because in his twenties and unmarried—just as the woman is—
he and even she fall into the vice of sodomy, from which married men aren't even
able to abstain," *Sermones Dominicales*, 1:115-16. On the encouragement of prostitution to combat sodomy, see Richard C. Trexler, "La prostitution florentine au XVe
siècle: patronages et clientèles," *Annales: E-S-C* 36 (1981), 983-1016.

61. *Purity and Danger* (Harmondsworth: Penguin, 1970).

62. E. Motta, *Nozze principesche nel Quattrocento* (Milan, 1894), p. 41.

63. See Silla Zamboni, *Pittori di Ercole I d'Este* (Milan, n.d.), pls. 16-17, VII.

64. Umberto Dallari and Luigi Alberto Gandini, "Lo Statuto suntuario bolognese
del 1401 e il registro delle vesti bollate," *Atti e memorie della R. Deputazione de Storia
Patria per le Provincie di Romagna*, 3rd ser., 7 (1889), 8-22.

65. Cecilia M. Ady, *The Bentivoglio of Bologna* (Oxford, 1937), pp. 8-10 and *passim*.

66. It is edited by G. B. Comelli, "Di Niccolo Sanuti primo conte della Porret-
ta," *Atti e memorie della R. Deputazione di Storia Patria per le Provincie di Romagna*, 3rd
ser., 17 (1899), 148-52.

67. Edited by Luigi Frati, *La vita privata in Bologna dal secolo XIII al XVII*, 2nd
ed. (Bologna, 1928), pp. 245-48.

68. *Provisione novissima delle dote et dello ornato delle donne* ([Bologna], 1521), art.
XXI-XXIII.

69. D. Bergamaschi, "Gli Ebrei a Cremona," *Scuola cattolica* 34 (1906), 265.

70. See, for example, Umberto Eco, *A Theory of Semiotics* (Bloomington, 1976),
pp. 48-150.

71. Luciano Chiappini, *Eleonora d'Aragona* (Rovigo, [1956]), p. 14.

72. L. Chiappini, "Un bruciamento delle vanità a Ferrara nel 1474," *Atti e memorie
della R. Deputazione Ferrarese di Storia Patria* 7 (1952).

73. When Ercole d'Este fell fully under the Dominican's sway in 1496, he not
only issued an edict against blasphemy, sodomy, and uncontrolled prostitution,
he also marked Ferrara's Jews with a yellow sign (*Diario ferrarese*, p. 174); and see
generally Edmund G. Gardner, *Dukes and Poets in Ferrara* (New York, n.d.), pp.
295-339.

74. See most recently Richard A. Goldthwaite, *The Building of Renaissance Florence*
(Baltimore and London, 1980), pp. 69-112. During this brief return to republican
government in 1527, the old association between female extravagance in dress and
concupiscence was reestablished; and Jewish bankers were given twelve months
to leave Florentine territory: Cecil Roth, *The Last Florentine Republic* (New York,
1925), p. 64. On Savonarola's identification of his reborn Florence with the New
Jerusalem, see Donald Weinstein, *Savonarola and Florence* (Princeton, 1970), pp.
138-84.

75. Christiane Klapisch-Zuber, "Le complexe de Griselda: dot et dons de mariage
au Quattrocento," *Mélanges de l'Ecole Française de Rome: Moyen Âge / Temps Modernes*
94 (1982), 7-43.

76. *Le prediche volgari di San Bernardino da Siena nella piazza del Campo anno
MCCCCXXVII*, ed. Luciano Banchi, 3 vols. (Siena, 1880-1887), 2:207.

77. Ibid., 2:197.

78. See Richard C. Trexler, *Public Life in Renaissance Florence* (New York, 1980),
pp. 462-82.

79. Teodisio Somigli, "Vita di S. Giacomo della Marca," p. 406.

80. Rezasco, "Del segno degli Ebrei," 15:250-51.

81. Sherrill Cohen, "Convertite e Malmaritate. Donne 'irregolari' e ordini religiosi

nella Firenze rinascimentale," *Memoria* 5 (1982), 46–63.

82. Lagumina, *Codice diplomatico dei Giudei di Sicilia*, 3:77–99, 113–15.

83. Ferrara turned on the Marranos in 1581 in the wake of the denunciation to the Inquisition in Lisbon by a penitent New Christian of over 30 Marrano householders who were living openly in Ferrara as Jews. In Venice some Marranos had always lived among Christians. Among those who went to the Ghetto many, according to Roth, experienced Judaism for the first time: Cecil Roth, *A History of the Marranos*, 2nd ed. (Philadelphia, 1959), pp. 209–12.

84. For attribution and date, see *The Complete Paintings of Mantegna* (New York, 1967), p. 99.

85. Berenson's attribution of the work to Bellini has been generally accepted; see *L'opera completa di Giovanni Bellini*, Classici dell'Arte, 28 (Milan, 1969), p. 89, where dates between 1465 and 1470 are proposed.

86. I should like to thank Mark Epstein for verifying with the staff of the Biblioteca Querini-Stampalia that the apparent hole represents a piercing of the ear.

87. It evidently was left unfinished, but it became the inspiration, in the opinion of Giles Robertson, for a later series of compositions of the Presentation and Circumcision, none of which return, however, to the pierced ear: *Giovanni Bellini* (Oxford, 1968), p. 76.

88. Teodisio Somigli, "Vita di S. Giacomo della Marca," p. 402.

Fig. 1. Ambrogio Lorenzetti, Presentation, *1342. (Uffizi, Florence.)*

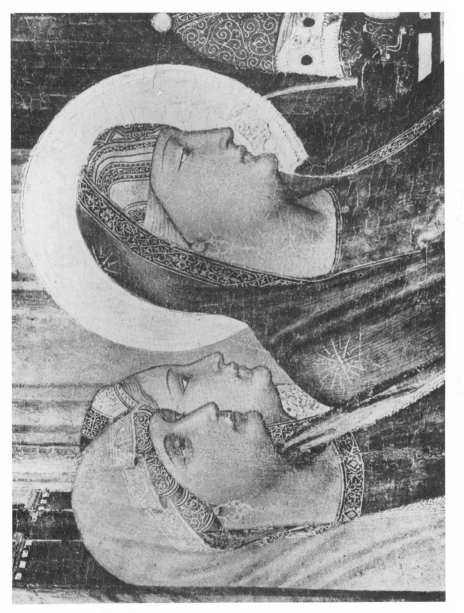

Fig. 2. *Ambrogio Lorenzetti,* Presentation, *detail.* (*Uffizi, Florence.*)

Fig 3.   Giovanni di Paolo, Presentation, *1447–1449. (Pinacoteca, Siena.)*

Fig. 4. *Andrea Mantegna,* La presentazione al Tempio.
(Ehemals Staatliche Museen, Berlin.)

Fig. 5. *Giovanni Bellini,* The Presentation in the Temple. *(Fondazione Querini Stampalia, Venice.)*

Fig. 6. *Andrea Mantegna,* La presentazione al Tempio, *detail. (Ehemals
Staatliche Museen, Berlin.)*

Fig. 7. *Giovanni Bellini,* The Presentation in the Temple, *detail. (Fondazione Querini Stampalia, Venice.)*

The Saint as Exemplar in Late Antiquity.

PETER BROWN

I n a discussion of a recent book, a reviewer raised the objection that its author

> may well have to defend himself against theologians who argue that applying the notion of 'classic' to persons has only a limited usefulness. Persons are not works of art, not pieces of literature, not paradigmatic actions ... By making them into classics, do we not neglect certain aspects of their lives and remove them from history?[1]

It might be helpful to begin any paper on the saint as exemplar in Late Antiquity by explaining briefly why such an eminently commonsensical remark would have impressed a Late Antique reader — pagan, Jewish or Christian — as the tacit abandonment of the *rationale* of their whole culture. For the Classics, a literary tradition, existed for the sole purpose of "making [persons] into classics." Classic books were there to produce classic persons; any other function was vaguely ridiculous.

> Two things can be acquired from the ancients — wrote Lucian of Samosata, attacking a *parvenu* who had made his money in the book trade — the ability to speak and act as one ought by emulating the best models and shunning the worst; and when a man clearly fails to benefit from them in one way or the other, what else is he doing but buying haunts for mice and lodgings for worms, and excuses to thrash his servants for negligence?[2]

We begin in the first and second centuries A.D. with a world whose central elites were held together by what Henri-Irenee Marrou has brilliantly characterised as "the civilization of the *paideia*." The Greco-Roman world, in which the saints later appeared, was a civilization of *paideia* in the same way as our own is a civilization of advanced technology. It invariably tended to opt for the necessary self-delusion that all its major problems could be both articulated and resolved in terms of that one major resource — in this case, by the paradigmatic behavior of elites groomed by a *paideia*, in which the role of ancient exemplars was overwhelming. I would suggest that the tendency to see exemplary *persons* as classics was reinforced by the intensely *personal* manner in which the "civilization of *paideia*" was passed on from generation to generation. Intensive male bonding between the generations lay at the heart of this "Civilization." No student ever went, as we do, to a university conceived of as an impersonal institution of learning — to "Cal.," to "SUNY" (how much these abbreviations speak of our desire to take the impersonality of learning absolutely for granted!). He would have always gone to a person — to Libanius, to Origen, to Proclus. The most poignantly expressed relation in the ancient and medieval worlds was that between teacher and pupil. From the farewell poem of Paulinus to Ausonius, his old master:

> Thee shall I behold, in every fibre woven.
> Shall I behold thee, in my mind embrace thee,
> Instant and present, there, in every place[3]

to Dante's encounter with Brunetto Latini in the *Inferno*, we are never very far from

> la cara e buona imagine paterna
> di voi, quando nel mondo ad ora ad ora
> m'insegnavate come l'uom s'eterna.[4]

Rather than be surprised by such an intensely personalized system, we should remember how long it survived unchallenged. Exemplars, if carefully sought out, if studied and remembered at appropriate moments, were still thought to add a strand of steel to the frail fiber of eighteenth century gentlemen: "Fancied myself Burke" wrote Boswell — admittedly one of the frailest — "and drank moderately."

If there is reason for surprise, it is two-fold.

First: we have here a culture that believed that the past had only become the past through the ever-remediable accident of neglect, not through any irreversible process of change and unidirectional evolution, which would render the moral paradigms of a man of the sixth century B.C. irrelevant to the behavior of a man of the fourth century A.D. Moral exemplars of a thousand years previously had no built-in obsolescence. What was good for them could be good for you. We are not in a world "condemned to history" by Hegel.

Second: the very real faith that a man can "mould" himself, like clay, can "carve and polish" himself, like a statue (I use the current images of late antique education and spiritual guidance) so as to slough off from the self those anomalous layers of the person that stood in the way of the emergence of the true patterns of exemplary behavior. Thus, neither distance of time, nor the resistant quirks of the individual character were regarded as reasons for not permeating the men and women of the "civilization of *paideia*" with the paradigms summed up in the exemplary figures of the ancient past.

The "ancients," therefore, already enjoyed the status of "human classics" in the late classical world. With late antique hagiography, however, this robust faith in the ability of the exemplar to internalise the values of the community and to pass these values on to others received the unprecedented additional momentum that came from the belief in providential monotheism. The past joined the present now through the active will of a God before Whose presence the righteous of all ages stood. The idea of a "community of the righteous," that linked Israel to its forebears and through these forebears to God Himself, has been rightly described as a "singular feature in [ancient] religious history."[5] It meant that the "man of God," the "righteous man" had a revelatory quality about him. The known presence of righteous men in Israel, it was believed, had the effect of bringing back God Himself from exile, in the hearts of those who doubted His abiding presence in a darkening world. The saints of Israel and of the Early Church are not guiding stars, set in a distant sky: they are a Milky Way thrown down from Heaven to earth; their presence expresses the purposes of a God who "wishes all men to be saved."

Furthermore, in late antique Christian thought, God Himself was proposed to man as the Exemplar behind all exemplars. The result of this view was to present history less as a reservoir of discrete "classic" persons, than as a sequence — a sequence of exemplars, each of which made real, at varying times and to varying degrees, the awesome potentiality of the first model of humanity, Adam, of human nature created "in the image of God" before the Fall. For, as Gregory of Nyssa puts it:

> in Moses and in men like him the form of that image was kept pure.
> Now when the beauty of the form has not been obscured, then is made
> plain the faithfulness of the saying that man is an image of God.[6]

In Christ, the original beauty of Adam had blazed forth again among men. For that reason, He was the pattern of the life of the holy man. The life of the holy man was a prolonged *imitation of Christ*. To imitate Christ, Gregory of Nyssa — and others less profound and idiosyncratic than himself — scanned the human race as a whole, finding in the righteous of all ages that shimmer of the original and future majesty of man, that Adam had borne and that Christ had brought back, evanescent, elusive but reassuringly the same, like the fleeting expression of a face cunningly carved (here Gregory was thinking of the ancient equivalents of those little anamorphic pictures — now available in plastic — which show different scenes when viewed from different angles) so that from one side the divine quality of man might appear, a sweet light smile playing across the whole face, while from the other all that could be seen was the hard frown of fallen man. The imitation of Christ, therefore, was to bring that elusive touch of the majesty of Adam back into the present age. Though the phrase does not, to my knowledge, occur among Late Antique Christian writers in precisely this context, *repraesentatio Christi*, "making Christ present by one's own life in one's own age and region,"[7] appears to be the aim and effect of the Early Christian Imitation of Christ.

> Indeed, the Christ-bearing man, having become forebearing, shines
> down on all men like the sun, showing to all the life of Heaven.[8]

Now it seems to me that the theological concept of *repraesentatio Christi*, "making Christ present" in a specific time and place, needs to be taken down off the rather high shelf on which it has been perched in standard histories of Early Christian spirituality, and looked at carefully and concretely. For it is an illustration of the process by which the identities of individual men and women were thought to have been charged, indeed saturated, with the values of their religious community, in such a way as to enable such persons (persons, as it were, "turned into classics") to bring these values to areas that had until then been ignorant of or indifferent to them. The exemplar does more than transmit: the saint reveals and re-enacts the basic Christian paradigm in every age and region. The holy man is a living *demonstratio evangelica*.

Before the conversion of Constantine and for centuries after, the Church should never be seen (as it is so often presented in maps) as a single wash of color spreading evenly and inexorably across the *orbis terrarum*: it was an archipelago of little islands of *central* values scattered across an "unsown sea" of almost total indifference.

Hence the crucial importance of the holy man as "Christ-carrying" exemplar. In almost all regions of the Mediterranean, from the third century onwards, he was far more than an exemplar of a previously well-organised and culturally coherent Christianity: very often, he quite simply *was* Christianity. Looking at Pachomius reading the Gospels in the little, newly-founded church in the deserted village of Tabennisi, noting that he "controlled his eye as he ought and that his mouth matched his mind," "men of the world, seeing the man of God in their midst, had even greater desire to become Christians and believers."[9] What all of them may not have known was that their exemplar as a Christian had come, only recently,

from a totally pagan village. Pachomius and many of his monks had to
learn their Christianity, as it were, "on the job," while acting as exemplars
to a body of laymen even less Christianized than themselves. We must look
out from the neat pages of standard histories of the church in order to catch
both the exciting prospects and flexibilities, but also the deep lack of cultural
and religious resources — amounting to a real cultural impoverishment —
of most Christian regions in Late Antiquity. A holy man, or the legend
and shrine later connected with him or her, could stand for a little drop
of the "central value system" of Christianity oozing tremulously to the surface in its locality. The well-to-do would be encouraged, on the day of the
saint, to give alms to the poor, "or to produce a book for the house of God
in his name or buy a Gospel and place it in the shrine."[10] A fresco, later,
perhaps, a little encaustic icon, might remind the passer-by of a touch of
beauty and unbroken harmony in a dirty, preoccupied world:

> And this boy Shenoufe was a fair person, more than them all; he was
> ruddy, with beautiful eyes, and hair entwined like clusters of henna
> blossom.[11]

Only we, who have hid for centuries behind books and machines for the
propagation of the Gospel, can afford to underestimate the crucial importance, in the frontier-life of the Early Church, of the human exemplar:

> I am convinced that God added to the length of their days — wrote
> the cultivated Constantinopolitan lawyer Sozomen of the wild holy
> men of Syria — for the express purpose of furthering the interests of
> religion.[12]

As pagan ladies of fifth-century Beirut said of Saint Matrona, lodged
in her cave near the city: "Let us go out, and look at the Christian."[13]

Let us conclude by looking at a few of the ways in which the holy man
was enabled to play the role of Christ made accessible to his fellows.

To begin with the holy man at his most particular, as the particular disciple
of a particular master: our starting point is a marble plaque discovered
in the ruins of a little church in central Anatolia. It is an inscription set
up by a certain Lucianus, the disciple of none other than the great martyr,
Saint Lucian of Antioch.

> Having lived without conceit,
> Having honoured as is due,
> Lucian the martyr,
> He who nurtured you.
> With him Christ made you
> A follower of Himself,
> A carrier of His Cross:

> A Cross dwelt on divinely in the mind,
> And touched by you (the martyr Lucian)
> In concrete pains (of death).[14]

Such language enables us to perceive at once the vigour of the early phases of the ascetic movement of the fourth century. In this movement, the intensity of a master-pupil relationship, that had ensured the continuity and the characteristics of the pagan "civilization of *paideia*," had been heightened to such an extent that literacy itself, both the medium and the *raison d'être* of traditional *paideia*, was vaporized in the intensity of face to face loyalty. Direct force of example was what mattered most; and the "Imitation of Christ," not mediated by any text or visual aid, was the logical extension to the divine Master of the tangible, almost pre-verbal adherence of the human pupil to his human model. A little later, the Pachomian monasteries grouped large bodies of men through the same hope of direct contact with a master: "knowing that, in listening to him, we make ourselves servants of Jesus." "Indeed," said the monks to their Patriarch, "when we look at you, it is as if we look upon Christ."

> Still another day, while our father Pachomius was praying somewhere alone, he fell into an ecstasy: all the members were in the *synaxis* [assembled for worship] and our Lord was seated on a raised throne, speaking to them about the parables of the holy Gospel.... From that day on, when our father Pachomius wished to address a word of God to the brothers, he would occupy the place where he had seen the Lord seated and speaking to the brothers.[15]

The world of early ascetic guidance has left us with some of the most vivid examples of a purely personal system of exemplary behavior ever preserved in the Christian church.

> Go and join a man who fears God: — advised Abba Poimen — just by remaining near him, you will gain instruction.[16]

But vertical transmission from master to disciple was not enough. Spiritual achievement had a revelatory quality for the world at large. The monk's journey moved on from such highly particularised loyalties. It took him out on to a plateau, surrounded by a mountain range of quite breath-taking immensity; for the greatest figures in the long history of the righteous on earth stood behind him. To be a "man of God" was to revive, on the banks of the Nile, all other "men of God" in all other ages. "The ascetic must observe most closely — said Anthony — the life and practice of the great Elijah." Occasionally, the lost countenance of Adam could blaze again among these humbled faces:

Just as Moses, while his face was glorified, took on the glory of Adam,
so the face of Abba Pambo shone like lightning, and he was like a
king sitting on his throne.[17]

It is Adam as we see him on the mosaic pavement of a fifth-century Syrian
church: man as monarch of the creation, sitting with Imperial serenity amidst
the wild beasts in Paradise. His quiet pose, like that of Pambo at his medita-
tions, captures the mighty order of man's first estate. Little wonder that
strong millennial hopes flickered around the persons of the holy men, and
around the walled monasteries of the Nile. The local populations flocked
to such figures. For his region, Abba Apollon was "like some new prophet
and apostle dwelling in our own generation."[18] The presence of the holy
man brought a touch of the ancient prophets and of the New Age into a
sinful, tawdry world.

The specifically Late Roman gusto for declaratory ceremonial heightened
these hopes by giving them visible form. It was possible for an adaptation
of the Imperial ceremonials of the *adventus*, the arrival in state, to make
the tiny relic-jar of the bones of the prophet Zachariah seem "*as if living
and present*" to the populations through which the cortège bearing the jar
passed on its way from Jerusalem to Constantinople.

Indeed, seen as a ceremonial re-enactment of Christ's coming among
men, the *repraesentatio Christi* could not happen without very real psychic
peril to the holy man. It is surprising how close to the surface in late Roman
hagiography we find the idea of the holy man as a "false Christ." These
dangers did not merely refer to a saint's inner struggles with his inflated
ego. Lay men (and more especially lay women) deliberately stylised their
relations with a man such as St. Martin as if he *were* indeed Christ among
them. We find the wife of the Emperor Maximus approaching Martin in
the same pose of adoration and service as those lavished by Martha and
by Mary Magdalen on the Lord. It was a form of access to him. Given
the known effect of a woman brushing, even by accident, against the foot
of an ordinary bishop, to treat the bishop of Tours as Christ Himself made
present was the only way in which the empress (as a woman) could gain
intimate contact with him. We have here an extreme example of the merciful "cushioning" of interpersonal contacts that late Roman men sought
in their elaborate codes of deportment and ceremonial. But the strain would
have been a real one for Martin and his circle. The great all-night "talk-in"
on the miracles of Martin, which even lay men had wished to attend,
gravitated insistently around those miracles by which Martin had been said
to have brought the presence of Christ into the woods and rivers of Gaul.
In these miracles, "he showed Christ working in him."[19] I think that it is
not merely a personal anxiety of Sulpicius Severus, but an essential element of the manner in which the exemplary quality of the life of Martin

was perceived, that the *Life* is overshadowed by stories that presaged the appearance of Antichrist. The Devil appeared to Martin himself, as an Imperial Christ, come down to Martin as the first believer honored to receive his Second Coming. It is an Imperial *adventus*, right down to the awesomely studied good cheer of the Imperial face, *ore sereno*, the rigid serenity of countenance such as was held by Constantius II for hours on end during his triumphal entry into Rome. There is also the very revealing tale of a young man in Spain who called himself Elijah and then Christ, and had been "adored" as such by a local bishop. Martin himself, we should always remember, might have looked no different to an observer who saw him "adored," who saw the empress fall at his feet in the manner of Mary Magdalen, and who saw a woman with an issue of blood reach for the hem of his cloak as he passed by.

This does not exhaust the problem of re-enactment. In the case of the holy man we are very far from a passive process, by which ceremonials of welcome, access and acclaim rendered his person benignly transparent to values wished upon him from the outside. If the holy man had what Clifford Geertz has called a distinctive "aesthetic of rule," this depended precisely on the degree to which the "master fictions" of a Christian society (again to use Geertz's terms) had been made fully his own.[20] But how did this happen? The Christian culture of late antiquity had none of the solidity of later centuries. We have to deal with the problem of the internalisation of a whole sacred literature and of a series of norms of behavior in a virtually illiterate and, by later medieval standards, a deeply underclericalised society.

The culture of Pachomius and his monks, for instance, was a thing of rags and patches. It is interesting to see how some of the most vivid anecdotes in the life of Pachomius emerge, and are arranged into a rough biographical sequence, from the long, intense discourses that he and his disciples held on the meaning of the Christian Scriptures, Scriptures which a very large proportion of them would have been reading for the very first time. The immediate context of the anecdotes often refers to attempts to understand a hitherto unknown Gospel in the light of their own experiences: Pachomius, for instance, learned how to meditate on the nails of Christ's Passion while treading barefoot among the terrible acacia-thorns to gather firewood for his new community. The idea of the growth of Christ in the soul can seem a doctrine veiled in a golden fog when we read it in the pages of even so exquisite an exponent of Gregory of Nyssa. It derived its unbroken vigor, in late antique society, from the heroic flounderings of men who had to find out what Christianity was in the very act of serving as Christian exemplars.

What were the main resources of such people? I would like to stress the overwhelming importance of liturgical prayer. A whole cultural situation, and indeed a whole art of memory, lies behind the Old Irish word for the good monk: *Psalmboc*, "Psalm-Mouth." The monk chewed through the Psalms and through a series of exclamatory prayers to Jesus, much as the village women, that Abba Macarius remembered, chewed on sticks of mastic to sweeten their breath. In so doing, the ascetic would be taken out of his own time and placed in the world of the prophets. For these were the *propheticae voces*, now heavy and potent in their own mouths. Christ was eternal, and could be addressed in all ages and places through them. So was the Devil. The "prophetic sound" of the Psalms drove him away, as Martin, a newly-consecrated exorcist, crossed the frightening Alps. There were "spirit-bearing fathers" who knew that the permanent enemy of the human race had a particular aversion to Psalm Sixty-Seven. Such certainties about essentials stood out like rocks in a sea of doubt and partial ignorance.

In the case of Martin himself, we can touch on a further layer in his appropriation of the new faith. He was made an exorcist long before he enjoyed any other clerical rank, such as might have brought him closer to a learned, clerical form of Christian culture. The long exorcistic prayers of the Christians were a "poor man's rhetoric." They required impressive feats of memory; and they were the occasion for virtuoso *cadenzas* of charismatic power. We should also remember that in this form they were, in themselves, a powerful preaching device: an exorcistic prayer brought into the present an awesome map of the cosmos, of its creation by God, of the place of the demons and the angels within it, and of the certain victory of the name of Christ. It had an effect as deep and subliminal as the regular "warning" of the *muezzin* in a modern Islamic land.

To a very large extent, the effectiveness of Martin in his re-enactment of Christ's impact on the world was judged by the degree to which he had internalised the world-view implied in such prayers. While the average clergyman might have to "raise a hurricane of words," Martin could rely on heavy and mute gestures. Faced by a berserk slave in Trier, it was enough for him to put his fingers into the man's throat, daring the Devil to chew on them. It is the approach, in silent and so in more palpable certainty, of the dread "fingers of God" that had first formed man and the universe, whose ancient power was appealed to and re-activated in the present by traditional exorcistic prayer.

Inevitably, the "re-enactment" of the presence of Christ carried with it also a *geographical* dimension of considerable importance in the early middle ages. As Clifford Geertz has remarked in his model study of the function of royal progresses, "Centers, Kings and Charisma": each royal arrival reactivated a sense of the availability of "central values," with their solemn and power-bring associations, in regions and among groups among which such a sense was usually in abeyance. But this reactivation depended on an ability to act out with gusto and with rightness of touch an "aesthetic of rule." In this "aesthetic of rule" the successful re-enactment of exemplary gestures of power counted for quite as much as the power itself. In this case, Geertz suggests, it is easy to imagine situations where manifestations of *"charisma"* might run loose at the arrival of a figure who can condense vividly central values that appear spasmodically in the locality:

> its most flamboyant expressions tend to appear among people at some distance from the center, indeed often enough at a rather enormous distance, who want to be much closer.[21]

With such a remark it is possible to write a whole chapter of the turbulent history of the relation between early medieval hagiography and the Christian missions. Hagiography was, in many ways, the special preserve of the provincial societies of the Byzantine world. This was not (as has often been suggested by scholars of Hellenic disposition) because mere provincials — Copts, Syrians, Armenians, and later the Irish and the Slavs — were capable of nothing better. Rather, it was because, in the lives of their saints, those on the peripheries of Christendom could sense the majestic tread of the center of the Christian world moving among the villages of Egypt, along the sandbanks of the Loire, finally, even, beside the wooden palisades of Kiev:

> *The generation of the upright shall be blessed* said the prophet *and their seed shall be for a blessing.* Now this is what took place not long before these events, when the sole rulers of all the land of Rus' was Volodomir, son of Svjatoslav and grandson of Igor.[22]

The *repraesentatio Christi* shrunk the huge cultural and social gulf between Galilee and a sub-Scandinavian Russia of the eleventh century.

With this we can conclude. The manner in which a late classical "civilization of *paideia*" felt able to permeate the individual with the exemplary values of the distant past gave place, in Christian circles, to a more dynamic concept, the "revelatory" function of the righteous. It was a notion more concerned to facilitate expansion than mere transmission. The Early Christian emphasis on the *repraesentatio Christi* enabled a holy man to bear in his own person the central paradigm of the Christian community. Bearing Christ in his person, he very often *was* Christianity in his region; and, as we have seen, the full resources of a late Roman zest for declaratory ceremonial made this tangible and even dangerously real to a man such as Martin and his followers in the fourth century. The idea that the great and good happenings of the mighty past were always available in any region, to be re-enacted by new Christian heroes, provided an imaginative map of Europe and the Near East in which it was possible, in the course of the early middle ages, to add to the Christian world provinces unimaginably distant, in reality, from the Mediterranean centers of the Early Church.

The history of the Christianization *of* Europe, as distinct from a history merely of the growth of the Christian Church *in* Europe, remains to be written. It is not until we allow ourselves to travel a little more widely in our minds, to think of the possible meanings of exemplars, of transmission, and of re-enactment in societies where modern Western modes of communication were totally absent, that we can return home, as if after a spell of residence abroad, to see, with the clarity that can come from an instant of unfamiliarity, some of the central problems of an over-familiar topic — the mission and expansion of Christianity in the ancient and medieval worlds.

Notes

1. J. B. Cobb, Jr., *Religious Studies Review* 7 (1981): p. 287. An elaboration of the present paper may be found in *Representations* 1 (1983): 1–25.

2. Lucian, *The Ignorant Bookseller* 17: tr. A. M. Harmon, *Loeb Classical Library* (Cambridge, Mass., 1969), 3:195.

3. Paulinus, *Poem* 10. 54–56: tr. H. Waddell, *Wandering Scholars* (London, 1927), p. 11.

4. *Inferno*, canto XV, lines 83–85.

5. A. Goldberg, "Der Heilige und die Heiligen: Vorüberlegungen zur Theologie des heiligen Menschen im rabbinischen Judentum," in *Aspekte Frühchristlicher Heiligenverehrung*, Oikonomia 6 (Erlangen, 1977), p. 19.

6. Gregory of Nyssa, *De hominis opificio* 8.

7. Ps. Athanasius, *De passione et cruce Domini*: *P. G.* 28, 237A.

8. Ibid.

9. *Vita Pachomii Graeca Prima* 29: tr. A. A. Athanassakis, Society of Biblical Literature (Missoula, Montana: Scholar's Press, 1975).

10. Sozomen, *Historia Ecclesiastica* 6:34.

11. E. A. E. Reymond and J. W. Barns, *Four Martyrdoms from the Pierpont Morgan Coptic Codices* (Oxford, 1973), p. 194.

12. Sozomen, *Historia Ecclesiastica* 6:34.

13. *Vita Sanctae Matronae* 22, Acta Sanctorum, November 3, 801B.

14. S. Eyice-J. Noret, "S. Lucien disciple de S. Lucien d'Antioche," *Analecta Bollandiana* 91 (1973): 365.

15. *V. Pachom*, c. 144.

16. *Apophthegmata Patrum*: Poimen 65, cited in P. Rousseau, *Ascetics, Authority and the Church* (Oxford, 1978), p. 21.

17. *Apophth*. Pambo 12. See M.Y. and P. Canivet, La mosaïque dans l'église syriaque de Ḥuārte, *Cahiers archéologiques* 24 (1975): 49–60.

18. *Historia Monachorum* vii, 8.

19. Sulpicius Severus, *Dialogi* III. 10, P.L. 20, 217C.

20. "Centers, Kings and Charisma: Reflections on the Symbolics of Power," in *Culture and its Creators*, ed. J. Ben David and T. N. Clarke (Chicago, 1977), now in Clifford Geertz, *Local Knowledge* (New York, 1983), p. 146.

21. Ibid., p. 144.

22. *The Narrative, Passion and Encomium of Boris and Gleb*, now translated by M. Kantor, *Medieval Slavic Lives of Saints and Princes* (Ann Arbor, Michigan, 1983), pp. 165–67.

Entre le texte et l'image:
les gestes de la prière de Saint Dominique.

JEAN–CLAUDE SCHMITT

Bien que les historiens en aient fait traditionnellement peu de cas, il me semble qu'un des changements importants qui se produisirent au XIIè siècle, en Occident, concerne les attitudes à l'égard du corps. Cette mutation est marquée notamment par une attention nouvelle portée aux gestes. J'ai montré ailleurs comment les occurrences croissantes du mot "*gestus*" dans toutes sortes de textes, avec une valeur positive (*gesticulatio* restant au contraire attaché à la description des gestes jugés désordonnés et mauvais des jongleurs et des démons), temoignaient de cette évolution.[1] Au même moment une définition du mot "geste" est donnée, en tête d'une véritable théorie de la gestualité, la première du genre: elle est l'oeuvre du théologien parisien Hugues de Saint Victor, dans son *De Institutione Noviciorum*:[2] "*gestus est motus et figuratio membrorum corporis, ad omnem agendi et habendi modum.*" "Le geste est le mouvement et la figuration des membres du corps dans le *but*, mais aussi suivant la *mesure* et une *modalité* propres à réaliser toute action et attitude." Cette traduction volontairement contournée montre la richesse d'une telle définition, sur laquelle il convient de s'arrêter un instant.

Le geste est d'abord compris comme une catégorie particulière de la notion plus générale de *mouvement*, qui joue un rôle central dans le renouveau philosophique et scientifique du XIIè siècle. Le mouvement n'est plus conçu comme un attribut de chaque corps, mais comme le résultat de l'interaction de tous les éléments de la nature. Rapportée au corps humain, cette idée de l'interdépendance du mouvement de ses membres est essentielle; elle relie d'autre part ces mouvements coordonnés du corps humain aux mouvements de l'Univers, dans une vaste harmonie de la nature (*concor dia*) et de la société. Ainsi Hugues de Saint Victor compare-t-il le corps humain à la *respublica*, dont les *officia* sont partagés entre tous ces membres sans qu'aucun puisse usurper l'office de son voisin: il en va de même pour le corps (par exemple, on doit parler avec la bouche, et non avec les mains, dont *l'officium* est différent), afin de garantir la concorde de tous les membres (*concordia universitatis*).

La notion de "*figuratio*" souligne la dimension visuelle de cette théorie: les gestes manifestent en effet à l'extérieur du corps (*foris*) la qualité de l'âme intérieure (*intus*). Ainsi chaque novice dans le monastère soumet-il ses gestes au regard, et aussi au jugement moral de son voisin. Mieux encore, cette notion de figuration, en même temps que celles de mouvement et de concorde, rattache le geste aux idéaux esthétiques du moment: au milieu du XIIè siècle la représentation du corps humain dans la sculpture des tympans suit de nouveaux modèles qui influencent aussi la maîtrise des gestes des hommes.

La locution "*ad modum*" exprime d'abord une idée de but, de finalité matérielle et morale de la "discipline" (*disciplina*) des gestes, qui présidera bien plus tard à la notion de "techniques du corps" de Marcel Mauss.[3] Au XIIè siècle nous la trouvons aussi présente dans un opuscule de Pierre Le Chantre sur la prière: les membres du corps humain y sont présentés comme des instruments (*naturalia instrumenta*), et l'homme qui prie comme un ouvrier: "*Artifex est orator.*"[4] Mais la notion de "*modus*" me paraît comporter une dimension supplémentaire: l'idée de mesure, que Hugues de Saint Victor identifie au juste milieu qui résulte de l'opposition de deux gestes vicieux de sens opposés: par exemple le geste vertueux est à la fois gracieux et sévère, mais gracieux sans relâchement, ce qui serait signe de lasciveté, et sévère sans trouble, ce qui signifierait l'impatience.[5] La norme gestuelle n'est donc ni une règle rigide, ni une qualité unique, mais la résultante dynamique et instable des contraires. Une tension habite en permanence cette définition de la mesure, et elle constitue la *modalité* du geste, troisième sens de "*modus.*"

Cette oeuvre de Hugues de Saint-Victor fut souvent citée aux XIIIè-XIVè siècles, parce qu'elle a eu une certaine influence sur les traités d'éducation monastique et les manuels de prédication. Mais cette tradition documentaire n'est pas unique. Il en existe une autre, plus spécialisée puisqu'elle concerne les seuls gestes de la prière, mais qui jette un éclairage complémentaire sur les notions de "mouvement," de "mode," et surtout de "figuration"; elle associe en effet la représentation iconographique des gestes à leur description texteulle.

Le plus ancien de ces textes est un opuscule *De Oratione* faisant partie du *De Penitentia* de Pierre le Chantre († 1197): il décrit sept "modes" de prière, accompagnés de figures correspondantes dans un grand nombre de manuscrits.[6] Pour ma part, je considérerai ici un document sensiblement

postérieur: le *De modo orandi corporaliter sancti Dominici*, généralement cité
comme *Les Neuf manières de prier de Saint Dominique*, écrit par un frère prêcheur
anonyme de Bologne, vraisemblablement entre 1280 et 1288.[7] Ce texte
ayant été associé à la *Vie* de Saint Dominique écrite par Thierry d'Apolda
a joui d'une large tradition manuscrite, mais les manuscrits comportant
des miniatures sont rares et ont subi les injures du temps. Trois d'entre
eux sont datés du XIVé siècle; celui de Carcassone, encore mentionné au
XVIIè siècle, mais perdu depuis lors, faisait partie des matériaux relatifs
à Saint Dominique rassemblés par Bernard Gui au dèbut du XIVè siècle
et utilisés bien plus tard par J. Echard pour son édition; celui du Vatican
(*Codex Rossianus* 3), écrit en latin et comportant 9 modes de prière; de Madrid
(couvent des Soeurs Dominicaines), écrit en castillan et qui présente le même
nombre de modes de prière et de figures correspondantes.[8] Un manuscrit
plus récent était conservé au couvent des Prêcheurs de Bologne, d'où il a
disparu récemment. Il avait été écrit en italien avant 1470 et comportait
quatorze modes de prière au lieu de neuf.[9]

Par le texte et l'image, tous ces documents confirment le changement
des attitudes à l'égard des gestes amorcé au XIIè siècle par Hugues de Saint
Victor et Pierre le Chantre. Ils confirment aussi le rôle dans cette évolution joué par les groupes les plus dynamiques de l'Eglise: chanoines vic-
torins, maîtres parisiens, religieux mendiants, tous acteurs du chantier in-
tellectuel urbain, qui ont su définir de nouvelles manières de penser et d'agir
aussi bien qu'un nouveau type d'apostolat.

I

La nature hagiographique de ce document est évidemment essentielle,
et elle le distingue d'emblée de l'opuscule de Pierre le Chantre, même si
l'un et l'autre relèvent des mêmes procédures d'analyse. Les modes de la
prière de Saint Dominique ne sont pas des types abstraits, fondés en droit
par des citations bibliques, des "*auctoritates*," comme dans l'oeuvre de Pierre
le Chantre.[10] Ils montrent les gestes et les mouvements d'un unique
"héros," qui est à la fois un saint et le fondateur d'un ordre religieux. Il
est d'ailleurs vraisemblable que l'opuscule a été compilé à partir des dépositions des dominicains de Bologne au procès de canonisation, tant sont nom-
breux les parallèles entre les descriptions de la prière du saint dans l'un
et l'autre documents. L'influence des *Vitae Fratrum* de Gérard de Frachet,
et même celle des *Miracles de Saint Dominique* dictés entre 1272 et 1288 par
soeur Cécile à soeur Angélique, au couvent des dominicaines de Sainte Agnès
à Bologne, sont également sensibles. L'opuscule sur la prière de saint Dominique est une compilation regroupant de manière systématique un ensemble d'informations provenant de cette tradition hagiographique composite.

Le prologue situe d'abord l'ouvrage dans la longue tradition des écrits sur la prière et sur les manières de prier (*de modo orandi*). Il rattache ainsi saint Dominique à la tradition patristique, commençant à saint Augustin (dont les Prêcheurs suivent par ailleurs la "règle"). Sont ensuite mentionnés Grégoire le Grand, Hilaire, Isidore, Jean Chrisostome, Jean Damascène puis Bernard de Clairvaux et "d'autres très pieux docteurs grecs et latins." La mention simultanée de Pères grecs et latins est remarquable, dans le contexte encore vivant de l'Union espérée au concile de Lyon de 1274. Un autre intérêt de cette énumération est de ranger saint Bernard parmi les Pères de l'Eglise, donc aussi de souligner la rupture entre le monachisme traditionnel, dont il est le dernier grand représentant, et les nouveaux Ordres, celui des Prêcheurs surtout, fondé par saint Dominique. Celui-ci s'inscrit donc dans une tradition mais inaugure en même temps une nouvelle période illustrée cette fois par des noms de contemporains, tous dominicains: Thomas d'Aquin († 1274), Albert le Grand († 1280) et Guillaume Péraud († 1271) cité pour sa *Summa de virtutibus*.

Pères et théologiens, selon l'auteur, s'accordent à souligner l'interaction des mouvements de l'âme et du corps: "*anima movens corpus moveatur a corpore.*" Cette émulation de l'âme et du corps peut conduire celui qui prie avec ferveur jusqu'à l'extase (*in extasim*), comme saint Paul, ou au ravissement de l'âme (*in excessu mentis*), comme le prophète David. La prière de saint Dominique n'était donc pas seulement rattachée à une tradition lettrée patristique et scholastique, mais au courant mystique et prophétique. Sa dévotion reproduit celle "des saints de l'Ancien et du Nouveau Testaments": comme eux le saint était animé d'une force spirituelle qui lui arrachait des larmes et qui soustrayait son corps à sa volonté (*in tantum ut in eo cohiberi non posset, quin devotionem membra corporis manifestarent certis indiciis*). Selon le texte italien plus tardif, l'exaltation spirituelle et physique du saint, qui poussait de vrais "mugissements," allait jusqu'à l'empêcher de célébrer la messe.

Selon le prologue, l'opuscule ne décrit pas les grands mouvements de ferveur qui "ravissaient" le saint lorsqu'il disait la messe ou chantait les psaumes, soit dans le choeur soit en voyage. Sans que cela soit dit explicitement, son objet semble plutôt de montrer la prière commune du saint hors du contexte liturgique, quand Dominique était seul face à face avec Dieu. Mais on va voir que cette prière n'excluait pas les transports mystiques comme si la tension d'une communication "secrète" avec Dieu avait le même effet d'entrainement que l'exaltation collective de la liturgie.

Dominique s'adressait au Christ, comme si celui-ci était "réellement et personnellement présent" dans le symbole de la Croix placé sur l'autel.[11] Mais il n'était jamais complètement seul avec Dieu; des frères l'observaient secrètement, l'épiaient par "curiosité,"[12] ou encore, à défaut de le voir, écoutaient ses paroles secrètes et ses gémissements.[13]

La description textuelle des modes de prière recèle, comme chez Pierre le Chantre, une foule de citations bibliques: procédé bien connu de légitimation par l'autorité de la Bible, d'autant plus nécessaire que ce type d'ouvrage ne se rattachait à aucune tradition livresque ancienne. Ces citations ont une autre fonction encore: bien souvent elles sont les paroles mêmes du saint, la part vocale de sa prière, donnée ainsi en même temps que sa part gestuelle. Sur 29 citations (texte latin), 22 proviennent de l'Ancien Testament, dont 17 des Psaumes. La part des Psaumes est proportionnellement plus forte encore dans le texte italien, qui compte 15 citations bibliques, dont 13 des Psaumes. L'importance de ces derniers souligne le caractère solitaire de cette prière, dans la tradition de la psalmodie monastique ou canoniale.[14]

Cependant la Bible n'est pas la seule source de légitimité de cette prière: la propre hagiographie du saint en est une autre, dans la mesure où plusieurs épisodes de sa *Vita* interferent avec la description de certains modes de prière. Par exemple, du mode VI (des mss. de Rome et Madrid), debout les bras en croix, il usa pour ressusciter à Rome le jeune Napoléon (à l'imitation d'Elie ressuscitant le fils de la veuve); il fut même soulevé au-dessus du sol selon le témoignage de soeur Cécile.[15] Il usa du même mode de prière pour sauver des pélerins anglais près de Toulouse.[16] Dans le ms. de Bologne, deux modes de prière renvoient pareillement à la biographie du saint: le mode 7, debout les yeux levés vers le ciel, dont il usa pour évoquer le démon sous la forme d'un gros chat noir devant les femmes hérétiques de Fanjeaux[17]; il priait suivant le mode 13, à genoux devant l'autel, mains jointes, lorsque le démon chercha un jour à le tuer à coups de pierre; le texte ne mentionne pas cet événement, que rapportent les *Vitae Fratrum*.[18] Mais le démon et les pierres sont présents dans l'image correspondante. L'entrecroisement de l'hagiographie et de cet opuscule donne à celui-ci une dimension historique qui s'ajoute à la valeur anhistorique qu'il tire de l'autorité biblique; il lui confère une légitimité supplémentaire au service de sa fonction pédagogique.

En effet, spécialement pour les quatre premiers modes, le texte précise que Dominique les enseignaient à ses frères. A propos du mode III (Le saint se donne la discipline), l'Ordre dominicain est présenté, comme le relai de cette pédagogie; pour que l'exemple de son fondateur soit imité, il a statué que tous les frères recevraient la discipline les jours de féries, après complies. Mais cet enseignement et cette imitation ne vont pas toujours de soi: ainsi, sans le prohiber absolument, saint Dominique n'exhortait pas les frères à prier selon le mode VI, dont il avait usé pour accomplir deux miracles, et qu'il réservait aux moments où il savait que "quelque chose de grand et de merveilleux allait se produire." Le document est ainsi traversé par une tension entre un but pédagogique — qui vise à imposer aux frères l'imitation des gestes de la prière du fondateur de l'Ordre — et le caractère

extraordinaire, inimitable de cette prière, son inspiration prophétique, les
pouvoirs miraculeux du saint. D'un côté, il convenait donc de témoigner
de cette prière et de l'imiter, de l'autre de préserver son secret. Le rôle assigné
aux frères tient compte de ces deux exigences contradictoires: ils n'observent le saint qu'à la dérobée, tendent l'oreille pour percevoir ses
gémissements, parfois sans pouvoir saisir ses paroles, mais ils en savent
assez pour être ses témoins au procès de canonisation, comme le frère Isidore
mentionné dans le manuscrit de Bologne.[19]

La description textuelle des gestes de prière pouvait s'appuyer en partie
sur une "grammaire gestuelle" établie au milieu du XIIIè siècle par le Maître
Général de l'Ordre dominicain Humbert de Romans.[20] Mais Humbert de
Romans ne retient que les attitudes générales de tout le corps, sans prêter
attention à la position des bras, des mains, de la tête, des yeux, à l'inverse
de notre document. Il distingue six *"humiliationes"* ou *"inclinationes,"* c'est-à-
dire six manières d'incliner le corps; les deux premières, nommées *"inclinationes"* dans un sens restreint, supposent l'inclinaison du buste seulement
(*ad renes*), soit à l'oblique (*semi-plena* ou *minor*), soit à angle droit (*plena*). Les
deux suivantes sont des génuflexions (*genuflexiones*), le buste étant droit (*cum
corpore erecto super genua*), ou incliné à angle droit (*genuflexio proclivis*). Cette
dernière position s'identifie à la première *prostratio* (*idem quod genuflexio proclivis*); pour la seconde *prostratio* (*venia*), le corps est entièrement étendu sur
le sol.

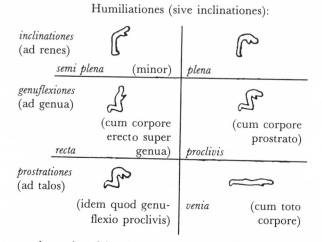

Humiliationes (sive inclinationes):

inclinationes (ad renes)			
	semi plena (minor)	*plena*	
genuflexiones (ad genua)			
	(cum corpore erecto super	(cum corpore prostrato)	
recta	genua)	*proclivis*	
prostrationes (ad talos)			
	(idem quod genu- flexio proclivis)	*venia* (cum toto corpore)	

Aucune place n'est faite dans cette grammaire au mouvement. Seules
sont décrites des attitudes statiques. Le traité de Pierre le Chantre au contraire contient à la fois une grammaire des gestes, avec l'énumération et
l'illustration de sept modes de prière (dont une *inclinatio plena* et une *genuflexio
recta*),[21] puis la description, comme un mouvement continu, de la prière

réelle, scandée par des prépositions temporelles qui en marquent les étapes.[22] Quant à l'opuscule sur la prière de saint Dominique, il ne comporte aucune grammaire gestuelle, mais seulement la description de mouvements, soit linéaires (avec un changement continu d'attitudes) soit alternatifs (comme dans le cas de la discipline). Surtout, la grammaire gestuelle d'Humbert de Romans ne concerne que la prière rituelle, liturgique, commune des frères, sans cette irruption du surnaturel, de l'extraordinaire, qui caractérise aussi notre document et s'intensifie au fil de son développement. C'est pourquoi des neuf (ou quatorze) modes de prière de saint Dominique, seuls les deux premiers se rapprochent de la grammaire d'Humbert de Romans; le mode I est une "*inclinatio minor*" (*plena* dans le mode 1 de Bologne); le II (et 2) est une "*prosternatio venia*"; le mode 3 de Bologne est une "*genuflexio proclivis*," et, de nouveau, le mode 13 de ce manuscrit présente une "*genuflexio recta*." Mais pour tout le reste et dans tous les manuscrits, les gestes du saint échappent très vite à la codification préétablie des inclinaisons, et suivent leur propre développement.

Les modes II, III et IV (Rome et Madrid) sont explicitement liés dans une succession chronologique. Ayant prié face contre terre, le saint "se relevait pour se donner la discipline" (III), puis (*post hec*) priait alternativement debout et à genoux (IV). Le mode V est en lui-même une séquence de positions différentes. Le saint est toujours debout, bien droit et sans appui, mais ce sont les positions de ses mains qui changent: elles sont tantôt "étendues devant la poitrine à la manière d'un livre ouvert," tantôt "jointes et fortement unies devant ses yeux clos," tantôt "levées à hauteur des épaules, comme le fait le prêtre qui célèbre la messe, comme s'il voulait tendre l'oreille pour mieux entendre quelque chose qui lui aurait été dite depuis l'autel." Selon le mode VI, présenté comme exceptionnel, le saint priait debout, le corps bien droit, les bras en croix. Le mode VII est comme une extension du précédent: les bras se dressent au dessus de la tête, les mains sont jointes ou légèrement ouvertes "comme pour recevoir quelque chose du ciel." Son corps en extension est comparé à une flèche prête à être décochée vers le ciel; cette élongation physique est le signe d'un "accroissement de grâce," l'âme est ravie "jusqu'au troisième ciel," le saint est "vraiment comme un prophète," mais pour quelques instants seulement (*non diu stabat*). Les sept modes de prière décrits de manière statique par Pierre le Chantre, se retrouvent parmi les modes de la prière de saint Dominique, y compris le dernier cité. Mais ces gestes sont insérés ici dans un contexte différent, où la prière commune se transforme rapidement en exaltation spirituelle réservée au saint. Les gestes ne tirent pas leur signification de leur forme mais de leur usage social, du contexte dans lequel ils sont accomplis.

Avec le mode VII, la description de la prière de saint Dominique atteint un véritable sommet, après lequel elle revient à des modes plus communs et plus paisibles. Suivant le mode VIII, Dominique s'asseyait parfois, solitaire, "dans une cellule ou ailleurs," pour lire "quelque livre ouvert devant lui"; lecture "active," véritable dialogue, à voix haute ou en pensée, avec le "compagnon" (*cum socio*) qui lui parlait à travers le livre. Il "vénérait son livre, s'inclinait vers lui, le baisait avec amour," d'autres fois il détournait le visage, le voilait de sa chape, le mettait dans ses mains ou se couvrait un moment la tête de son capuce." Puis, "il s'élevait médiocrement en faisant une inclinaison de tête, comme s'il eût voulu remercier quelque grand personnage pour un bienfait reçu." Satisfait, il reprenait alors sa lecture. Admirable description des attitudes du lecteur solitaire aux XIIIè–XIVè siècles, (également illustrée peu après par Fra'Angelico à San Marco), et aussi, dans le dernier passage cité, d'un geste de gratitude d'un inférieur à un supérieur (Dieu ici, mais quelque noble ailleurs). Le geste est sans doute emprunté aux usages du temps, et même à la société laïque.

Le mode IX est différent des précédents puisqu'il était exclusivement réservé aux voyages du saint (*eundo de patria ad patriam*) à l'inverse du mode V par exemple où le voyage (*in itinere*) est seulement envisagé comme une possibilité. Ici le saint est décrit plongé dans ses prières tout en marchant à l'écart de son "*socius*," derrière lui de préférence; il semblait chasser de la mains des "mouches importunes," et faisait le signe de croix, comme pour repousser les agressions démoniaques qui se déchaînent en plein air.

Ce dernier mode de prière est seulement présent dans les manuscrits de Rome et Madrid. Tous les autres sont présents dans tous les manuscrits, mais parfois à des places différentes en raison de l'insertion à Bologne, de cinq et même six modes originaux.

II

Les images de chaque manuscrit forment une série, dont la relative uniformité est le trait dominant. Cette double caractéristique de notre corpus iconographique permet de mettre en valeur les éléments structuraux des images de chaque manuscrit, puis le développement dynamique de chaque série, pour enfin comparer ces séries entre elles.

Dans le manuscrit du Vatican, l'image est dans huit cas sur neuf, comme une fenêtre s'ouvrant dans la page sur l'espace intérieur d'une chapelle. L'architecture de celle-ci, identique dans sa structure, mais dont les motifs diffèrent dans chaque cas, sert à la fois de cadre à l'image et de dais pour le saint. Parfois, les murs latéraux de la chapelle se referment partiellement sur l'image, laissant voir leur face externe (IV, VIII). Jamais saint Dominique ne sort de ce cadre.

Dans le manuscrit de Madrid, le cadre se réduit à une double ligne, dans la totalité des images. La relation entre le saint et le cadre est remarquable: de I à IV, les pieds du saint sont simplement au contact de la ligne in-

Tableau des concordances entre les modes des divers manuscrits

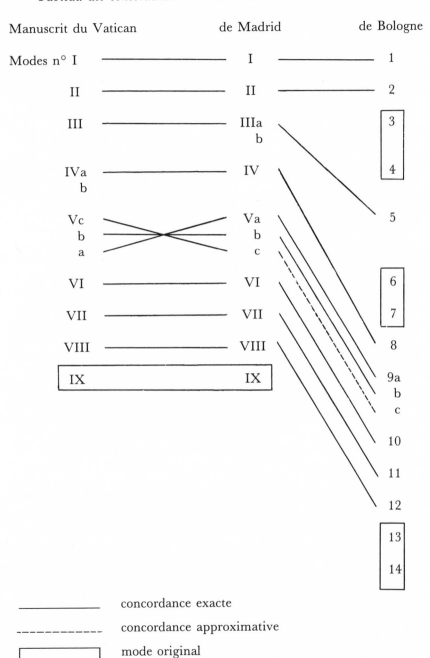

Manuscrit du Vatican   de Madrid   de Bologne

concordance exacte

concordance approximative

mode original

térieure. Le saint la franchit ensuite soit vers le haut, par son auréole (V) puis ses mains (VII), soit vers le bas, par ses pieds (V, VI, VII, VIII). En VII, au comble de son exaltation spirituelle et de l'extension de son corps, ses mains tendues atteignent, du bout des doigts, la ligne extérieure du cadre. En IX, c'est sur cette ligne que le saint marche pieds nus, se servant du cadre de l'image comme d'une route (*in itinere*).

La même relation entre l'intensité de la prière et le traitement du cadre s'observe à Bologne, ou le saint, en 11 (qui correspond au mode VII des autres manuscrits) sort même du cadre de l'image.

Le "mobilier" des images est particulièrement riche à Rome. Sur le mur du fond se croisent généralement des lignes verticales — qui redoublent la position dominante du saint et structurent l'espace qui le sépare du Christ en croix (III, IV) — et des lignes horizontales, une bande médiane notamment, qui dans tous les cas prolonge le bois transversal de la croix et met en relation le saint et le Christ (VI notamment).

A cet enchaînement des deux figures concourt aussi le dessin géométrique du pavement, par des lignes obliques qui se croisent et parfois même convergent vers le centre de l'image (VI). La bande horizontale du mur du fond donne par ailleurs la mesure de l'inclinaison et du redressement du saint: en I elle est tangente à l'auréole; en IV elle épouse l'axe qui sépare très exactement les deux positions successives de sa tête.

Enfin, le mur du fond est généralement percé d'ouvertures qui suggèrent que ce lieu secret est pourtant traversé par des regards, et peut être est aussi — car ces fenêtres sont vides — soumis à une écoute. En VIII, la fenêtre, et même une porte, s'ouvrent sur le jardin du cloître, image du "jardin mystique" auquel la lecture pieuse donne accès; ce spectacle est en même temps une invite à sortir à l'extérieur, ce que réalise la dernière image.

A Madrid, le fond de l'image est un dessin géométrique qui présente des variations sur une même trame orthogonale. A Bologne, le mur du fond apparaît comme un vaste écran, qui suggère une ouverture vers le ciel, sur lequel se détachent "l'étoile du soir"[23] et l'ange. Celui-ci volette dans toutes les images autour du saint à l'intérieur de l'espace de la chapelle: ou bien il y pénètre, à moitié caché encore par le panneau latéral de l'autel. Il est une présence intermédiaire entre le saint et Dieu, complice d'une dévotion solitaire qu'il semble parfois encourager du geste (image 9).

A Rome l'autel est toujours à droite de l'image, tourné de trois-quart à la fois vers le saint et vers le spectateur. Les positions relatives du Christ et du saint sont inversées à Madrid et Bologne. Ce qui importe donc, c'est l'orientation interne de chaque système d'images, qui ne dépend ni d'une orientation géographique *absolue* (l'autel est en principe tourné vers l'Est, qui n'est pas nécessairement représenté à droite comme sur une carte moderne), ni du sens de l'écriture qui accompagne ces images. L'orientation interne des images, ses retournements éventuels dans le cours de chaque série, doivent donc être tenus pour des éléments hautement signifiants.

Saint Dominique n'est pas toujours le seul personnage représenté: à Rome, le Christ est figuré sur la croix, où sa présence "réelle," soulignée par le texte, est manifestée par le sang qui gicle de sa plaie en direction du saint. En IX, il est en compagnie de son "*socius.*" A Madrid (III), il donne la discipline à un frère, à Bologne (14), c'est un frère qui la lui donne. Dans chaque image de ce dernier manuscrit l'ange semble apporter au saint un objet symbolique (lys, phylactère, etc). Le diable est également présent une fois (13).

Le dédoublement ou le triplement de la figure de saint Dominique dans certaines images des trois manuscrits constituent l'un des traits les plus remarquables de cette iconographie. Ils permettent la représentation du mouvement qui caractérise la description des modes de la prière de saint Dominique et la distingue de l'opuscule de Pierre le Chantre, où les modes sont statiques et les figures correspondantes toujours uniques.

Ce procédé, en Rome IV, exprime le mouvement alternatif du saint qui tantôt s'agenouille, tantôt se relève. En Rome V, Madrid V, Bologne 9, il permet de distinguer les trois positions successives des mains, en relation avec un changement de position de la tête non spécifié par le texte.

Selon ce dernier, le saint avait d'abord les mains ouvertes comme un livre, puis jointes fortement serrées devant les yeux, (ou, précise le texte de Bologne, à la manière de la Mère de Dieu pleurant son fils crucifié près de la croix), et enfin élevées à hauteur des épaules, comme le fait le prêtre disant la messe (ce qui peut s'interpréter comme une allusion à la lecture de la Préface, à la prière du *Pater Noster*, ou des Dernières Collectes). Si, dans les images du manuscrit de Rome, où l'autel est toujours à droite, l'artiste avait suivi l'ordre du texte pour représenter successivement les trois figures du saint, la dernière, où le saint imite le prêtre disant la messe, eût été au plus près de l'autel; cette proximité aurait pu donner l'impression que saint Dominique était en train de dire la messe, et non de se livrer à une prière secrète. L'inversion de l'ordre de la représentation iconographique par rapport à l'ordre de la description textuelle n'a-t-il pas permis d'éviter cette confusion? L'hypothèse paraît vérifiée a contrario par le manuscrit de Madrid, où l'autel est à gauche: l'ordre du texte n'avait pas ici à être inversé puisque la troisième figure du saint était ainsi la plus éloignée de l'autel. A Bologne enfin, le texte mentionne bien ce troisième geste (*le mane expante agli omeri*), mais sans référence à l'attitude du prêtre disant la messe, et comme pour interdire tout rapprochement avec cette attitude, l'image représente tout autre chose que ce que dit le texte: les bras de saint Dominique sont figurés baissés, légèrement écartés du corps.

Grâce aux dédoublements ou triplements de la figure du saint, nous comptons au total, dans les trois manuscrits, 42 images de saint Dominique: 14 à Rome (dans 9 images), 12 à Madrid (dans 9 images également), 16 à Bologne (dans 14 images). Les indices retenus pour une description aussi exhaustive que possible de ces figures sont les suivants:

1–L'orientation du corps dans l'image, selon qu'il est de face ou tourné principalement vers la droite ou vers la gauche.

2–La position du corps:

>   —prosterné sur le sol
>   —à genoux, buste incliné
>   —à genoux, buste droit
>   —à genoux / debout (Cf. Bologne, 8)
>   —assis
>   —debout, buste incliné
>   —debout, buste droit
>   —marchant.

3–Le degré de "rotation" du corps:

>   —profil
>   —profil / trois quarts (Cf. Madrid IV ou Bologne, 5)
>   —trois-quarts
>   —trois-quarts / face (Cf. Madrid, Va)
>   —face

Plusieurs figures associent plusieurs attitudes, dans un remarquable mouvement de torsion du corps.

4–La position de la tête

>   —redressée à l'extrême et tendant même à se renverser en arrière (Rome et Madrid VII)
>   —redressée
>   —droite
>   —inclinée en avant
>   —profondément inclinée

5–La position des bras et des mains, en distinguant les cas où ils sont invisibles des deux côtés, ou d'un seul côté; les 9 cas où la ou les mains tiennent un ou deux objets (fouet, livre, bâton); et enfin, quand les deux mains sont visibles et dépourvues d'objet (15 cas différents), en notant la hauteur des mains, la position des doigts, etc....

Le recensement de toutes ces variables garantit l'examen attentif des images, astreint à une analyse rigoureuse. Il permet ensuite de constater que les variables appartenant aux divers registres de la description ne sont pas toutes compatibles; une minorité seulement de leurs associations est effectivement réalisée: il y a par exemple 8 positions différentes du corps et 24 positions différentes des mains (lorsqu'elles sont visibles), soit logiquement 192 associations possibles, à s'en tenir à ces deux variables seulement. Or, seules 39 associations sont effectivement réalisées.

La prière les mains jointes à hauteur de la poitrine, doigts étendus, est la plus fréquente. Cette attitude n'est plus nouvelle au XIIIè siècle.[24] Dans nos images, elle apparaît 7 fois en association avec 6 positions différentes du corps.

La prière debout, et non à genoux, est la plus fréquente. Elle renvoie, selon Pierre le Chantre, à une conception "militante" de la prière: un combattant ne lutte pas assis, mais debout. La position debout est compatible ici avec toutes les positions des bras et des mains (à l'exception, pour des raisons physiques, des mains jointes sur les genoux); on la trouve associée en particulier avec les vastes mouvements des bras, écartés comme ceux du Christ sur la croix, ou dressés au dessus de la tête.

Cependant, l'analyse de ces variables et de leurs associations en des gestes de prière complexes et à chaque fois différents, serait sans intérêt si ces gestes n'étaient situés dans la double série, textuelle et iconographique, des modes de prières, dans chacun des manuscrits.

III

Dans tous les cas, le saint est d'abord debout et incliné; puis il se jette sur le sol, avant de se relever progressivement, se mettant d'abord à genoux, puis debout (redressement que concrétisent bien les deux figures de Rome, IV, et qui se réalise plus lentement á Bologne, de 3 à 8). Il garde ensuite sa position debout, mais avec une extension croissante des membres et de tous le corps qui culmine en VII à Rome et Madrid, en 11 à Bologne. Il revient ensuite à des positions plus basses, sinon plus paisibles, celle de la lecture par exemple. Cependant, les deux premiers manuscrits et celui de Bologne s'achèvent de manières différentes: à Rome et Madrid il marche à l'extérieur du couvent, à Bologne il demeure à l'intérieur et y reçoit la discipline.

Tous les aspects de la représentation iconographique forment, dans chaque image, un tout structuré; ainsi marquent-ils ensemble dans les images VII de Rome et Madrid et 11 de Bologne, le sommet de la dévotion du saint: c'est le moment où, à Madrid, un bâtiment à fenêtre géminées, d'allure ecclésiastique bien qu'il ne comporte ni clocher ni croix, remplace l'autel habituel; peut-être ce bâtiment figure-t-il le couvent, ou bien le "troisième ciel" évoqué par le texte, la Jérusalem céleste que le saint, dans son extase, paraît alors atteindre. Ce moment est aussi dans la série de tout ce manuscrit, celui d'une réorientation de l'image de la gauche vers la droite: jusqu'alors l'autel était sur la gauche, et le saint parfois tourné vers lui; dans l'image

VIII, l'édifice qui paraît désigner la cellule du saint est à droite et c'est vers la droite aussi que se dirige le saint dans la dernière image. Cette réorientation concerne au premier chef la figure du saint, principalement tournée de trois quarte gauche dans les quatre premières images, de face dans les images V à VII, de trois quarte droite dans les deux dernières images. L'image VII, dont le saint, en totale extension, transgresse doublement le cadre, marque à tous points de vue un tournant, une rupture.

Cette rupture n'est pas moins sensible dans le manuscrit de Bologne, même si elle s'exprime différemment. Ici aussi le corps du saint atteint dans l'image 11 (qui correspond à l'image VII des autres manuscrits) le maximum de son extension, et il paraît même s'envoler hors de l'image "comme si, appartenant à la cité céleste, il était étranger en ce monde," dit le texte.

Cette rupture dans la série iconographique comme dans la description textuelle des modes de prière marque l'intrusion du merveilleux hagiographique dans le document, qu'il sous-tend tout entier, mais sans s'exprimer plus tôt avec tant de force. L'équilibre entre les deux fonctions, hagiographique et pédagogique, du texte est ici rompu, un bref instant, au profit de la première. Dans le manuscrit de Bologne, qui est le plus tardif, la métaphore du voyage céleste est représentée de manière réaliste comme un cas de lévitation. Sans doute trouvons-nous ici l'illustration des modèles de piété de la fin du Moyen Age, mettant l'accent, notamment dans les Vies de saints, sur les effets extraordinaires, spirituels et physiques, de l'identification au Christ.[25] L'évolution des modèles de piété se remarque aussi aux allusions faites par ce manuscrit à la dévotion mariale, soit dans le texte (mode 9), soit dans l'image, par les inscriptions *"Ave Maria"* et *"Gratia"* (*plena*) sur le devant de l'autel, généralement au dessus du monogramme du Christ. Mais l'originalité du manuscrit de Bologne réside surtout dans la manière dont s'y achève la série des modes de prière.

La fin des manuscrits de Rome et de Madrid se conforme à l'idéal apostolique de la route, du voyage, caractéristique des Ordres Mendiants à l'origine. Saint Dominique marchant pieds nus entre deux bouquets d'arbres stylisés, dans la dernière image du manuscrit de Madrid, évoquerait presque le *Poverello* d'Assise....[26] A Rome, l'importance attachée à ce dernier *"modus"* est soulignée par le format exceptionnel de l'image, qui comprend deux registres superposés, et en fait trois scènes différentes qui se font suite. A Bologne au contraire, la dévotion du saint reste jusqu'à la fin enfermée dans la même chapelle, et son aspect pénitentiel est rappelé dans la dernière image, où le saint reçoit la discipline des mains d'un frère.

Cette différence essentielle entre les deux types de manuscrit doit s'expliquer historiquement par un affaiblissement de l'idéal Mendiant de la route (du reste déjà sensible, dès le XIIIè siècle, par exemple dans les remaniements de la *Vie* de saint François) au profit d'une dévotion individuelle et pénitentielle privilégiant la fustigation et aussi la récitation de prières répétitives (Ave Maria, Rosaire, etc). Mais la manière différente dont finissent les deux types de manuscrit permet aussi de poser la question fondamentale de la fonction de ces images.

IV

Les images n'ont pas ici pour fonction de rendre intelligible à des *illiterati* incapables de lire ce que le texte dit de chaque mode de prière. Il est vraisemblable que ces documents étaient destinés à l'usage interne des couvents, sous leur double forme écrite et imagée. L'écriture en langue vernaculaire, dans deux cas sur trois, s'explique par le fait qu'il ne s'agit pas de documents hagiographiques officiels comme l'étaient les *Vies* du saint (encore que des *Vies* de saint Dominique aient été traduites en langue vulgaire dès le XIIIè siècle), et surtout par le fait qu'ils étaient destinés à la dévotion "privée" des frères. On ne peut manquer d'assimiler tous les gestes de prière à une sorte de gymnastique, à un système d' "expression corporelle" et de méditation, que les pays occidentaux redécouvrent aujourd'hui à travers la spiritualité hindoue. Le texte lui-même souligne expressément que saint Dominique avait recours à ces gestes de prière "comme à son art et à son ministère particulier" (*quasi ad quandam suam artem et suum singulare ministerium*), expression qui rappelle l' *"artifex orator"* dont parlait Pierre le Chantre. Ces documents offraient donc une sorte de manuel pratique, de guide où les images rendaient plus exacte la description des gestes et surtout du mouvement à imiter. Mais surtout, l'usage de la langue vulgaire et la présence des images augmentaient le degré d'intimité entre chaque frère et le saint, permettaient par dessus tout l'identification de l'un à l'autre. Chaque frère, scrutant du regard l'image du saint participait déjà à son extraordinaire dévotion, avant même de s'essayer à la reproduire dans son propre corps.

Identification au saint, mais aussi au fondateur de l'Ordre des Prêcheurs, au Père et au patron de tous les frères. Il ne s'agissait donc pas seulement d'approfondir la piété de chaque frère, mais de construire une identité collective, en même temps qu'individuelle. D'où le paradoxe de cette omniprésence des frères dans le document, bien qu'ils soient le plus souvent invisibles dans les images; mais celles-ci suggèrent, et le texte souvent note, les regards furtifs qu'ils posent sur le saint, l'oreille qu'ils tendent au moindre de ses gémissements. En dépit des apparences, saint Dominique n'était jamais seul. En particulier, dans tous les manuscrits, l'image finale le montre associé à un frère, mais de deux manières différentes.

Au mode III des manuscrits de Rome et Madrid, le texte dit que saint Dominique *se donnait* la discipline, avec une chaîne de fer, ce pourquoi l'Ordre dominicain avait prescrit que chaque frère *recevrait* la discipline avec des verges de bois, tous les jours de férie, après complies. L'image III de Rome illustre la première partie de ce texte: saint Dominique à genoux, se donne la discipline en face du crucifix. A Madrid, l'image correspondante associe, de part et d'autre d'une colonne qui rappelle celle de la Flagellation du Christ, à gauche saint Dominique se donnant la discipline au moyen de chaînes, et à droite le même saint (identifiable à "l'étoile du soir") administrant la discipline à un frère avec un fouet, et incarnant l'Ordre qu'il a fondé. Si le texte explique historiquement l'origine de cette coutume, instituée en mémoire de la dévotion du saint, l'image personnalise le lien entre l'Ordre et son fondateur, elle abolit le temps et convertit une tradition historique en une relation physique intense, celle de la souffrance, entre deux personnes.

Ce lien personnel apparaît encore plus fort à Bologne, où la discipline concerne deux modes différents de prière: le mode 5 correspond partiellement au mode III des autres manuscrits, puisqu'il montre saint Dominique se donnant la discipline avec une chaîne de fer. Le texte précise qu'il se frappait une fois pour ses propres péchés, une fois pour les pécheurs encore en vie et une fois pour les âmes du purgatoire; mais il ne fait pas allusion à la coutume instituée par l'Ordre. Cette précision est au contraire donnée au mode 14, qui rappelle que saint Dominique *se faisait donner* la discipline par un frère, nommé Ispano. C'est aussi ce que représente l'image correspondante.

Le mode 14 de Bologne renvoie donc partiellement au mode III des autres manuscrits, dans la mesure où il évoque l'origine d'une coutume de l'Ordre dominicain. Mais en même temps il innove totalement puisque ce n'est pas (comme à Madrid III b) saint Dominique qui donne la discipline à un frère, mais au contraire lui qui la reçoit. Saint Dominique et le frère ont donc échangé leurs positions; du même coup est rétablie la valeur historique du document: la figure du saint représente bien ici Dominique lui-même et non l'incarnation de l'Ordre, de même que le frère Ispano, est nommé; mais d'un manuscrit à l'autre s'affirme la réciprocité de la relation physique qui unit saint Dominique et ses frères, par une sorte de don et de contredon des coups de verges.

En ce sens, les deux types de manuscrits ne sont pas aussi différents qu'il peut sembler, y compris dans la manière dont ils s'achèvent. La dernière image du manuscrit de Rome comprend trois scènes: dans les deux scènes du haut, le saint marche avec son "*socius*," la direction de leur marche de la gauche vers la droite est conforme à l'orientation de la figure du saint dans toutes les images de ce manuscrit. Au contraire, au registre inférieur, le saint est tourné vers la gauche, face à son compagnon qui s'est agenouillé sur son manteau étendu sur le sol. De la main gauche, le "*socius*" lui tend ce qui semble être un livre, vers quoi il pointe l'index de sa main droite. Saint Dominique, debout, fait de la main droite un geste de bénédiction. Le texte ne donne aucune indication qui permette d'identifier cette scène, qui me semble pourtant pouvoir être interprétée en fonction de l'ensemble du document: saint Dominique n'est-il pas en train de confier leur mission apostolique aux Prêcheurs, en la personne de son compagnon agenouillé devant lui et de bénir les constitutions de l'Ordre, tenues (reçues?) par le frère? Dans cette hypothèse, le retournement du saint vers la gauche prend tout son sens car le frère figure ici à gauche, à la place qu'occupait saint Dominique lui-même face à l'autel; et c'est maintenant saint Dominique qui a pris la place du Christ en croix. La relation entre le saint et le Christ est tranformée en une relation homologue entre l'Ordre et son fondateur. Le texte ici se tait, au moment même où la dernière image fait accéder toute la série à l'ordre du divin qui légitime tout à la fois la pédagogie des modes de prière et l'identification physique de l'Ordre à son fondateur.

   L'analyse qui précède a tenu compte des caractéristiques essentielles du document — son caractère "sériel," c'est-à-dire la remarquable permanence des normes de la description textuelle de chaque "*modus*" (notices de longueur et de structure semblables) et de la représentation iconographique dans chaque manuscrit (stabilité de la structure de l'image). Ces permanences, la seconde surtout, ont rendu attentif à toutes les variations, souvent légères, mais toujours signifiantes, d'un "*modus*" à l'autre.
   — Son caractère "séquentiel": j'entends par là que ces modes de prière ne sont pas juxtaposés, mais liés l'un à l'autre, comme le texte le signale parfois explicitement. Certes, le document n'illustre pas le développement d'une seule prière à travers diverses étapes se succédant dans un ordre nécessaire; il est vrai que les mêmes dispositions spirituelles générales, avant tout la volonté de s'humilier devant Dieu, président à la plupart des modes de prière, qu'on pourrait donc considérer comme des variations gestuelles sur un même "thème." Cependant certaines circonstances imposaient un mode particulier de prière, et un seul: le mode VI lorsque le saint "savait que quelque chose de grand et de merveilleux allait se produire" c'est-à-dire un miracle; le mode VIII, auquel il se livrait "après les heures canoniales et après l'action de grâce commune qui suit les repas"; le mode IX lorsqu'il voyageait. Néanmoins, la présentation séquentielle de tous ces modes dans le document obéit à une sorte de "conjoncture," qui culmine en VII (ou 11), et qui donne sa signification à l'ensemble de ces manières de prière.
   — la possibilité d'une comparaison entre plusieurs manuscrits, qui met en évidence les singularités de chacun d'eux (par exemple concernant la dernière image) et permet d'introduire une dimension chronologique dans l'analyse historique (le manuscrit de Bologne étant sensiblement postérieur aux autres).
   — la double description, verbale et iconique, de chaque "*modus*," qui a permis notamment de juger du degré d'autonomie de l'image par rapport

au texte; (Bologne, 9). Il est admis que le texte a précédé les images, et celles-ci ne sont pas présentes dans tous les manuscrits. Les images paraissent pourtant indispensables à la pleine compréhension des gestes décrits, et certaines notices renvoient d'ailleurs aux images qui les accompagnent.[27] Enfin les images paraissent pouvoir servir, mieux que le texte, la fonction essentielle d'identification individuelle et collective des frères à leur saint fondateur.

Notes

1. J. C. Schmitt, *"Gestus - Gesticulatio*. Contribution à l'étude du vocabulaire latin médiéval des gestes,"* in *La Lexicographie du Latin médiéval et ses rapports àvec les recherches actuelles sur la civilisation du Moyen Age*, Paris, CNRS, 1981, pp. 377–390.

2. *PL*. 176, col. 925–952. Mise en doute par B. Hauréau, l'attribution à Hugues de Saint Victor ne paraît plus faire de doute. Voir en dernier lieu: Caroline Walker-Bynum, *Docere verbo et exemplo. An aspect of twelfth-century spirituality,* Missoula, Mon., Scholars Press, 1979 (Harvard Theological Studies, XXXI), p. 24, n. 18. Le traité a peut-être été écrit avant 1125. Je me suis contenté d'indiquer la richesse de cet ouvrage dans un bref article. "Le geste, la cathédrale et le roi," l'*ARC*, 72, 1978, pp. 9–12, et je me réserve d'y revenir plus en détail.

3. Marcel Mauss, "Les techniques du corps" (1936), réed. dans *Sociologie et Anthropologie*. Introduction de Claude Levi-Strauss, Paris, PUF, 1968, pp. 363–386.

4. Je remercie Richard C. Trexler de m'avoir communiqué sa transcription du Livre V du *De Oratione*, de Pierre le Chantre, dont il prépare l'édition. L'expression citée se trouve au troisième paragraphe de ce livre.

5. Voir analyse plus détaillée et schéma complet dans mon article cité, "Le geste, la cathédrale et le roi."

6. Cf. note 4.

7. Le titre latin est celui qu'adopte le P. Simon Tugwell, O.P. pour la nouvelle édition, en préparation, de ce texte, dont il a bien voulu me communiquer sa transcription. Celle-ci comporte, outre d'infimes variantes, le récit final d'un miracle qui ne se trouve pas dans l'édition due au P. I. Taurisano, O.P. dans *Analecta Sacri Ordinis Fratrum Praedicatorum* XXX, fasc. II, 1922, pp. 93–106, du ms. *Codex Rossianus* 3 de la Biblioteca Vaticana (avec les miniatures ici reproduites). Ce texte a fait l'objet en 1891 d'une mauvaise traduction française malheureusement reprise telle quelle dans le M. H. Vicaire, *Saint Dominique. La Vie apostolique*, Paris, Les Ed. du Cerf (Chrétiens de tous les Temps, 10), 1965, pp. 93–102. Le P. Vicaire date l'opuscule de 1260–1262 ou 1272–1288; je penche pour la datation la plus tardive en raison de la mention dans le texte du nom d'Albert le Grand, dont on peut penser qu'il était déjà mort quand le texte a été écrit, donc entre 1280 et 1288. Après cette date, l'opuscule aurait été apporté de Bologne à Thierry d'Apolda par

Conrad de Trebensee, en même temps que d'autres matériaux sur la vie de Saint Dominique, en particulier le récit des miracles du saint fait par soeur Cécile. Au titre retenu par le P. Vicaire, je préfère le titre latin des manuscrits étudiés par le P. Tugwell qui met bien l'accent sur la nature "corporelle" de la prière du saint. V. J. Koudelka, "Les dépositions des témoins du procès de canonisation de Saint Dominique," *Archivum Fratrum Praedicatorum*, XLII, 1972, pp. 62–63, signale aussi le manuscrit de Modène, Bibli. Estense, Campori, o. 3. 25. ff. 127–133 v, "De modo orandi corporaliter almi confessoris sancti Dominici." L'auteur indique à tort (p. 63, n. 41) que c'est ce manuscrit qui a été édité par I. Taurisano. Les illustrations ne paraissent pas concerner cette partie du manuscrit, d'après les indications qui m'ont été aimablement fournies par l'administration de la bibliothèque.

8. Edité par C. Alonso-Getino, "Los nueve modos de orar de señor Santo Domingo," *La Ciencia Tomista*, 70, Julio-Agosto 1921, pp. 5–19. Le texte est la traduction fidèle du texte latin précité. Je remercie le P. Domingo Ityurgàiz de m'avoir procuré des photographies des miniatures de ce manuscrit.

9. Le vol récent de ce manuscrit m'a été confirmé par le P. L.-A. Redigonda, O.P. Heureusement, le texte a été partiellement édité par E. Dupré Theseider, "Come pregava S. Domenico," *IL VII. Centenario di S. Domenico*, I-II, 1920–21, pp. 386–392, avec des photographies très réduites des miniatures. Plus visibles, les dessins ici reproduits proviennent de A. Collomb et F. Balme, *Cartulaire ou Histoire diplomatique de saint Dominique*, Paris, 1901, III, pp. 277–287 (où les images I et 3, 12 et 13, ont été inversées). L'auteur de ce texte se nomme lui-même = frère Bartolomeo de Modène.

10. Voir R. C. Trexler, "Legitimating Prayer Gestures in the Twelfth Century. The *De Penitentia* of Peter the Chanter," *History and Anthropology* 1 (1984), (dédié aux *Gestures* et présenté par J. C. Schmitt).

11. "ac si Christus per altare significatus, realiter et personaliter esset ibi, non tantum in signo..."

12. Cette "*curiositas*" dont il est fait vertu, est mentionnée dans le prologue de la version italienne (gli quali modi furono saputi dagli primi frati gli quali *curiosamente* observavano quello, ovvero anche furono soi compagni), comme dans le texte latin (VIII: Si aliquis *curiosus* voluisset eum videre latenter...)

13. Voir par exemple le mode IV, où ses frères l'entendent crier, puis ne perçoivent plus sa voix. L'habitude prise par les frères d'observer en cachette la prière du saint est attestée par l'un d'eux, témoin au procès de canonisation de Bologne. Cf. M. H. Vicaire, *Saint Dominique, sa Vie apostolique, op. cit.* pp. 47–48.

14. La pratique du Psautier est bien décrite en VI: "Illa vero verba, que in Psalterio mentionem faciunt, de isto modo orandi ponderose et graviter et mature proferebat, atque attente dicebat: *Domine Deus meus*, etc..."

15. Voir la description de ce miracle dans: M. H. Vicaire, *Saint Dominique, Sa Vie apostolique, op. cit.*, pp. 105–106.

16. Ce récit provient de Gérard de Frachet, *Vitae Fratrum*, ed. B. M. Reichert, Louvain, 1896, (MOPH, I), pp. 68–69, cap. III.

17. Miracle rapporté par une certaine Bérengère, lors des interrogations en Languedoc pour la canonisation du saint: Cf. J. C. Schmitt, "La parola addomesticata. San Domenico, il gatto e le donne di Fanjeaux," *Quaderni Storici*, 41, 1979, 2, pp. 416–439.

18. Gérard de Franchet *op. cit.*, p. 77, cap. XIV.

19. "Lo quartodecimo modo è che orava spogliato nudo et ingenocchiato, e

facevasi disciplinare ad uno frate, secundo che si crede nominato Ispano, lo quale fu uno degli examinatori ovvero de delegati di lo papa sopra la sanctitade di questo santo, in questo modo." Les réponses fournies par les frères lors de l'enquête de Bologne livrent en effet un grand nombre de détails sur la prière du saint.

20. "Expositio Magistri Humberti Super Constitutiones fratrum Praedicatorum," in *Humberti de Romanis Opera de Vita Regulari*, ed. J. J. Berthier, Rome, 1888–1889, II, pp. 160–171.

21. Voir la reproduction des images d'un des manuscrits dans Richard C. Trexler, *Public Life in Renaissance Florence*, New York, Academic Press, 1980, p. 23.

22. Voir le § "Qualis sit orandum ante altari": "... sed erunt sursum toto corpore erecti usque ad finem illius cantici.... Et *hinc* proicient se in terram.... *Postea* vero surgent et cantabant..." (souligné par moi).

23. P. H. Vicaire, "*Vesperus* (L'étoile du soir) ou l'image de Saint Dominique pour les frères au XIIIè siècle," in *Dominique et ses Prêcheurs*, Fribourg / Paris, 1977, pp. 280–302.

24. Voir notamment, Louis Gougaud, *Dévotions et pratiques ascétiques au Moyen Age*, Paris, 1925, p. 237. Gerhard B. Ladner, "The Gestures of Prayer in Papal Iconography of the Thirteenth and Early Fourteenth Centuries," in *Studies in honor of Anselm M. Albareda*, ed. Sesto Prete, New York, 1961, pp. 245–275. B. Neuheuser, "Les gestes de la prière à genoux et de la génuflexion dans les églises de rite romain," in *Gestes et Paroles dans les diverses familles liturgiques*, Rome Centro Liturgico Vincenziano, 1978, pp. 153–165.

25. A. Vauchez, *La sainteté en Occident aux derniers siècles du Moyen Age d'après les procès de canonisation et les documents hagiographiques*, Rome, Ecole Française de Rome, 1981, p. 499 et suiv.

26. L'habitude qu'avait saint Dominique de voyager pieds nus est en fait rappelée par un des témoins de Bologne: Cf. M. H. Vicaire, *Saint Dominique. La Vie apostolique, op. cit.*, pp. 48–49.

27. Rome, VI: "ut in figura patet"; Ibid., VII: "Quod ut melius intelligatur, subscripta figura docet."

Vatican

Fig. 1.

Fig. 5.

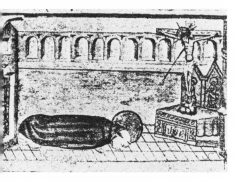

Fig. 2.

Fig. 6.

Fig.3.

Fig. 7.

Fig. 4.

Fig. 8.

Madrid

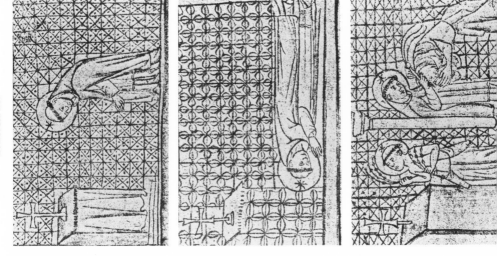

Fig. 1.

Fig. 2.

Fig. 3.

Vatican

Fig. 9.

Madrid

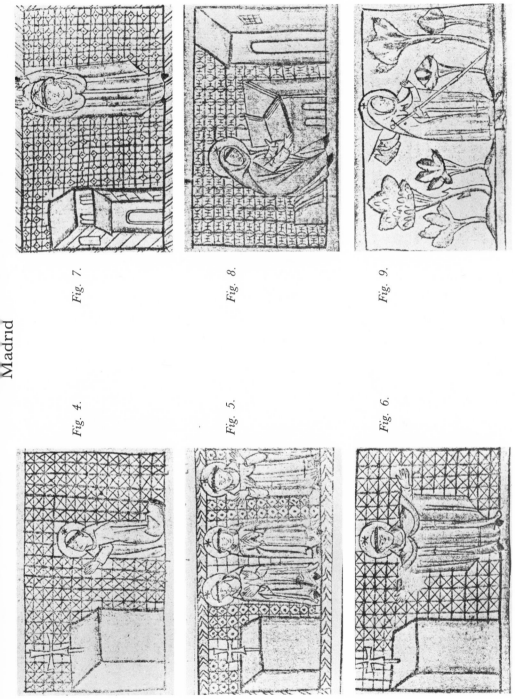

Fig. 4.

Fig. 5.

Fig. 6.

Fig. 7.

Fig. 8.

Fig. 9.

Bologna

Fig. 1.

Fig. 2.

Fig. 3.

Fig. 4.

Fig. 5.

Fig. 6.

Fig. 7.

Fig. 10.

Fig. 8.

Fig. 11.

Fig. 9.

Fig. 12.

Bologna

Fig. 13.

Fig. 14.

Identity and Censored Language: The Case of the Familists

JANET E. HALLEY

The Family of Love, a radical spiritualist sect, was founded in the 1540s by the Lowlands merchant Hendrick Niclaes. This heretical sect and the strong reactions against it make an important chapter in the religious and political history of the Netherlands, Germany, France, and England.[1] It is an appropriate place to study the relations between language and identity in a heretical group.

Personal identity is a very unstable quantity in Familist theology. Niclaes draws on the German spiritualist tradition, a mystical and quite noninstitutional movement that emphasizes the resignation of the individual will to God and an inner experience that replaces external forms of worship. This theology is rich in a paradoxy of selfhood: the "begodded man" acquires his real identity only when it is no longer his own but God's. Niclaes exacerbated this paradox in claiming that he personally had attained this divine identity. Any reader of Niclaes' exasperating texts recognizes that their difficulty results, in part, from the instability of his persona. As a self-defined prophet, Niclaes claims absolute authority to speak for God. Announcing his *Prophetie* (*sic*), Niclaes reports that "I gaue-fourthe the Sounde of the Voyce of the gratious Woorde of the Lorde.... And eauenso, out of the Loue of my God and Christ, *became* the gratious Woorde of the Lorde...."[2] Niclaes presents *himself* as the unequivocally authorized speaker, by defining his person as God's word. In attempting to transform the person into the word and to incorporate the word as a person, he implies that the only perfect text is the extralinguistic experience of the begodded individual. Written texts—even the New Testament, even the *Prophetie* itself—remain profoundly inequivalent to the experience they proclaim; here, as in many

radical Protestant sects, the text is in some way superfluous. The tasks assigned to writing, then, of proclaiming the authoritative experience and
asserting its truth, are quite problematic. The authority of the experience
and of the speaker seem both to deny and, after all, to rely on the authority of the text.

We might trace to this unresolved dependence on written language some
interesting contradictions between Niclaes' *dicta* about language and his actual
practice — for instance, between his reverence for silence as a perfect and
authorizing mode of expression and his unrestrained repetition of claims
to authority. But for Niclaes and his Continental and English followers,
these problems were probably experienced within the broader context of
social relations. First, of course, given its theology, the Family of Love encountered problems in identifying its own membership; and second, as a
heretical sect in an age of severe reaction, it faced the challenge of making
itself invisible to outsiders.

Niclaes strove to embody German spiritualism in a rigidly hierarchical
sect that would recognize him as an absolutely authoritative patriarch. The
private, autonomous spiritual experience of what Norman Burns calls "experimental religion"[3] runs athwart Niclaes' efforts to consolidate the Family
of Love as a cohesive social group. Because "experimental religion" relies
on individual experience to validate an inner impulse whose authority ex-
ceeds such other signs as law and Scripture, the franchise of authority cannot be limited: large sects tend to break up into smaller ones, small ones
tend to resolve into individuals. Niclaes responds to this challenge by attempting to make language identify true believers.

The *Proverbia H.N.*, a handbook of Familist doctrine and practice, declares
on its title page that "I will open my Mouth in Prouerbes or Similitudes"
and that

> To the Children of Loue and the vpright Disciples of Iesu Christ,
> it is geeuen to vnderstand the Mysterie of the heauenlie Kingdom:
> But to Such as are ther-without, it is not geeuen. For-that-cause, all
> thinges chaunce vnto them in Similitudes and Prouerbes.[4]

The problem of distinguishing the "Children of Loue" from "Such as are
ther-without" is not only the subject of this volume: it is its assigned function as well. Niclaes defines perfect Familist discourse as a silent mutual
recognition, possible only when *illuminati* recognize each other as identical:
the spiritual person can "be seene with all Eyes of the Sprit and . . . be hearde
with all Eares of the Spirit," though he or she is "inuisible before all Eyes
of the fleash / and also unheareable with all Eares of the fleash."[5] But it
appears that this silent discourse, however flawless as an ideal, does not
suffice in practice, for the *Proverbia* outlines some ways in which language
is to function to allow mutual recognition of Familists. Here as in many

other works, Niclaes propounds an elaborate hierarchy, of neophytes, disciples, and elders, in which one's spiritual identity is to correspond with one's status. Though he cannot make language signify, Niclaes does rarefy it as a way of articulating and enforcing this hierarchical order: the higher one's status in the Family of Love, the more talking one is allowed to do.[6] Loquacity is a privilege, a mark of rank, and therefore a mark of spiritual aptitude. These social practices mirror the contradiction between Niclaes' ideal of silent discourse and his sesquipedalian style.

But the point is not simply that the *illuminati* encounter God and each other — or God *in* each other — in silence, and discipline their subordinates by enjoining their silence in a torrent of words. Social relations among the Familists are orchestrated not only by how they speak but also by how they read. A key initiation rite described in the *Proverbia* indicates that one important function Niclaes assigns to written texts is that, though unable to distinguish between meanings, they should distinguish between readers by manifesting their interpretive strategies. The ritual crisis that transforms a disciple into an elder occurs when he is given a white stone inscribed with a unique and secret name. The ability to read the stone indicates that the initiate has attained membership: "And that is the Difference betwixt the true Beeing, which is remaining with the Elders / and the Images or Figures, which are administered vnto the Disciples, to an Introduction for them vnto the true Beeing."[7] Elders and disciples, looking at the same sign, see two different things. True believers read "the true Beeing" in the sign; that is, they see it as a perfectly transparent indicator, or rather the very substance of the truth. The stone is able to distinguish between readers, however, because of its simultaneous illegibility. It has a second structure as an image or figure, a signifier remote from its significance. The same could be said of the "Prouerbes and Similitudes" promised on the title page of the *Proverbia*, and, indeed of the *Proverbia* itself.

The problem that appears now is: how can the reader of the stone — or of the *Proverbia* — indicate his successful reading to the assembled community? What gesture signifies that an authoritative interpretation has taken place? Here all Familists become enmeshed in the problems of proof and testimony that plague the group's founder. If speech and interpretation are inadequate to their assigned tasks of proving spiritual authority, true membership cannot be ascertained. The safety of any forbidden group depends on its ability to identify its members, but the Family of Love is by its very theology highly permeable to hostile infiltration. Further, Niclaes and his followers express ambivalence about whether the Family of Love is a sect at all, claiming that it is both a sect outside of and opposed to a dominant cult, and a mystical association of true believers within it. Thus, theological problems merge with problems of group definition that are pre-eminently political. When a defector states, in 1651, that Familists in Surrey "hold y^t they ought to kepe silence amongst them selues, that the libertie they haue in the Lorde, may not be espied out of others,"[8] he effaces any boundary between internal and external political relations. If there is no "inside" to the Family of Love, discursive relations within it are never safe; the sect's heretical and outlawed status shapes all Familist discourse. The relations between Familist language and identity are relations between forbidden language and forbidden identity.

In England, Anglican and state authority struggled with Familists over the identity of persons and the status of their language. From the state's point of view, the central Familist heresy was the doctrine of the individual perfection of the true believer, who, in a moment of mental congruence with the divine, becomes "Godded with God" and thus attains perfect liberty. While still on the Scottish throne, James I perceived that this doctrine posed a political threat. His *Basilikon Doron* argues that Familists epitomize Puritanism "because they thinke them selues onely pure, and ... without sinne, the onely true church.... [B]efore that any of their grounds be impugned, let King, people, lawe & all be tred *[sic]* vnder foote."[9] Thus, both Elizabeth and James sternly repressed the sect. But heretics were never easy to detect. Lacking any positive confessional evidence, the authors of a report on suspected Anabaptists in the Guilford area, for instance, describe themselves as fearful, suspicious, doubtful, and uncertain:

> We are very doughtfull (yf yt may please you) of a certen heresy of Annabaptistry which we very muche feare that some of oure neighbors do holds. Not that we are able to accuse them particularly of any article touching the same secte. But by cause some of them hathe bin suspected thereof along tyme, and also by cause some other suspected in lyke case dothe frequent and use one anohers company styll.[10]

Official vigilance is obliged to collate old and new circumstantial evidence. It could be frustrated of proof by any sectary's readiness to say, with the suspect John Warner, "What I thinke of the magistrate I will kepe to *my selfe*" (emphasis mine).[11]

The autonomy and obscurity of the radical self is allied here with a refusal to speak out. In responding to this subversion, the English state engaged in two related attempts to control discourse: it insisted that speakers have unique personal identities, and that their language be clear. Michel Foucault suggests that the literary category "the author" may be the creation of law: "Texts, books, and discourses really began to have authors (other than mythical, 'sacralized' and 'sacralizing' figures) to the extent that authors became subject to punishment, that is, to the extent that discourses could be transgressive."[12]

Effective legal appropriation requires further that the attributed text also be a clear reproduction of its author's thoughts. The state's strategy leaves a rich textual trace in the many sixteenth-century Familist confessions, in which apprehended individuals charged with Familist belief or membership abjure heresy. In extracting confessions that meet its requirements for attribution and clarity, the state invited their deconstruction. From the very start, a confession is a compromised speech act. The accused speaker must divest himself or herself of heresy by shifting from one personal identity and discursive group to another. To effect this, the confessor must reproduce *not* the heretical beliefs themselves — for that would be to speak as a heretic — but their formulation in the dominant discourse. Any confession can render both authorial identity and linguistic reference problematic. The confession of one Leonard Romsey reveals his eager attempt to cooperate with the state's demand for what Foucault would call the "author-function." Niclaes' texts make many ambiguous predictions of the Last Day, and Romsey interprets them as a call for rebellion only with difficulty: "...the next day is [in?] my iugement sent vnto rebellion.... And that this their rebellion is to be looked for er it be longe this moueth me to think so because...."[13] The hesitant, doubtful gestures point to Romsey himself, the cooperative (read: nonrebellious) interpreter. But the full official programme in these confessions contradicts this very demand by insisting that the confessor dissolve the politically suspect *self* by merging his or her speech into that of the Elizabethan church and state. The 1575 confession of Robert Sharpe, printed as a broadside with a "joint" confession by four other men, is a good example.[14] Sharpe relates his fall into heresy and rescue by orthodoxy as a series of relations with advisors, authorities, and, especially, texts. The confession opens, for instance: "...I Robert Sharpe, haue hertofore vnauisedly, conceyued good opinion of certayne bookes of an aucthour" whom he identifies as Niclaes. The turn occurs "Now vppon conference wyth the Godly learned, (whereof some are in auctoritie)...," whose instruction he substitutes for Niclaes' books. Thus, he repeatedly abjures Familism by repudiating first the author and books and only secondarily the doctrines and the sect. Sharpe proceeds to renounce

> all other Errours and Heresies whatsoeuer contrarie to the Common, Nicene, and Athanasius Creedes, or to the holye Scriptures conteyned in the Bookes of the olde and the newe Testament. And [I] doe also forsake whatsoeuer is repugnant to the Doctrine nowe taught and publiquely *[sic]* set foorth in the Church of England, which Doctrine I acknowledge and confesse, to be the true and Catholicke Doctrine, agreeable to the Canonicall Scriptures....

As these dual abjurations and declarations leave behind specific matter to confirm disbelief and belief along an increasingly indefinite range of doctrine, the possibility of Sharpe's cognitive consent is lost; the self is effaced and merges with authoritative discourse.

The state therefore demands the author-function and sincerity at the cost of contradicting its intention of reabsorbing the individual self of the radical tradition. The Familist response to this contradictory challenge is Nicodemism, or dissimulation: a practice of saying all one is required to say and joining in all the required rituals while privately believing them to be meaningless images.[15] Official records, notably Queen Elizabeth's 1580 proclamation against the Familists,[16] join expressions of outrage at this policy with resolves to seize control of Familist texts — to forbid their publication, distribution and ownership; Familists then respond with repeated episodes of lying about their possession of or acquaintance with Familist *books*.[17] These episodes, like Sharpe's confession, make textual authority the terrain of political struggle. The interrogator pits his authority against Familist books, and the Familist's lie — his announcement that he has not read or does not own such books, indeed, the mere possibility that he does not mean what his words say — deprives language of meaning in the very process of surrendering it to his inquisitor.

Several confessions perform this gesture in the most acute way by naming and renouncing the Familist policy of lying. Corresponding with the state's contradiction is a contradiction in the Familist's response: the confessor's statement that Familists may lie belongs to the required pattern of submissively retailed information, but at the same time it perversely suggests that the confession itself may be a lie. The confession points out that it may be deliberately opaque — a mask of language that, instead of revealing, hides the speaker's meaning. It thus refers to its own status as a predetermined, immutable programme, and belies the authoritative claim that its language *can* be clear and univocal.

It would appear that, by refusing to cooperate with state demands for linguistic clarity, the Familist rescues a detached and opposed personal identity. The situation would appear to exemplify the Derridean argument that textuality subverts ideology, that the text's polysemy can undercut a dominant ideology that relies, in the Western essentialist tradition, on a philosophy of presence and on enforced linguistic transparency. Familist Nicodemism, verbal equivocation, indifference to ritual, *et cetera*, are profoundly subversive in this fashion. But this subversive textuality is always embedded within the discourse it undercuts. Just as the Family of Love was not able to draw a boundary separating itself from an antagonistic world, so its discourse is penetrated by the discourse it opposes. An episode among the Surrey Familists illustrates this point. "They did prohibit bearing of weapons, but at the length, perceiuing them selues to be noted and marked for the same, they haue allowed the bearing of staues."[18] To understand this episode, we may turn to Henry Ainsworth's attack on Niclaes' *Terra Pacis*: Ainsworth objected that Niclaes' pacifist and communist utopia placed in question the magistrate's right to the sword and, with it, all magistracy.

Likewise, the Surrey Familists' refusal to carry weapons would indicate that no one should, that the magistrate should not have the power of physical force over anyone.[19] By inverting an accepted signification, the gesture subverts the hierarchy it implies. But any justice of the peace could read the inverted sign, fix its meaning, and then proceed to wield unimpaired power. Obliged to resume bearing weapons, the Familists double the possible meanings of this act — it can now mean either submission to or protest against a weaponed prince — and thus render it illegible, meaningless in the sheer surplus of possible meanings. But at the same time we must note that they had no recourse outside of the prevailing system of signs. In attempting first to reverse and then to destabilize a socially fixed signification, they continue to be captured in it: their staves also "mean" submission. The subversive self has, to preserve itself, spoken its own prohibition.

We have before us a complex discursive system in which heretical subversion and orthodox regulation interact to preserve and dissolve identity. Terry Eagleton has argued that dominant and oppressed cultures mutually constitute one another, as each develops both ideology and textual practice in response to and in the material context of its opposition. According to Eagleton, *langue*, or the fixed structure of language, is not bound to ideology, and *parole*, the unfixed, arbitrary speech act, is not the unique property of textuality, for these elements operate reciprocally at each specific ideological "conjuncture," or material setting. All discourse, whether dominant or oppressed, "constantly is trying to captivate *langue*-meaning and constantly is being captivated by it." Closure "in place" anywhere may at any time be opened and dispersed; polysemy "in place" anywhere may become trapped and fixed.[20] On both sides of a putative orthodox / heretical borderline, individual utterance *and* fixed social forms of discourse are always at risk.

To borrow Eagleton's terms, Familist and orthodox discourse are diacritical as well as antagonistic.[21] The state responds to the contradictory Familist notion of a divine human identity by generating its contradiction between legally fixed personal identity and the absorption of persons into an official credal programme. Familists reciprocate by displaying the state's contradiction, itself a subversive act. However, their cooperative gestures simultaneously specify and dissolve Familist groups and Familist persons: in a sense, identity is named in order to be abandoned, and abandoned in order to be preserved. And, while Familists specify their own separateness by silent dissent from the discursive forms they reproduce, they have nonetheless placed that very separateness within a system that proceeds to affect its definition. Finally, Familists rescue an identity whose outlines have been limned, in part, by the state's antagonistic formulation of it.

Notes

1. Scholars arguing the importance of Familism in Reformation history include Herman de la Fontaine Verwey, "The Family of Love," *Quaerendo* 6 (Summer, 1976), 219–71, and "Trois Heresiarches dans les Payes-Bas du XVIe Siècle," *Bibliothèque d'Humanisme et Renaissance* 16 (1954), 312–30. Alastair Hamilton's *The Family of Love* (Cambridge, Eng.: James Clarke, 1981) provides primary and secondary bibliographies that supercede most earlier ones, though scholars interested in English Familism should also consult the bibliography supplied by Joan Dietz Moss, "Variations on a Theme: the Family of Love in Renaissance England," *Renaissance Quarterly* 31, No. 2 (1976), 186–87n.

2. Hendrick Niclaes, *The Prophetie* [sic] *of the Spirit of Loue Set-fourth by HN: And by him perused a-new, and more distinctlie declared* (Cologne: 1574), fol.4v; emphasis mine.

3. Norman T. Burns, *Christian Mortalism from Tyndale to Milton* (Cambridge, MA: Harvard Univ. Press, 1972), p. 58.

4. Niclaes, *Proverbia HN. The Prouerbes of HN. Which hee in the Dayes of his Olde-Age, hath set-fourth as Similitudes and mystical Sayings* (Cologne: 1575?).

5. Niclaes, *Proverbia*, fol. 7v.

6. Niclaes, *Proverbia*, fols. 43r–v.

7. Niclaes, *Proverbia*, fol. 32r.

8. The confession of Thomas Chaundler and Robert Sterte is available complete only among Sir William More's papers in the Folger Shakespeare Library, Loseley MS L.b.98. This essay depends on a slightly abbreviated version that John Rogers printed in *The Displaying of an horrible Secte of grosse and wicked Heretiques, naming themselues the Family of Loue* (London: 1578), sig. I1v–H2v. The present quotation is to be found on sig. H2r.

9. *The Basilikon Doron of James VI*, ed. James Craigie (Edinburgh and London: William Blackwood and Sons, 1944), pp. 15–16.

10. Folger Library, Losely MS L.b.99, reprinted in J.W. Martin, "Elizabethan Familists and other Separatists in the Guilford Area," *Bulletin of the Institute of Historical Research* 51 (1978), 92–93.

11. Folger Library, Losely MS L.b.99; Martin, "Elizabethan Familists," 93.

12. Michel Foucault, "What Is An Author?", in *Textual Strategies: Perspectives in Post-Structuralist Criticism*, ed. Josué V. Harari (Ithaca: Cornell Univ. Press, 1979), p. 148.

13. Moss prints the entire confession and provides a very cogent commentary on its difficulties, 190–91 and 191–95.

14. *The confession and declaration of R[obert] Sharpe, and other of that secte, tearmed the Familie of Loue, at Pawles Crosse in London the xij of Iune. An. 1575* (London: 1575).

15. See Carlo Ginzberg, *Il Nicodemismo: Simulazione e dissimulazione religiosa nell' Europa del '500* (Turin, 1970); Moss, "The Family of Love and English Critics," *The Sixteenth Century Journal* 6 (April, 1975), 41–43; Moss, "Additional Light on the Family of Love," *Bulletin of the Institute of Historical Research* 47 (1974), 103–5; Leon Voet, *The Golden Compasses* (Amsterdam, 1969–72), I.29–30.

16. Queen Elizabeth, Proclamation 652, "Ordering the Prosecution of the Family of Love," in *Tudor Royal Proclamations*, ed. Paul Hughes and James F. Larkin (New Haven: Yale Univ. Press, 1969), II, 474–75.

17. Anecdotes are related in Romsey's confession (Moss, 191), and by William Wilkinson, in *A Confutation of Certaine Articles Delivered by HN unto the Familye of Love* (London: 1579), fol. 61v.

18. Rogers, sig. I6v–I7r.

19. Niclaes, *Terra Pacis. A true testification of the spirituall Lande of Peace, which is the spirituall Lande of Promise, and the holy Citee of Peace or the heauenly Ierusalem: and of the Holy and spirituall People that dwel therin: as also of the Walking in the Spirit, which leadeth therunto. Set-foorth by HN: and by Him newly perused and more-playnly declared* (Cologne: 1575?), fols. 14r and 41r–56; Niclaes, *An epistle sent unto two daughters of Warwick from H.N. the oldest Father of the Familie of Love. With a refutation of the errors that are therin; by H. A(insworth)*. (Amsterdam: 1608), fols. 51–54.

20. Terry Eagleton, "Test, Ideology, Realism," in *Literature and Society*, ed. Edward W. Said, Selected Papers from the English Institute, NS 3 (1978), pp. 149–61.

21. Eagleton, p. 165.

Personal Perceptions, Collective Behavior: Twelfth-Century Suffrages for the Dead

A certain brother at the abbey [of Marmoutier], by the name of Ulric, was versed in the knowledge of temporal things. His abbot established him as the steward of the priory of Tavant. But Ulric was hard and inhumane, in such a way that he endeavored, at various times, to diminish the income that was established for the brothers. And indeed, in as much as no one could be found who demanded from him the benefits for the dead, he freely defrauded them. And therefore it happened that two brothers who had been freed from the body appeared to him in a dream and rebuked him with very harsh words for this injury to the dead. But he was hardened and considered what he had seen as nothing, as if it were a dream. Appearing to him once more they announced that punishment for his contempt was imminent. Nonetheless, he remained uncorrected. Having returned a third time, they gave him so many floggings that he remained in bed for half a year tortured by the most severe pains. In time he barely recuperated, but he was never able to recover his original vigor.[1]

Ulric's experience was not unique in the twelfth century. Indeed, around the time of Leo IX—in the mid-eleventh century—the dead began to pay more frequent visits to the living. They came to voice their complaints and to make their petitions: knights who had enlarged their patrimonies through unjust means returned to request that their heirs dispose of the properties; contrite sinners appeared to recount deeds overlooked in their final confessions; repentant usurers came to insure that the debts still owed to them were given, instead, to the church.[2]

This resurgence of ghost stories—which drew on earlier models, such as the *Dialogues* of Gregory the Great—coincided with the rise of a new, more personal and interior spirituality. Indeed, through their stress on the fate of the individual soul and on the role of interior contrition, the ghost stories helped spread that spirituality.[3]

But the account of Ulric is exemplary of a group of stories that concerned not only interior, personal experience, but also corporate behavior. Those stories dealt with monastic suffrages for the dead, and their value lies in the fact that they combined corporate and individual, external and internal concerns.

The prescriptive quality of the other sources for monastic ritual—custumals and charters of confraternity—has led many historians to characterize Benedictine ritual as impersonal and external, and to associate it with the period that preceded the spiritual and intellectual awakening of the late eleventh and twelfth centuries.[4] But the monastic ghost stories indicate that the black monks and their rituals evolved along with the rest of society. The stories suggest that while twelfth-century monks continued to engage in collective, vicarious suffrages, they had begun to perceive their participation in the rituals in personal ways.

A number of prominent monks—Peter the Venerable, Peter Damian, Othloh of St. Emmerman—wrote such ghost stories.[5] However, the anonymous author of Ulric's story—a monk from the Abbey of Marmoutier—was unusual because he included his ghost stories in a collection of spiritually edifying tales that dealt almost entirely with monastic assistance for the dead and dying. That collection, the *De rebus gestis in Majori Monasterio*, provides the focus for this paper.[6]

Several salient characteristics of the *De rebus*, and of the monastic ghost stories in general, point to personal and interior perceptions of monastic ritual. The rhetorical nature of the genre itself reflects a preoccupation, which one does not find in monastic custumals, with motivation. Moreover, the punishments of individual monks—such as Ulric—suggest that the ties between the living and the dead could be personal, with consequences for the individual monk, rather than for the corporate group. And finally, the *De rebus* restricted the community of the living and the dead to an intimate group of men who knew each other's names and faces, and it implied that in addition to participating in the corporate monastic community, each monk formed his own network of relationships which constituted for him a personal, unique community.

The flowering of the ghost stories suggests that writers were exploring, through rhetorical genres, the art of persuasion. The rhetorical purposes varied: Peter the Venerable employed ghost stories to discourage nobles from harming ecclesiastical property, to refute heretics, to demonstrate the efficacy of confession and suffrages for the dead, and, finally, to demonstrate the virtue of the monks of Cluny.[7] The author of the *De rebus* also wished to propagandize the services that his abbey could offer to the world. However, more than Peter the Venerable, he directed his work toward his brothers. He appealed to the individual monk, attempting to sway him by stimulating his internal fears and motivations.

The author of the *De rebus* wanted to persuade the monks to fulfill their calling, and that calling largely entailed, for him, collective behavior. Over half of his stories involved rituals described in monastic custumals — prayers and benefits for the dead, rites for the dying, joining the abbey *ad succurrendum*.[8] However, while custumals outlined the actions themselves, the *De rebus* described the consequences of the actions: the rewards that some monks had incurred for conforming to their abbey's practices and ideals, and the punishments that others incurred for diverging from them.

The persuasive force of the stories lay in their credibility, in the author's ability to convince his audience that the rewards and punishments had really occurred, and that they could occur again. Specific detail — references to familiar names and places — helped establish that credibilty. The author associated four abbots of Marmoutier with the ghosts. Moreover, he referred to other monks by name, and he sometimes identified the office that they filled and the place where they filled it. Ulric was purportedly the steward of the nearby priory of Tavant; Hildebrand was a confessor at Marmoutier; Herveus was a priest from St.-Epain who joined Marmoutier shortly before his death.[9]

Specific detail enhanced the credibility of the stories, but the author still needed to establish the connections between the individual examples and the general experiences and motivations of his monastic audience. Chronological imprecision, and references to familiar routines helped create this connection; they left the impression that extraordinary and supernatural events could interrupt the monastic life at any moment. Ulric's ghosts came "while he was sleeping," two others visited abbot Bartholomew, "at some time," while he was saying his private orations, and another came to the confessor Hildebrand, "in the middle of the night when the brothers were resting in their beds."[10]

Short prefaces or conclusions also served to draw general truths from the specific examples. But the author sometimes went further, as when he concluded Ulric's story with a direct address to the reader:

From this you should infer, reader, that if someone who had not yet departed from the temporal life deserved to be flogged in such a way,

vengeance is imminent in the future for those defrauding the obligations to the dead.[11]

In his discussion of the punishments that monks could incur for their
actions, the author from Marmoutier, as well as other monastic authors,
developed an idea that was not in the models provided by Gregory the Great:
that the dead could punish the living. Ulric's punishment was physical, in
the here and now. Other accounts, though, inspired fear of punishments
in the next life. The two ghosts who visited abbot Bartholomew, for instance, sent a warning to those monks who were not "zealous enough for
their dead brothers" that each monk owed a debt to the dead, which he
had to pay off before his own death. Otherwise, the suffrages that were
performed in his behalf would benefit not him, but the dead to whom he
was still indebted.[12]

These punishments, which constituted the second characteristic of the
ghost stories, simultaneously underscored personal and vicarious aspects
of the monks' relationship with the dead. On the one hand, they indicated
that the consequences of a monk's behavior were personal. Although the
suffrages for the dead were largely corporate, and the dependence of the
dead on the living was vicarious, living monks were responsible for rendering
vicarious assistance as individuals. Each monk ran a personal risk of in-
curring punishment, each accumulated or paid off his own debt to the dead.

On the other hand, the fact that the ghosts themselves inflicted the
punishments indicates that monastic spirituality was intensely relational.
These were the retributions of other men, not divine retributions, and they
demonstrated, therefore, that each monk was responsible not only for his
own standing before God but also for that of his brothers. The monks were
to "bear one another's burdens,"[13] and the dead themselves had the power
to insure that their burdens were indeed taken up by the living. This emphasis on the sharing of spiritual burdens belied the claims of critics, such
as the Augustinian canons, that monks endeavored only for their own personal salvation.[14] Interrelatedness was at the center of the spirituality of
the Benedictine ghost stories.

The third salient characteristic of the *De rebus* — its portrayal of the corporate community as an intimate family of living and dead brothers who
knew one another's names and faces — also distinguished the work from
Gregory the Great's *Dialogues*. Gregory's ghosts, who tended to frequent
the public baths, did not necessarily appear to men who knew them, or
who even recognized that they were dead; but the ghosts in the *De rebus*,
all monks from Marmoutier, tended to visit their living brothers, who
recognized them.[15] Moreover, the portrayal of an intimate community
distinguished the *De rebus* from custumals and charters of confraternity,
which prescribed suffrages for hundreds of strangers — monks from other

abbeys, secular canons, laymen.[16] Those suffrages for outsiders continued, even at Marmoutier, in the twelfth century, but the *De rebus* focused on relationships within the abbey. Only one of its stories mentioned an arrangement of confraternity with an outsider.[17]

The emphasis on suffrages for fellow monks was tied to the author's interest in a practice that was gaining popularity in the twelfth century—that of joining a monastery at the end of one's life, *ad succurrendum*.[18] Through this practice, the monks were able to serve the world by serving their own intimate community: the suggestion of the author of the *De rebus* was that the monastery did not have to offer impersonal prayers for strangers. Rather, it could invite outsiders to cease being strangers, to join in the abbey's discipline and prayers, to end their lives as members of a monastic community.

The man who joined the abbey *ad succurrendum* benefited from the abbey's intimate vicarious assistance. He would die in that holy place surrounded by the other monks, whose prayers—at that critical moment when the soul left the body—would "confirm" the strength of the convert's own faith, and even chase away demons.[19] And after his death, the monks would do for him as they would for any member of the abbey—they would complete whatever satisfaction he still owed for his sins.

The promise of vicarious assistance was balanced, however, with an emphasis on the responsibility of the individual for his own spiritual welfare. The monks could aid only those who had shed tears of contrition—their role was to help him pay off his satisfaction once he had been absolved of his sins. Moreover, those who were able could themselves begin, before their death, to make satisfaction. The case of a monk who had disavowed the monastic life and become a secular priest illustrates this sense of personal responsibility. Like Ulric, the former monk was "versed" in the knowledge of worldly things. He accumulated much wealth, and he lived with a concubine, who bore him several children. His soul might have been lost, except that God sent a warning—the concubine and the children died, the renegade monk fell ill, and at last, "he returned to himself"—he repented and asked to be readmitted to Marmoutier, where he could do satisfaction by undergoing the discipline of flogging. After making this decision, the repentant sinner had a vision in which Saint Martin and Saint Benedict disputed with the devil over their rights to the man's soul. Martin's successful argument—a favorite phrase of twelfth-century theologians—was that "in whatever hour the sinner sighs, all his iniquities will be handed over to oblivion."[20]

The renegade monk's experience conformed to the new theology of penance. He earned his salvation by feeling true contrition, but he still had to make satisfaction for his sins, and Marmoutier offered him, as well as other secular priests and laymen, the opportunity to make that satisfaction in this life rather than the next. The sinner's contrition and part of the satisfaction for his sins were personal, the suffrages in his behalf, and sometimes even the completion of the satisfaction for his sins, were vicarious, and they were performed by an intimate community of monastic brothers.

In addition to assuming this intimate corporate community, the *De rebus* also suggested that each monk was at the center of another community, which resulted from the special ties that he as an individual formed with other individuals. Those ties could be familial, affective or contractual. At Marmoutier, for instance, a monk who died in England appeared to a member of the abbey who was his natural brother, another dead monk came to his confessor, and a third sent a message to a man who was bound to him by a financial debt. Other monastic sources told of dead monks who visited men who were related to them through close ties of personal friendship. In all of these cases, the authors suggested that the dead were particularly dependent on men with whom they had formed or inherited special relationships while they were alive.[21] They implied, moreover, that each monk had his own community, which overlapped with, but differed from, the monastic community as a whole; each developed his own set of obligations and affections which distinguished him from his brothers.

The ghost stories from Marmoutier are illustrative of the simultaneous existence of interior and exterior, personal and corporate, concerns. Some aspects of the stories indicate that the author was able to balance these contrasting concerns. However, others—especially the language and rhetorical approach of the stories—reveal tensions.

The author's intent was to move the monks emotionally, but the persuasive force of his stories lay in their credibility, not in the emotional or poetic power of the language. His prose was stark, concrete; he employed only a few figurative expressions. A graphic description of the changes in a monk's appearance, for instance, communicated the intensity of his struggle with invisible demons:

> His eyes swelled with bloody veins, and offered, as they twisted around, a horrible appearance. His distorted mouth vomited forth foam colored with blood, while his limbs enjoyed no rest.[22]

Passages such as this certainly had the power to evoke emotional response. There is a paradox, though, in the fact that the author attempts to move his audience internally with prose that depicts subjective experience only through external signs. Bitter tears and sighs signify sincere contrition, weeping signifies despair, shaking signifies fear.[23]

A stress on external behavior emerges, as well, from the theme that monks who fail to conform to the abbey's customs incur punishments. However, even here the author is not indifferent to attitude. In the introduction to the *De rebus* he points to the monks who resided at Marmoutier in the eleventh century as models, and he emphasizes that those monks carried out their corporate vicarious responsibilities with zeal and love:

> Whenever one of the brothers had recently died, his confessor was questioned in public regarding the penance imposed on him. And when it was heard, you would have seen the burden of the dead brother eagerly taken up with wondrous compassion by the brothers. This one seized for himself psalms, this one masses, another fasts, and another disciplining with whips. Truly with a wondrous ardor of love that apostolic saying was fulfilled, "Bear one another's burdens and thus you will fulfill the law of Christ."[24]

The author also stresses external behavior in his depictions of monks whose sanctity brought them spiritual rewards. These were men — or boys — whose actions exceeded the demands of the abbey's customs: they filled the lavatories in the middle of the night, washed walls, engaged in extensive private prayers. But the appearance and behavior of at least one monk — his *gravitas*, his eyes, his tears — pointed to an inner life behind those actions.[25] The author never attempted to penetrate that inner life, but he suggested that it was there.

There were tensions, then, between the purpose of the *De rebus* — to sway the monks by appealing to their interior motivations — and its rhetorical method. Nevertheless, the work suggests that corporate behavior is not incompatible with individual perceptions and motivations. By demonstrating this point, the *De rebus* addresses not only the issue of the differences and continuities between Benedictine monasticism of the tenth and eleventh centuries and the new spirituality of the twelfth century, but also the general question of how historians can and should approach the study of ritual.

Because we usually see rituals from the outside — from sources describing or prescribing their form — we often assume that whatever meaning we find in the symbolic behavior of the group as a whole applies equally to all of the members of that group. One conclusion drawn from this view of ritual has been that the society of the tenth and eleventh centuries, in which corporate religious behavior was so prominent, was impersonal and external in nature. We know, however, that the men and women of the twelfth century, like those of the Renaissance, had internal and personal concerns, and we know as well that corporate ritual played a vital role in those two societies. The challenge posed by this juxtaposition of internal concerns with external and corporate behavior is to find a way to interpret ritual adequately, without reducing the symbolic behavior of groups to external and impersonal interpretations, without assuming that rituals represent corporate consensus and an absence of individual motivation. The monastic ghost stories offer only a small response to that challenge. They indicate that the participants in, and advocates of, monastic suffrages for the dead were themselves aware that men had, or needed, personal motivations for joining in those rituals.

Notes

1. "Eodem in cenobio frater quidam Ulricus nomine temporalium callebat pruden-
tia, quem in cella que Tavent nuncupatur procuratorem pater monasterii con-
stituerat. Erat autem durus admodum et inhumanus ita ut fratribus constitutam
annonam aliquotiens imminuere niteretur. At vero defunctis beneficia statuta tanto
licentius defraudabat quanto minus inveniebatur qui hec ab eo exigeret. Contigit
igitur ut ei dormienti duo fratres a corpore soluti per somnium apparerent, et pro
hac defunctorum iniuria durrissimis eum verbis increparent. Induratus ille quasi
somnium nichili pendit quod viderat. Cui denuo apparentes illi pro contemptu vin-
dictam sibi imminere denuntiant. At ille nichilominus incorrectus permansit. Ter-
cio reversi tantis eum verberibus affererunt ut per annum dimidium lectulo decubans
gravissimis doloribus torqueretur. Vix tandem convaluit, quamvis pristinam corporis alacritatem nullatenus recuperare potuerit," *De rebus gestis in Majori Monasterio
saeculo xi*, no. 10, ed. Jean Mabillon and Luc d'Archery, *Acta sanctorum Ordinis Sancti Benedicti*, 9. vols. (Venice: Coletti and J. Bettinelli, 1733–38), saec. vi, pt. 2,
p. 400. Where it differs from the printed edition, I have followed the only known
twelfth-century manuscript: Bibliothèque Municipale de Charleville, ms. 117, fols.
116v–117. For the date of the *De rebus* (between 1137 and 1200), see Louis Halphen
and René Poupardin, *Chroniques des comtes d'Anjou et des seigneurs d'Amboise* (Paris:
A. Picard, 1913), p. xiii; and Joseph van der Straeten, "Le recueil de miracles de
St. Martin dans le ms. 117 de Charleville," *Analecta Bollandiana* 94 (1976), pp. 89–92.

2. Peter the Venerable, *De miraculis* 1:23, ed. J. P. Migne, *Patrologiae cursus com-
pletus. Series latina* (Paris: 1844–) (Hereafter, PL), 189:891–94; Othloh of St. Emmerman, *Liber visionum*, chap. 7, PL 146:360–61; *De rebus*, no. 8, p. 398.

3. On the genre in general, see Jacques Le Goff, *La naissance du purgatoire* (Paris:
Gallimard, 1981), pp. 24 ff.; and J.-C. Schmitt, "Les revenants dans la société
féodale," *Le temps de la réflexion* 3 (1982), pp. 285–306.

4. See, for instance, R. W. Southern, *Western Society and the Church in the Middle
Ages* (Middlesex, England: Penguin Books, 1970), pp. 227–31.

5. See notes 2, 7, 21.

6. Eleven of the 16 paragraphs (nos. 1,2,3,4,5,6,8,9,10,11,16) deal with care
for the dead and dying. All of the ghost stories are about dead monks: 5 (nos.
2,4,8,9,10) involve one or two dead monks; 2 others (nos. 11,17) involve a large
group of dead monks. Paragraph no. 15 of the printed edition is not in Charleville
117, so I have not included it in the total. *De rebus*, pp. 395–405; Charleville 117,
fols. 108v–124v.

7. Peter the Venerable, *De miraculis* 1:9,11,23,27,28, PL 189:871–73, 874–76,
891–94, 900–908.

8. See notes 6 and 18.

9. *De rebus*, nos. 2,4,8,10,17, pp. 395–96, 398–400, 404–5.

10. "Dormienti ei," "aliquando in oratione posito," "mediae noctis libramine quies-
centibus adhuc fratribus in lectulis," *De rebus*, nos. 10,2,4, pp. 400, 395–96 (the
last passage follows the variations in Charleville 117, fol. 111v).

11. "Hinc conice lector quod in futuro vindicta mortuorum debita defraudantibus
immineat si sic flagellari meruit qui nondum temporali decesserat vita," *De rebus*,
Charleville 117, fol. 117. This is slightly different from the printed edition, p. 400.

12. "qui pro fratribus suis defunctis non satis solliciti sunt," *De rebus*, no. 2, p. 395. Other stories about ghostly punishments include William of Malmesbury, *Gesta regum anglorum* 3:293, PL 179: 1262; and Othloh, *Liber*, chap. 16, PL 146: 372.

13. *De rebus*, no. 1, p. 395. See note 24.

14. R. Foreville and J. Leclercq, "Un débat sur le sacerdoce des moines au xii s.," *Studia Anselmiana* 41 (1957), pp. 117–18.

15. Two of Gregory's three ghosts appeared in the baths, one to a stranger: Gregory the Great, *Dialogues* 4:42, 57, trans. O. J. Zimmerman (New York: Fathers of the Church, Inc., 1959), pp. 249–250, 266–270. Only one of the dead monks in the *De rebus* appeared to someone outside the monastery, to a priest who recognized him, and only one of the stories—concerning a large group of ghosts—mentioned a need for identification: the living monk asked a dead monk whom he knew to identify the others, *De rebus*, nos. 8, 17, pp. 399, 405.

16. J. Wollasch, "Die Überlieferung cluniacensischen Totengedächtnisses," *Frühmittelalterliche Studien* 1 (1967), p. 400.

17. *De rebus*, no. 12, p. 402. Other twelfth-century references to relationships of confraternity include: *Cartulaire de Marmoutier pour le Perche*, ed. Barret (Mortagne, 1894), p. 80; *Marmoutier, Cartulaire Blésois*, ed. Charles Métais (Blois: Impr. E. Moreau, 1889–91), p. 137.

18. J. P. Valvekens, "Fratres et sorores 'ad succurrendum,'" *Analecta Praemonstratensia* 37 (1961), pp. 323–24; Louis Gougaud, *Dévotions et practiques ascétiques du moyen âge* (Paris: Desclée de Brouwer et cie:, 1925), p. 133. Four of the 16 paragraphs in the *De rebus* (nos. 5,6,8,11, pp. 396–401) concern monks who joined the abbey "ad succurrendum."

19. "Quantum fides propria possit, comprobat aliena," *De rebus* no. 3, p. 396.

20. "in se reversus ... In quacumque hora ingemuerit peccator, omnes ejus iniquitates oblivioni tradentur," *De rebus*, no. 11, pp. 400–401. On the frequent use of this phrase, see Paul Anciaux, *La théologie du sacrement de pénitence au xii s.*, (Louvain: E. Nauwelaerts, 1949), p. 52, n. 2,3.

21. *De rebus*, nos. 4,8,9, pp. 396, 398–400; Peter Damian, *Epistolae* 8:20, PL 144:403–404. Schmitt ("Revenants," pp. 295–97) outlines four categories of relationships between living and dead—familial, feudal, economic and spiritual—and mentions that the spiritual (monastic) relationship can overlap with the others. However, I do not know of any story in which a spiritual relationship overlaps with a feudal relationship.

22. "oculi venis intumescunt sanguineis, et versati terribilem praebent intuitum; os distortum in partes spumas sanguine infectas evomit, cum membra ejusdem nulla quiete fruantur," *De rebus*, no. 5, p. 397.

23. *De rebus*, nos. 8,11; pp. 398–99, 401.

24. "Cum enim aliquis fratrum nuper obisset, confessor eius in communi super indicta ei penitentia inquirebatur. Qua audita, mira compassione videres certatim a fratribus defuncti fratris onus suscipi: hic psalmos, ille missas, alius ieiunia aliusque disciplinas verberum sibi rapiebat. Implebatur profecto miro caritatis ardore apostolicum illus: "Alter alterius onera portate, et sic adimplebitis legem Christi (Gal. 6:2),'" *De rebus* no. 1, p. 395, following variations in Charleville 117, which are printed in van der Straeten, "Le recueil," p. 90.

25. *De rebus*, nos. 7,14,17, pp. 398, 402–3, 404–5.

Burying and Unburying the Kings of France

ELIZABETH A. R. BROWN

etween 1180 and 1270 there occurred in France a profound change in attitude to the royal dead, a change whose repercussions have not yet completely disappeared. Royal tombs with effigies representing the individuality of the dead began to be erected; royal bodies began to be divided and their different parts separately interred; churches chosen as royal mausoleums began to devote special attention to the royal bodies — or parts of them — that they sheltered. These practices reveal not only generally increased concern with the material world and with the corporeal remains of once-living individuals, but also the increased attention paid to royalty and their earthly remains, attention similar to that long accorded the bodies of the saints. For, like the saints, the kings and the members of the royal lineage were becoming first quasi- and then fully public persons and their bodies thus, in a sense, the possessions of their own faithful, the subjects whom they ruled. The elevation of the spiritual status of the kings of France, which was fully developed by the mid-fourteenth century, in part accounts for the changed attitude to the king's earthly body. Further, respect for royal remains signalled the increased reverence for the king and crown which emerged in the later Middle Ages, and also the greater impressiveness of the king's power over the kingdom, reflected both in his legislative authority and the ceremonial of the court. At a time when intellectual activities were coming to be marked by greater emphasis on reason and greater confidence in the power of abstractive thought, these new practices demonstrate the persistence of deep-rooted beliefs regarding the importance of the body, living and dead, and the strength of the ties believed to link soul and body, even after death. These beliefs, centuries earlier,

Augustine had attempted to discourage, but nonetheless, however firmly denounced by theologians and philosophers, they have subsequently manifested themselves with remarkable insistence.[1]

Before the twelfth century individuals were concerned about the treatment they and their bodies would receive after their deaths — where they would be buried and how their memories would be celebrated. In the early Middle Ages, however, elaborate tombs calling attention to the unique individuality of the dead person were rarely erected. Charles the Bald, for example, chose burial near one of the altars of the abbey church of Saint-Denis, and his grave, according to Suger, was distinguished not by any memorial to himself but rather by the seven lamps that burned continually before the altar and by the three especially venerated relics that were set into it. The proximity of these spiritual and symbolic comforts were evidently thought to provide earthly solace sufficient for the dead emperor.[2]

The attitudes of Abbot Suger are particularly significant, for the abbey of Saint-Denis, which he ruled from 1122–51, sheltered the bodies of Dagobert, the abbey's reputed founder, and various other Merovingians and Carolingians; even more important, it was the traditional burial place of the Robertian and Capetian line. Beginning with Hugues le Grand, count of Paris and father of Hugues Capet, all the Capetians save Philip I, buried at Fleury in 1108, had been interred at the abbey, and Suger held that burial of kings at Saint-Denis occurred "quasi jure naturali." By Suger's time, most of the anniversary services instituted by and for the royal dead of Saint-Denis had come to be neglected, and Suger's concern for the royal bodies the abbey held was focused on reviving these services and thus promoting the royal souls' eternal welfare, concern which is evident in the provisions he made for himself in his own testament. Consonant with these attitudes was his firm belief that the dead should rest in peace for eternity. Although he sympathized with the desire of Louis VI to be buried between the altars of the Trinity and the Holy Martyrs, Suger flatly refused to move the royal bodies that occupied this space in order to accomplish the king's wish. "It is neither proper nor customary," he declared, "to exhume the bodies of kings." Whereas Louis VI believed that burial in the area he had designated would, through the intervention of the saints and the prayers of those visiting the two altars, win the persons interred there forgiveness for their sins, Suger paid less heed to such materially-grounded means of reassurance. After Louis' death in 1137 a spot for his body was found between the altars, but, following customary practice and doubtless with Suger's approval, the grave was marked simply with a slab indicating that beneath it rested "the king of the Franks, son of King Philip," a marker hardly likely to elicit the special intercessions for which Louis VI hoped.

In these respects, as in others, Suger's opinions were conservative. They contrasted with the attitudes of contemporaries in Normandy and England, where, by his time, several rich tombs had been installed in the churches that housed rulers' bodies. Suger must have known, not only of these monuments, but also of those erected in the 1140s for two of the last Carolingian kings, Louis IV and Lothair, who were buried at Saint-Remi of Reims. Neither these memorials nor those installed before 1163 for the Merovingians interred at Saint-Germain-des-Prés, however, moved Suger or his successors at Saint-Denis to commission similar monuments for the rulers buried at the abbey.

As the memorials to the royal and ducal dead in churches of England and France other than Saint-Denis demonstrate, the bodies of dead rulers were coming to be especially valued by those who had survived them. For descendants and successors, imposing tombs dedicated to their ancestors and predecessors served as testimony to dynastic greatness and redounded to their own temporal welfare. Further, the cult of the ancestral dead served to shore up feelings of insecurity harbored by those whose claims to the authority they had inherited were questionable. As to the religious establishments where the rulers' bodies were interred, striking memorials testified to the continuing presence of the distinguished dead within their walls and thus won the houses both renown and also the prospect of donations from those drawn to view and venerate the monuments.

Fig. 1. Gisant of Louis VII at Barbeaux (Aubin-Louis Millin, Antiquités nationales, *5 vols. [Paris: Drouhin, 1790–98], 2: art. XIII [Abbaye de Barbeau], pl. 3–1).*

Funerary monuments depicting the individual dead also had appeal for those who, like Louis VI, were convinced of the special efficacy of the prayers of visitors at their gravesites. An impressive tomb was more likely to attract their attention than was the stark slab over Louis VI's grave. The memorial installed at Montmartre for Adelaïde de Maurienne, wife of Louis VI and mother of Louis VII, after her death in 1154, bears the likeness of a queen strikingly similar to the representation of Fredegunde on the mid-twelfth-century tomb erected in her honor at Saint-Germain-des-Prés. This suggests that her son, doubtless involved in the project, was impressed by the new fashions. Even more persuasive evidence of Louis VII's sentiments is found in his decision to be interred not at Saint-Denis but rather at Barbeaux, the Cistercian monastery he had founded. He thus gained, on his anniversary, the prayers of the entire Cistercian order; further, and perhaps more important, the move enabled his widow, Adèle de Champagne, to commission in his honor and have installed before the main altar of Barbeaux a grand tomb adorned with gold, silver, and precious stones, and the effigy of a king. The splendor of the tomb contrasted strikingly with the rude simplicity of his father's slab at Saint-Denis, with the starkness of the church of Barbeaux, and also with the sentiments expressed in his epitaph. This announced that although other kings of France had sought burial in places lofty and regal, he had chosen to lie "in poverty in this poor company" and "to be impoverished in this poor house, so that the poorest will remember me, poor as I am" (figure 1).[3]

The monks of Saint-Denis were impressed by the tomb of Barbeaux. Of it Rigord, the Dyonisian historian of Philip Augustus's deeds, wrote, "Such work, of such subtlety, has not been seen since Solomon's day." The more general interest Rigord and his fellow-monks took in royal burial places is indicated in his preface to the short history of the Franks which he composed for the monks of Saint-Denis. There he said that for each king who had reigned over the Franks he would give not only his name and origin, but also the location of his tomb. Rigord made no reference to tourists to the abbey who might, like the monks, have been interested in the stories of the kings he had collected, and when he wrote, at the end of the twelfth century, those interested in royal monuments would have had little reason to visit the abbey, since, save for Dagobert's, the graves of the monarchs buried there were either unmarked or, like Louis VI's, designated by simple inscriptions.

This situation changed during the following century, and it is not surprising that the preamble to an early edition of Guillaume de Nangis' short chronicle of France, written at Saint-Denis soon after Philip the Fair's accession in 1285, stated that the history had been composed to satisfy the avid curiosity of those visiting the church where "the greatest part of the kings of France lay buried, who wanted to know the origins of these rulers." By this time a splendid array of royal monuments adorned the abbey.

When Guillaume de Nangis wrote, gold and silver tombs had been erected to commemorate Philip Augustus and Louis VIII, Louis VII's successors, in the transept directly before the main altar. An impressive bronze tomb commemorating Charles the Bald had been set at the entry to the monks' choir, and an equally imposing stone monument to Dagobert and Nantilde had been erected near the main altar.[4] Further, in the 1260s, and surely with the approval of the reigning king, Louis IX, occurred a dedicated search through the abbey for all the royal remains to be found there. By 1267 there had been installed in the transept two rows of tombs, flanking the monuments of Philip Augustus and Louis VIII. The abbey's Merovingians and Carolingians were aligned on one side, its Capetians on the other (figure 2).

Fig. 2. Gisants of Robert the Pious and Constance of Arles, Saint-Denis.
(Photographic Credit: Elizabeth A. R. Brown.)

These developments took place, it seems clear, in response to the threat to the abbey's primacy as royal mausoleum posed by Louis VII's desertion of its precincts and the installation of his splendid tomb at Barbeaux. Further, Suger's successors were doubtless more affected than he by the impulses that had moved other ecclesiastics in France and England to erect tombs to honor their royal dead. Nor could it have seemed fitting to the kings who succeeded Louis VII that their ancestral mausoleum should be bare of such monuments as those that decked so many other churches. Indeed the meticulous arrangement of the thirteenth-century tombs of Saint-Denis suggests that they were installed to convey to those who viewed them a specific and carefully-calculated message regarding the Capetian dynasty and the relationship of that dynasty to those that had preceded it.

The tombs of the crossing of Saint-Denis gave monumental expression to an idea first advanced in the late twelfth century and subsequently espoused by Vincent de Beauvais and incorporated into the historical tradition of Saint-Denis. Through the marriage of Philip Augustus to the Carolingian princess Isabelle de Hainaut, it was held, a return to the Carolingian line was accomplished in the person of their son Louis VIII and the durability of the hybrid line confirmed through the accession and reign of Louis IX. Thus was resolved the ideological threat posed to the Capetians by a prophecy, first recorded in the eleventh century, that, having received their power by God's special dispensation because of their services to his saints and church, the Capetians would reign for seven generations — and no more. The position of Philip Augustus's tomb close to the Capetian line, of Louis VIII's in the center of the crossing, and the space left for Louis IX's to the south, near the Carolingian line, provided a concrete illustration of this theme (figure 3). Its importance in the historiographical traditions of Saint-Denis is signalled by its inclusion in the short history which Guillaume de Nangis wrote for the abbey's tourists, who presumably heard the tale from their guides.

This interpretation of Capetian legitimacy — hardly flattering or reassuring to the descendants of Hugues Capet — found favor in the eyes of the pious Louis IX, persuaded as he was of God's power to move kingdoms as he wished. It both challenged and threatened those who, like Philip the Fair, were impressed by the importance of blood descent as warrant of dynastic legitimacy. On the other hand, the movement of royal remains that had been sanctioned by the grand translations of the 1260s provided a means of dealing with the problem.

Following his death on crusade in 1270, Louis IX's remains were buried next to his father's, in the crossing of the abbey. The saintly king's clearly-stated intention that the abbey be reserved as royal burial place for kings alone was frustrated by the crusading deaths of many of his relatives and followers, whose remains were also interred at Saint-Denis. The essential pattern established in the transept in the 1260s, however, remained intact, then and in 1298, when Philip the Fair had the remains of his recently canonized grandfather translated to the abbey's main altar. One of the anticipated consequences of canonization is translation, as well as division, of the beatified remains, but Philip the Fair's wish to transport the greater part of Louis' bones to the Sainte-Chapelle (and thus, through the physical proximity of his remains, to associate his saintliness with the royal administration of justice in the adjacent palace) was frustrated by the monks' determined opposition.

By accomplishing the canonization and translation of Louis IX, Philip the Fair provided the monarchy and the people of France with a saintly hero. Philip's subsequent actions show, however, that more was needed to assuage his insecurities regarding his lineage's legitimacy. In 1306, the same year in which he secured Saint Louis' head, minus a portion of his jaw, for the Sainte-Chapelle, the king ordered a rearrangement of the tombs of the crossing of Saint-Denis. These alterations resulted in a mingling of the monuments of the three royal lines and thus indicated that there was no essential difference or break among them. The tombs of Philip the Fair's mother and father were installed in the formerly Merovingian and Carolingian line, and a place for his own body was left between his father's tomb and the original resting place of Saint Louis' remains (figure 4).

In the early 1300s changes were introduced in the official Latin history of the kings of France, kept at Saint-Denis, which suggest the deeper significance of Philip the Fair's actions. Doubtless with royal approval, this history was reworked to eradicate any suggestion of Capetian usurpation by divine dispensation or limitation of Capetian rule to seven generations. The new version established that, from their early beginnings, the royal houses of France had been directly linked, one to another, by blood ties resulting from the marriages of two obscure princesses. Later, toward the end of his reign, Philip the Fair installed in the Grand' Salle of the royal palace in Paris a series of statues depicting all rulers of France from the mythical Pharamond to himself, an ensemble which indicated even more explicitly and clearly than the rearranged tombs of Saint-Denis the unbrokenness of descent of the Capetians from their royal predecessors.[5]

After Philip the Fair's death in 1314, the Grand' Salle continued to receive monumental statues representing the successive monarchs of France until, when it burned in 1618, it held fifty-eight of them. The abbey of Saint-Denis was, however, a more important focus for the aspirations of the monarchs and the display of their glory, since it received not merely the simulacra but rather the actual earthly remains of the kings, as well as those of many of their relatives.

In the mid-fourteenth century a fresh attempt was made by Philip VI of Valois or his son John II to restrict royal burial at Saint-Denis to kings. The importance then accorded burial at the abbey is shown by the elo-

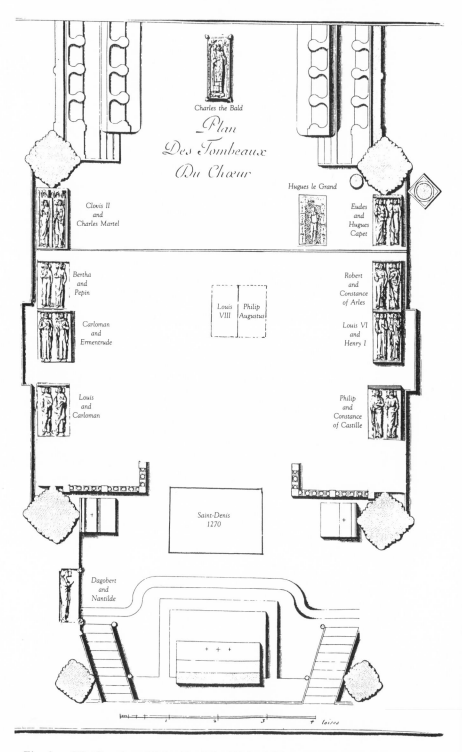

Fig. 3.   The Crossing of Saint-Denis in 1270, A Schematic and Partial Reconstruction. (Elizabeth A. R. Brown, based on Félibien, Histoire, plate facing p. 550.)

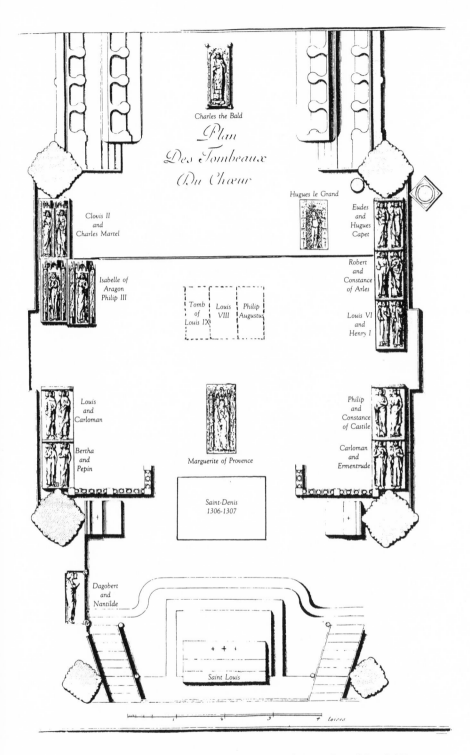

The labels within the plan:

Charles the Bald

Plan
Des Tombeaux
Du Chœur

Hugues le Grand

Clovis II
and
Charles Martel

Eudes
and
Hugues
Capet

Isabelle of
Aragon
Philip III

Robert
and
Constance
of Arles

Tomb
of
Louis IX | Louis
VIII | Philip
Augustus

Louis VI
and
Henry I

Louis
and
Carloman

Philip
and
Constance
of Castile

Bertha
and
Pepin

Carloman
and
Ermentrude

Marguerite of Provence

Saint-Denis
1306-1307

Dagobert
and
Nantilde

Saint Louis

loises

Fig. 4.   The Crossing of Saint-Denis in 1306–07, A Schematic and Partial Reconstruction. (Elizabeth A. R. Brown, based on Félibien, Histoire, plate facing p. 550)

quent and successful efforts of the future Charles V, while still duke of Normandy, to secure his father's dispensation to permit his interment at Saint-Denis should he die before ascending the throne. Charles V not only planned the special chapel where his remains were to lie and the monument that was to cover them, but he also encouraged the faithful Bertrand du Guesclin to be buried at his feet — as Saint Louis' chamberlain had been interred near his master.[6] Portions of the royal bodies were buried elsewhere, but the bodies of the Capetian line of kings, except for that of Louis XI, were interred at Saint-Denis.

The royal funerary monuments installed at Saint-Denis in the late fifteenth and sixteenth centuries expressed not only the monarchs' awareness of the transitoriness of human fortune and life, but also the political and military glory they had achieved at home and abroad.[7] Catherine de Médicis saw to the construction of the imposing Rotonde des Valois (figure 5) north of the abbey church, and there she and her husband Henry II and many of their offspring were buried and rested until the destruction of the Rotonde in 1719. Plans for a similar monument to house the bodies of the Bourbon family, drawn up in the 1660s, were never executed, and the bodies of the Bourbons were, from the early seventeenth century, placed in simple coffins in the abbey's crypt. There they were arranged in solemn lines, the entry to their common resting place guarded by the coffin of the king who had most recently died.[8] These simple memorials contrasted strikingly with the monuments that filled the church above them, and there may be some connection between the change in sepulchral style at Saint-Denis and the fate suffered in 1562 by the mausoleum and remains of Louis XI and his wife, buried at Notre-Dame of Cléry. There the Huguenots demolished the monument, cast the monarch's remains into a coal-heap near the church, and then played ball with his head.[9] As this showed, and as future events would make abundantly clear, there were dangers associated with display and magnificent memorials.

By 1780 the cult of the royal funerary monuments seems to have become less important to the religious of Saint-Denis, Maurists since 1663. In 1781 the prior, Dom Malaret, proposed the removal of the abbey's tombs to the church's chapels and crypt. The monuments installed during Saint Louis' reign were mutilated, he said, and had fallen into irremediable disrepair; the "hideous representations," he declared, "served only to testify to the barbarism of the centuries which had produced them." They interfered with services and, in addition, obscured and damaged the pavement of the church — which Dom Malaret was in the process of replacing. Malaret's plans were in some quarters opposed, but it seems likely that, in the end, he would have won the day had not other events intervened.[10]

These events were, of course, those of the revolutionary years after 1789, and they demonstrated that Dom Malaret's aesthetically detached attitude

Fig. 5. The Rotonde des Valois, Saint-Denis. (Cabinet des Estampes, Bibliothèque nationale.) (Photographic Credit: Bibliothèque nationale.)

toward the tombs of the abbey was not widely shared. Artistic monstrosities he may have considered them, but their intimate relationship to the Capetian line that was being overthrown meant that they and the remains they covered became the foci, on the one hand, for the passionate hatred of the monarchy's many vocal enemies, and, on the other, for the devotion to the monarchs, nostalgia for the past, and dissatisfaction with the current regimes felt by others in that time of cataclysmic change.

For many people in France — at all levels of society and whatever their attitudes to the Revolution — the monarchs lived on in the earthly remains that were sheltered by their tombs. Sixteen days after Louis XVI's execution on 21 January 1793, a poem published in *Le Moniteur* revealed the still-vital power exercised by "the despots who wanted to reign over the French even in the rottenness of their tombs" (as officials of Saint-Denis put it the following September). The poem was a call to arms:

> Let us purge the soil of the patriots,
> Still infected by kings.
> The land of liberty
> Rejects the bones of the despots.
> Let all the coffins of these divinized monsters
> Be broken open!
> Let their memory be condemned!
> And with their errant shades,
> Let the cadavers of these tyrants
> Leave the breast of the fatherland.[11]

The future of the tombs and royal bodies of Saint-Denis — like that of Marie Antoinette and the royal children — hung in the balance. The fate of the royal line, living and dead, was decided at the same time, on 1 August 1793. After proposing "to reduce the children of Louis the Conspirator to what was strictly necessary for two simple individuals and to abandon Marie Antoinette to the public prosecutor," Bertrand Barère de Vieuzac, in the name of the Committee of Public Safety, proposed that, to celebrate the taking of the Tuileries on 10 August 1792, "the ostentatious mausoleums of Saint-Denis" should be destroyed. "Under the monarchy," he said, "even tombs learned to flatter the kings. Royal pride and vain-show could not be subdued in this theater of death, and the sceptre-wielders, who visited such evil on France and on humanity, seem still, even in their tombs, to glory in vanished grandeur. The hand of the Republic must mercilessly efface these haughty epitaphs and demolish these monuments, which recall the terrible memory of the kings." His impassioned pleading carried the day.[12]

Between 6 and 8 August 1793 occurred the systematic removal and defacing of the stone funerary monuments of Saint-Denis; metal slabs and statues had already been removed.[13] But this did not satisfy those intent on seeing "the entire demolition of the tombs of the ancient tyrants." Protests in the Convention led to the events that took place between 12 and 25 October, a poignant accompaniment to the execution of Marie Antoinette on the 16th. During those fourteen days the royal tombs were opened and their contents thrown into two pits, termed the *fosses* of the Valois and of the Bourbons, to the north of the abbey church. Finally, quick-lime was poured over the contents of the two pits.[14]

In mid-October, despite the stench that filled the church, numerous people wanted to view and participate in the proceedings, conducted carefully by the government's delegates. The Commune ordered, to aid the workers and "for reasons of health," that none save those involved in the operations should be admitted to the church, but its decree was frustrated by the eagerness of the many people anxious to be present.

Some came to mock. Soldiers cut off the beard of Henry IV; a woman struck his cadaver; some workers pulled out his hair; another took two of his teeth; yet another cut a sleeve from his chemise and, carrying it like a banner, paraded through the church. Others, inspired by scientific curiosity, made a cast of his head. Still others, moved by profound awe of their former rulers, surreptitiously sought for themselves relics of the dead kings. Indeed, the remains snatched wantonly from the corpse of Henry IV were preserved by one of the guards and presented, mounted in a *tableau*, to Louis XVIII soon after his accession. Alexandre Lenoir, the architect who founded the Musée des Monuments français where many works threatened with destruction were somehow saved, took for himself Hugues Capet's shoulderblade, ribs of Philip the Fair and Louis XII, Charles V's femur, and a tibia and some vertebrae of Charles VI—together with other souvenirs. M. Manteau, librarian of Laon, left a vivid account of his visit to the site on 15 October. On that day, he said, many spectators climbed down ladders into the pit where the bodies of Henry IV, Louis XIII, and Louis XIV were thrown; he followed them and, although fearing the glance of a woman who sat writing on a nearby rock, succeeded in detaching from the bodies fragments which he guarded and which, in 1824, were deposited in the church's crypt. Thus revolutionary rage did not motivate all who observed the events of the October days at Saint-Denis, and the body of Saint Louis' wife, Marguerite of Provence, escaped the workers in the church because those who knew where it lay hidden—under the steps before the main altar—kept silent.[15]

Some of the tombs taken from the church were used in the construction of a short-lived *Montagne* erected at the entry to the town in honor of Marat and Le Peletier de Saint-Fargeau, dead heroes of the Revolution (figure 6). The rest were scattered in the northern courtyard of the church, near the *fosses* of the Valois and the Bourbons.[16] Representatives of the govern-

Fig. 6.   The Montagne of Saint-Denis, a drawing by Alexandre Lenoir. (Louvre, Album Lenoir, RF 5287, fol. 18.) (Photographic Credit: Réunion des musées nationaux.)

ment who visited the church in late January 1794 regretted that the memorials had not been left in place until some "truly Republican use" for them could be found; their report suggested that many might yet be employed in the Colossus which, in the preceding November, the painter and regicide Louis David had proposed should be erected in place of the statue of Henry IV that had dominated the Pont Neuf. This project, designed to enlist in the service of liberty such "Gothic effigies" as the toppled kings of Notre-Dame's facade, proved abortive, and most of the monuments of Saint-Denis were taken to Alexandre Lenoir's museum in Paris. There, sometimes identified, they were displayed with other remnants of the royal and feudal past within the walls of the museum or in the garden behind it.[17] These operations, like the dislodging of the kings of Notre-Dame, were expensive, and by early 1794 the enterprising *marbrier*, Citizen François-Louis Scellier, was already asking some 90,000 *livres* for his work in transporting monuments from one site to another.[18]

During the last years of the century, Saint-Denis stood desolate and open to the elements, its lead roof removed and melted. Proposed for use as a military hospital, it was employed as a storehouse and theatre, and it narrowly escaped demolition. The havoc of the 1790s had not, however, effaced the memories and traditions associated with the church—nor those linked either with the royal remains lying in the two *fosses* north of the church or with their monuments. Napoleon succumbed to their appeal, and in 1806, "perhaps to link his dynasty to that of the kings of France," as a shrewd observer later commented, he decreed that the church of Saint-Denis should become the burial place of the emperors and that chapels should be established in the church to honor those who had once been interred there. Their ancient tombs, however, were to be lodged in the church of Sainte-Geneviève, perhaps to insure that at Saint-Denis chief attention would be focused on him and his imperial successors. To effect these operations he allocated two and a half million *francs* for the work at Saint-Denis. By 1811, perhaps surer of his own line's destiny, he ordered the restoration of the royal tombs to Saint-Denis, but when he abdicated they still remained at Lenoir's museum in Paris.[19]

With the restoration of Louis XVIII in 1814, the sentiments of devotion to the dead kings so harshly treated just twenty-one years earlier found open expression. In that year, before the monarchy determined to restore the abbey church to its traditional position of eminence, a sepulchral mound was created "by the piety of the inhabitants of Saint-Denis, on the spot where they believed the mortal remains of the kings had been interred." A few months later, by royal decree, the bodies of Louis XVI and Marie Antoinette were exhumed from the cemetery of the Madeleine where they had been buried and taken with great pomp to the crypt of Saint-Denis. By the end of 1816 the decision had been made to restore the royal tombs to the church that had once housed them and, more important, to reinstate the royal remains within the basilica.[20]

By 10 January 1817 the plans for the exhumation of the remains from the courtyard of Saint-Denis had been completed and the ceremonial to celebrate their reinterment determined; lists of those whose remains had been violated were established and marble slabs recording their names readied for installation. No difficulties were anticipated, and the ceremony was confidently scheduled for the morning of 20 January. It was carefully coordinated with other services: on 16 January the burial of the body of Louise of Lorraine, wife of Henry III, to be brought from Père Lachaise; on 21 January, a service in honor of Adelaïde and Louise, daughters of Louis XV, whose bodies had been transported from Trieste to Toulon and were being escorted to Paris; finally, at noon on the same day, an anniversary service for Louis XVI.[21]

In preparation for the exhumation of the royal remains, depositions were taken from those who had witnessed or possessed information about the events of 1793, and the enterprising Scellier produced a plan to guide the workers. When the digging began, early on the morning of 13 January, the workmen and their supervisors were sure that their efforts would soon be crowned with success. The next day they were less confident; additional witnesses were heard at the *Mairie* and the archives of Saint-Denis searched for plans. A steady rain commenced and continued throughout the next days; the work began early and ended, by torchlight, late at night. Stray skeletons were found, but not the *fosses*. Finally, late in the morning of the 18th, the sites were located, and the systematic transfer of the remains to waiting coffins commenced.

No use was found for the individual coffins that had been readied for single bodies. As the *procès-verbal* of the proceedings reports, the workers could find "nothing entire and in its natural order except for the lower parts of three bodies; the bones ... were dessicated and had been thrown into the *fosses* in total disorder." Thus the mingled remains were placed in five great coffins. "Four of large dimensions were filled with bones from the *fosse des Valois* and an enormous coffin contained the bones found in the *fosse des Bourbons*." M. de Geslin, Second *Aide des Cérémonies*, wrote that at the end of these labors, which ended at midnight, "an inexplicable mixture of sentiments of joy, grief, and respect moved all who were present." A *chapelle ardente* illuminated by candles and decorated with the royal arms was hastily contrived near the *fosses*, and, accompanied by members of the royal chapter of Saint-Denis, garbed in their vestments, "the coffins were carried in the greatest silence and with the most profound respect to rest in the chapel (figure 7). The only sound was the voice of the priest who, reciting prayers, seemed to call the august shades to abandon the depths of the pits to which they had criminally been relegated." The following day, under the supervision of the Chancellor of France, the coffins were consigned to the crypt of Saint-Denis.[22]

No representative of the royal family attended the formal services, which were held as planned on the morning of 20 January, and, in the end, as the Grand Master of Ceremonies reported, they amounted to very little.[23] The 90,000 *francs* invested in them testify, however, to the monarchy's recognition of their symbolic importance.[24] As significant as Saint Louis' act of piety in gathering the bones of dead crusaders and seeing to their interment, the reburial of the royal remains at Saint-Denis demonstrated the restored monarchy's respect not only for the dead in general but, more specifically, for the monarchs who had ruled before Louis XVII. The awe which the ceremonies occasioned provides ample testimony to the respect which the dried remains of France's former rulers continued to command.

In succeeding years, the funerary monuments in Lenoir's museum were returned to Saint-Denis, together with royal memorials that he had gathered elsewhere. François Debret, the architect who presided over Saint-Denis from 1813 until his forced departure in 1846, gladly received them. Dedicated to the grandeur of the church and France's past, but hampered by his limited intelligence and lack of scholarly ability, Debret treated the monuments with enthusiastic and unfortunate abandon. Most of them he arranged in the crypt to provide a complete series of representations of the

Fig. 7.   The Exhumations at Saint-Denis, 18 January 1817, a drawing by François-Joseph Heim. (Musée de Versailles, MV 5652. des. 179) (Photographic Credit: Réunion des musées nationaux)

rulers of France. As the Baron de Guilhermy wrote in 1847, "Having tallied up the statues and monuments they had, those charged with arranging them decided that each marble king should have a queen of the same species to share the ennuis of the tomb. The actual status of the princesses, their attachments, their legitimate affections posed no obstacle to the arrangements. Princes of lesser rank were condemned willy-nilly to yield their spouses to the kings unless, by chance, a woman was not needed. There resulted singular incests in stone and the worst sort of marble adultery. It was a scandal to make the venerable pillars of the crypt blush. One can scarcely imagine the archeological immoralities committed beneath the dim vaults of Saint-Denis."[25] Nor were all the identifications of the kings' monuments correct, despite the effort Debret claimed to have invested in the work. Having arranged the memorials, Debret simply proceeded, between 1838 and 1841, to canonize his actions by bringing in artisans to carve on the monuments in Gothic letters the inscriptions he believed they should bear. The monuments suffered, not only from the crypt's humidity, but also from souvenir-hungry tourists. Nor was the fate of the memorials too large for the crypt much happier. Dagobert's huge tomb, for example, was split in two to provide symmetrical monuments for the narthex.[26]

It was not his treatment of the royal monuments but rather his restoration of the northern tower's *flèche*, struck by lightening in 1837, that brought about Debret's downfall (and the demolition of the *flèche* as well). However inept Debret's efforts, his attention to the royal tombs, the funds that were appropriated to support his work, and the crowds which, for better or worse, his installations attracted to the crypt of Saint-Denis all testify to the appeal of the royal monuments. Similarly, the royal funeral and anniversary services held at Saint-Denis and, even more, the pomp of Napoleon's second funeral and interment at the Invalides in December 1840 demonstrate how deeply the French continued to venerate the earthly remains of their rulers, royal and imperial.[27]

In 1846–47 Eugène Viollet-le-Duc and his iconographic adviser, the Baron de Guilhermy, replaced Debret at Saint-Denis, and their advent occasioned no slackening of interest in the memorials of the royal dead. Both men were determined to restore the basilica to the conditions they believed had once prevailed within it. From the outset, one of their chief goals was the correct identification of the royal monuments and their removal from the crypt to appropriate settings in the transept. This they largely accomplished by 1868, ten years before Viollet-le-Duc's retirement from Saint-Denis and eleven years before his death. By the time of his retirement he had spent some two and a half million francs on his restoration work at the abbey.[28]

During the regime of Viollet-le-Duc and Guilhermy at the abbey the interest taken in Saint-Denis as repository of royal monuments and remains was more then merely antiquarian or aesthetic. Portions of the royal bodies that had been taken from the *fosses* in 1793 were restored to the church, as were the remains of the royal hearts which, at the height of the Revolution, had been taken from their coffers at Val-de-Grâce and portioned out — one or two to a painter wanting to use them to produce the sepia hue that others were obtaining from mummies in the Levant. In 1846 was installed in the crypt of Saint-Denis an *armoire des coeurs* fitted with boxes containing the hearts (or parts of them) of Marie de Médicis, Henry IV, Louis XIII, Louis XIV, and Louis XVIII — and one whose precise identity was unknown. One space was left empty, perhaps awaiting the heart of Charles X, who died in exile. In the same year, on 23 and 24 November, a certain M. Richer held a sale at Saint-Denis at which were offered, in addition to furniture, paintings, and a reliquary, various royal remains gathered during the violation of the abbey's tombs — bones of Pepin, Philip III, and Jean Tristan, son of Saint Louis, a hand of Louis XII, hair of Marguerite of Provence (whose body, it will be remembered, was apparently never exhumed), a piece of the gown of Louise of Lorraine, and the skull of the Abbot Suger.[29]

Since the days of Viollet-le-Duc and despite the political vicissitudes which have occurred in the intervening years, interest in the royal monuments and remains at Saint-Denis has remained strong. By 1956 the tombs of the French kings had once again undergone restoration, this time at the hands of Jules Formigé, who in 1952 submitted a request to the government for more than six million *francs* to undo the work which Viollet-le-Duc and Guilhermy had accomplished ninety years earlier. Some of his requests were modified, but most of them were approved, and thus the tombs were taken from their nineteenth-century mountings, carefully modeled on pre-Revolutionary drawings, cleaned, and placed on starkly simple blocks of stone. The last ten years have also seen great activity: a northern collateral chapel opened as a showcase for royal funerary robes used in the nineteenth century; a special chapel created in the southern part of the crypt to shelter the bodies, hearts, and other remains of princes and princesses that have found their way to the abbey since the Restoration; the erection in the courtyard east of the church of the huge funeral monument of the Duc de Berry; in the central crypt, Hilduin's chapel, the installation of six marble tombs and the transfer to them of the royal bodies formerly housed in the southern chapel of the crypt. Even now are being incised on their surfaces inscriptions announcing that beneath them lie Louis VII, Louise of Lorraine, Louis XVI, Marie Antoinette, and Louis XVIII; the sixth, empty, awaits the remains of Charles X, still interred in Yugoslavia. These developments are all the more noteworthy in light of the radical political sentiments that prevail in the town of Saint-Denis, for the municipality, as well as the state and the *département*, has supported these new projects at the basilica.[30]

In scale and significance the alterations of monuments and the movements of royal remains that have taken place in recent years at Saint-Denis are unlike those that occurred in the thirteenth and fourteenth and the eighteenth and nineteenth centuries. They and the tourists who continue to throng the basilica show, however, what power is still possessed by monuments linked with a distant and radically different past. The emotions the monuments and remains arouse in those who view them are matters for speculation: curiosity, nostalgia, admiration, envy, and, perhaps, vestiges of the devotion and respect and of the fear and hatred they provoked in previous centuries. One thing seems certain: no more than in the past are they considered objects of indifferent importance, to be disregarded and neglected.

The interest shown in Saint-Denis, the care lavished on the monuments and remains it houses confirm the sagacity of those who in the thirteenth and fourteenth centuries gauged the effects which funeral memorials honoring the royal dead might have on those who viewed them. The current evidence indicates that contemporary reactions are more closely linked to those of the people of the later Middle Ages than to the attitudes of disinterest and even scorn that characterized Abbot Suger and many of his contemporaries. It suggests cognitive and emotional continuities that historians who focus on change and revolution too easily disregard. Those who study modern France, as well as its medieval and Renaissance past, would do well to attend to the comings and goings and the changes in the basilica of Saint-Denis — the modernists for evidence of conservative sentiments often dismissed as unimportant, the students of earlier periods for observable analogues of the reactions experienced by those people, long dead, whose ways of thinking and feeling they seek to comprehend.

Equally interesting, for similar reasons, is another group of monuments located some two hundred kilometers southeast of Paris, between Bar-sur-Aube and Chaumont. There too visitors flock to view a tomb which, in its simplicity, resembles the first memorial that sheltered the remains of Saint Louis. As pilgrims once collected and treasured dust from Saint Louis' tomb, so, it is said, visitors to this memorial gather dirt and pebbles that lie near it. Beside it is another monument — a cross — at whose foot are placed plaques like those often seen in churches graced with the relics and memorials of saints; here they testify to gratitude and veneration, if not to the miraculous cures once attested by the offerings and waxen images laid on Saint Louis' tomb at Saint-Denis. Over the site towers a giant cross of Lorraine (figure 8), which would dwarf the impressive cross that once stood before Saint Louis' remains at Saint-Denis. The form of this monument to Charles de Gaulle suggests that the resonances of the memory of the hero buried there are different from those created by the monuments honoring Saint Louis, his predecessors, and his descendants. Nonetheless, like the new black marble tombs at Saint-Denis, like the continually refurbished medieval and Renaissance monuments in the basilica, the memorials that dominate the village of Colombey-les-Deux-Eglises and the tourists who visit them serve as visible testimony to the effects exercised today, as in the past, by the images and monuments of the royal dead — whether formally crowned or not.

*Fig. 8.   Cross of Lorraine,   Colombey-les-Deux-Eglises.
(Photographic Credit: Frank M. Turner.)*

Notes

1. The portions of this article dealing with the Middle Ages will be more fully treated in a study of the royal tombs and historiography at Saint-Denis on which I am now engaged. Many of the conclusions presented here depend on sources which I have discussed in three articles: "Philippe le Bel and the Remains of Saint Louis," *Gazette des Beaux-Arts* 95 (1980): 175–82; "Death and the Human Body in the Later Middle Ages. The Legislation of Boniface VIII on the Division of the

Corpse," *Viator* 12 (1981): 221–70; and "La notion de la légitimité et la prophétie à la cour de Philippe Auguste," *La France de Philippe Auguste. Le temps des mutations*, Colloques internationaux CNRS, No. 602. I have also delivered papers on different aspects of the topics I treat here in the seminar of Georges Duby at the Collège de France ("Politique funéraire et manipulations symboliques à Saint-Denis," 13 March 1980), at the first Caltech / Weingart Humanities Conference ("Royal Tombs and Myths of Descent at the Abbey of Saint-Denis: The Capetian Dynasty's Creation of its Past," 2 April 1981), and, most recently, at a conference on Legitimation by Descent at the Maison des Sciences de l'Homme, Paris ("The Quest for Ancestry in Later Medieval Europe: Myths of Origin and Genealogies in Capetian France and the Anglo-Norman and Angevin Dominions," 7–9 July 1982); I am grateful for the many useful comments and suggestions I received from those who were present at these meetings. My studies of the Oxford Collection of Gaignières drawings of the royal tombs and of the restorations of the tombs of Saint-Denis in the nineteenth century will soon be published.

Although my conclusions are not always the same as their authors', I have found invaluable the following works, which provide excellent bibliographical information: Georgia Sommers Wright, "A Royal Tomb Program in the Reign of St. Louis," *Art Bulletin* 56 (1974): 224–43, and her doctoral dissertation (Columbia University, 1966), *Royal Tombs at St-Denis in the Reign of Saint Louis* (Ann Arbor, Michigan: University Microfilms, Inc., No. 67–809); Alain Erlande-Brandenburg, *Le roi est mort. Etude sur les funérailles, les sépultures et les tombeaux des rois de France jusqu'à la fin du XIIIe siècle*, Bibliothèque de la Société française d'archéologie, No. 7, (Geneva: Droz, 1975); Jean Adhémar, "Les tombeaux de la Collection Gaignières. Dessins d'archéologie du XVIIe siècle," *Gazette des Beaux-Arts* 84 (July–September 1974), 88 (July–August, September 1976), and 90 (July–August 1977); Gabrielle M. Spiegel, *The Chronicle Tradition of Saint-Denis. A Survey*, Medieval Classics, Texts and Studies, No. 10 (Brookline, Massachusetts and Leyden, 1978); Marc Du Pouget, "Recherches sur les chroniques latines de Saint-Denis. Edition critique et commentaire de la *Descriptio Clavi et Corone Domini* et de deux séries de textes relatifs à la légende carolingienne," Thèse, Ecole Nationale des Chartes, 1978; Andrew W. Lewis, *Royal Succession in Capetian France. Studies on Familial Order and the State*, Harvard Historical Studies, No. 100 (Cambridge, Massachusetts and London: Harvard University Press, 1980). For their generous assistance and advice I am deeply grateful to the staffs of the Archives nationales and the Bibliothèque nationale, of the Cathedral of Saint-Denis, of the Archives et Bibliothèque de la Direction du Patrimoine, and of the Centre de documentation of the Musée de l'Ile-de-France at Sceaux, and to Françoise Bercé, William W. Clark, Richard C. Famiglietti, Anne Lombard-Jourdan, Yves Metman, Patrick Périn, Hervé Pinoteau, Georges Poisson, Nancy B. N. Rash, and Frank M. Turner.

2. Clovis, the first Christian king of the Franks, buried with his wife Clotilde and some of their children at the Church of the Holy Apostles (Sainte-Geneviève) in Paris, apparently did not have a funerary monument before 1220–30, the date of the tomb figure now installed at Saint-Denis: Erlande-Brandenburg, *Le roi est mort*, 6, 133–34. No evidence of any memorial erected to Clotilde or the children has survived.

3. For the epitaph, see Robert Barroux, "Recueil historique en français composé, transcrit et enluminé à Saint-Denis vers 1280," *Mélanges d'histoire du livre et des bibliothèques offerts à Monsieur Frantz Calot...*, Bibliothèque elzévirienne, n.s., Etudes

et documents; (Paris, Librairie d'Argences, 1960), 29.

4. On this monument, see Maryse Bideault, "Le tombeau de Dagobert dans l'abbaye royale de Saint-Denis," *Revue de l'art* 18 (1972): 27–33.

5. Jean Guerout, "Le Palais de la Cité à Paris des origines à 1417. Essai topographique et archéologique," *Mémoires de la Fédération des Sociétés historiques et archéologiques de Paris et de l'Ile-de-France* 2 (1950): 128–38, and Sabine Salet, "La sculpture à Paris sous Philippe le Bel," *Document Archéologia*, 3 (1973): 44–46.

6. Paris, Archives nationales, K 49B, no. 74, an exemplification of Prince Charles' act of October 1362 in an act of 25 October 1362. See also K 49B, nos. 71 and 72 for the act of September 1362 in which John II gave permission to Charles to found the chapel of Saint John the Baptist at Saint-Denis. In October 1373 Charles V, then king, provided for the celebration of his anniversary at Saint-Denis: Jacques Doublet, *Histoire de l'abbaye de S. Denys en France* (Paris: Jean de Heuqueville, 1625), 1028–32. See also Paris, Archives nationales, LL 1177, a cartulary containing acts connected with Charles V's foundation. For the chapel of John the Baptist and its effigies, see Claire Richter Sherman, *The Portraits of Charles V of France (1338–1380)*, Monographs on Archaeology and the Fine Arts, No. 20 (New York: New York University Press, 1969), 65–71, and also Michel Félibien, *Histoire de l'abbaye royale de Saint-Denys en France ...* (Paris: Frederic Leonard, 1706; repr. Paris: Editions du Palais Royal, 1973), 555–59.

7. On these tombs, see Kathleen Cohen, *Metamorphosis of a Death Symbol. The Transi Tombs in the Late Middle Ages and the Renaissance*, California Studies in the History of Art, No. 15 (Berkeley, Los Angeles, and London: University of California Press, 1973), 133–81.

8. Félibien, *Histoire* 555, 565–68; Jules Formigé, *L'abbaye royale de Saint-Denis. Recherches nouvelles* (Paris: Presses Universitaires de France, 1960), 153–57.

9. Félibien, *Histoire* 365. On Louis XI's burial at Cléry and the fate of his tomb, see Michel Caffin de Mérouville, "A la recherche de tombeaux perdus," *Gazette des Beaux-Arts* 56 (1960): 185–94, and Timothy Verdon, *The Art of Guido Mazzoni*, Outstanding Dissertations in the Fine Arts (New York: Garland Publishing Co., 1978), 126–28. See also Max Billard, *Les tombeaux des rois sous la Terreur* (Paris: Perrin, 1907), 94–95; this book is useful for the history of the tombs and their fate in the centuries following their construction.

10. Jules-Joseph Guiffrey, *Un chapitre inédit de l'histoire des tombes royales de Saint-Denis d'après les documents conservés aux Archives nationales, avec un plan et deux fac-simile de dessins du temps. 1781–1787* (Paris: Henri Menu, 1876), also published in *Le Cabinet historique* 22, part 1 (1876), 1–31, 49–77, 97–149 under the title "Les tombes royales de Saint-Denis à la fin du XVIIIe siècle."

11. The journalist Lebrun published the poem on 6 February 1793; it is quoted in Abel Hugo, *Les tombeaux de Saint-Denis ou Description historique de cette abbaye* (Paris: F.-M. Martin, 1825), 107; see also Louis Réau, *Histoire du vandalisme. Les monuments détruits de l'art français*, 2 vols. (Paris: Bibliothèque des Guides bleus Hachette, 1959), 1:226, and, for other events of the Revolution related to the royal monuments, 1:226–31, 306–7, 363–64, and 2:47–50, 107–9, 162–67.

12. Billard, *Tombeaux* 7–8, and also Paris, Bibliothèque nationale, nouv. acq. fr. 6121 (Collection Guilhermy; Notes historiques et descriptives sur l'abbaye et basilique de St. Denis), fol. 4.

13. Paris, Archives nationales, AE I 15, no. 12 ("Rétablissement des sépultures royales à Saint Denis 1817, 48 pièces et I inventaire. La pièce I, 2: AE II 1383"), no. 8h.

14. In addition to the sources cited above, see, for the events of 1793 and 1794, the proceedings of the governmental commissions which oversaw the work at Saint-Denis: *Procès-verbaux de la Commission temporaire des arts*, ed. Alexandre Tuetey, 2 vols. (Paris: Imprimerie nationale, 1912–17), and "Procès-verbaux de la Commission des monuments," ed. Louis Tuetey, *Nouvelles archives de l'art français*, 3rd ser., 17–18 (1901–1902). In 1980 the Archives nationales acquired (AB XIX Entrée 2832) a near-contemporary copy of the "Journal historique de l'Extraction des Cercueils de plomb des Rois, Reines..." (12 October–12 November 1793), which contains an interesting and unique (although inexact) diagram of the abbey church's tombs and the *fosses* dug in 1793 on the northern side of the church.

15. Particularly informative regarding these events and those of later years are the following works: Billard, *Tombeaux*, passim; Georges d'Heilly [Edmond-Antoine Poinsot], *Extraction des cercueils royaux à Saint-Denis en 1793* (Paris: L. Hachette, 1868), passim; Fernand Bournon, *Histoire de la ville et du canton de Saint-Denis* (Paris: Charles Delagrave, 1892), 43–88; and Georges Poisson, *Evocation du Grand Paris*, 3 vols. (Paris: Editions du Minuit, 1956–61), 3: 63–81. See also the clipping preserved among the papers of the Baron de Guilhermy, Paris, Bibliothèque nationale, nouv. acq. fr. 6121, fol. 24, from *L'Union* of 25 October 1872, and the extracts from the contemporary diary of the organist of Saint-Denis, Ferdinand-Albert Gautier, in *Le Cabinet historique* 21, part 1 (1874) and 22, part 1 (1875) (published, without attribution, as "La ville de Saint-Denis pendant la Révolution. Récit contemporain"), especially 21, part 1, 118–34; the diary ("Recueil d'anecdotes et autres objets curieux relatifs à l'histoire de l'Abbaye royale de Saint Denys en France pour faire suite à l'histoire de Dom Félibien") is found in Paris, Bibliothèque nationale, fr. 11681.

16. Paris, Louvre, RF 5282 (Album Lenoir), no. 18 (1793), and Paris, Bibliothèque nationale, Cabinet des Estampes, Yb 4 671 quarto (Notes d'Albert Lenoir, Dossier 4, Statues), 154; see also Gautier's diary, in *Le Cabinet historique* 20, part 1 (1874): 291, 299–300, and 21, part 1 (1875): 118–19, 125; and the papers of the Baron de Guilhermy, in Paris, Bibliothèque nationale, nouv. acq. fr. 6121, pièce 328.

17. For an excellent survey and bibliography, see Alain Erlande-Brandenburg, "Alexandre Lenoir et le Musée des Monuments français," in *Le "Gothique" retrouvé avant Viollet-le-Duc* (Paris: Caisse Nationale des Monuments Historiques et des Sites, 1979), 75–84, 160–61.

18. See the papers of the Baron de Guilhermy, in Paris, Bibliothèque nationale, nouv. acq. fr. 6122, pièce 328; *Procès-verbaux de la Commission temporaire des arts* 1:57, n. 4; and Paris, Archives nationales, F 17 1231, dossier 5, no. 269.

19. *Bulletin des lois de l'Empire français*, 4th ser., 4 (Paris: Imprimerie impériale, June 1806), 280–82; Paris, Archives de la Direction du Patrimoine, Eglise royale de Saint-Denis, no. 5842 (Album Debret; François Debret, "Notice historique sur l'origine et les diverses moments de la construction de l'Eglise Royale de St Denis"), fol. 71, and, in the same archives, the plans for the restoration of the abbey resulting from Napoleon's mandate of 24 February 1811, in Album Debret, Caveaux Nos. 22–23 (5794–95) and Plans Généraux Nos. 3–3 bis (5772–5772 bis) and No. 4 (5773). See also Paris, Archives nationales, F 13 1295, no. 469D, for estimates of the expenses that would be necessitated by the movement of tombs. Particularly useful for these events and for the history and condition of Saint-Denis to 1825 is P. de S.-A. (*sic*), *Promenade aux sépultures royales de Saint-Denis et aux Catacombes ...*, 2nd ed. (Paris: C.-L.-F. Panckoucke, 1825), 63–99; this book includes a detailed

description of the exhumation of the remains of Louis XVI and Marie Antoinette and of the funeral of Louis XVIII (71-77, 81-99).

20. For these and earlier events, see A.-P.-M. Gilbert, *Description historique de l'église royale de Saint-Denys, avec des détails sur la la cérémonie d'inhumation de Louis XVI et de Marie-Antoinette* (Paris: Plancher, 1815), and Gabriel Vauthier, "L'église abbatiale de Saint-Denis (1802-1817)," *Bulletin de la Société de l'histoire de Paris et de l'Ile-de-France* 52 (1925): 142-48. On the so-called "tertre tumulaire" of 1814, see the account of the exhumations of January 1817 written by M. de Geslin, *2e Aide des Cérémonies*, in Paris, Archives nationales, O 3 527, Liasse "Exhumations" ("Relation des Travaux Exécutés dans le Cimetière de L'ancienne Abbaye Royale de St. Denis pour L'exhumation des Dépouilles Mortelles des Rois, Reines . . ."), fol. 4v.

21. See the dossiers in Paris, Archives nationales, AE I 15, no. 12, particularly nos. 1-8a and 9-13.

22. Ibid., no. 7a, and the account of M. de Geslin, in Paris, Archives nationales, O 3 527, Liasse "Exhumations."

23. See the narrative accounts of the events of 20 and 21 January 1817 prepared by M. le Ministre de Dreux Brézé, *Grand Maître des Cérémonies*, in Paris, Archives nationales, O 3 527, Liasse "Exhumations" ("Relations des Cérémonies funèbres du 20 Janvier 1817. Rétablissement des Sépultures Royales," and "Relations des Cérémonies funèbres des 20 et 21 Janvier 1817. Transport des Corps des Mesdames Adelaïde et Victoire de France de Toulon à St. Denis").

24. See the accounts of expenses connected with the exhumations and the services ("Exercise de Monseigneur le Duc d'Aumont" and related documents), in Paris, Bibliothèque nationale, nouv. acq. fr. 21252 (Phillipps MS. 22192), fols. 15-22, 28-41, 48-54. For the somewhat fanciful painting of the exhumations, based on a sketch made by François Debret, which François-Joseph Heim executed between 1820 and 1822, see Josette Bottineau, "Le décor de tableaux à la sacristie de l'ancienne abbatiale de Saint-Denis (1811-1823)," *Bulletin de la Société de l'histoire de l'art français*, 1973: 255-81, and especially 276.

25. François, Baron de Guilhermy, *Monographie de l'église royale de Saint-Denis. Tombeaux et figures historiques* (Paris: V. Didron, 1848), 105.

26. See the Baron de Guilhermy's report to the Ministre des Travaux publics, in Paris, Bibliothèque nationale, nouv. acq. fr. 6122, pièces 332-33, and the copy of the report in Paris, Archives de la Direction du Patrimoine, Eglise royale de Saint-Denis, Dossier de l'administration 1841-76; in the same *fonds*, Dossier de l'administration, Correspondance administrative, 1836-51, "Observations critiques sur la restauration de l'Eglise Royale de St Denis" dated 21 June [1841], and the report of the Baron de Guilhermy dated 24 July 1837; and, in the Dossier de l'administration 1841-76, reports dated 10 June and 14 October 1841. Particularly interesting is Debret's reply to the criticisms of the Commission des Monuments historiques, dated 14 January 1842, in the same *fonds*, Dossier de l'administration 1841-76. See also the proceedings of the Commission des Monuments historiques for 3 June 1842, when Debret's "système déplorable de restauration . . . à St-Denis" was discussed: *Les premiers travaux de la Commission des Monuments historiques 1837-1838. Procès-verbaux et relevés d'architectes*, ed. Françoise Bercé, Bibliothèque de la Sauvegarde de l'art français (Paris: A. et J. Picard, 1979), 213-14.

27. For Napoleon's second funeral, see particularly M. A. Titmarsh [William Makepeace Thackeray], *The Second Funeral of Napoleon, in Three Letters to Miss Smith of London, and The Chronicle of the Drum* (London: Hugh Cunningham, 1841), and,

for the veneration of the Emperor, *La légende napoléonienne 1796–1900*, ed. Jean Adhémar (Paris: Bibliothèque nationale, 1969), especially 62, 67, 69; and Jean Lucas-Dubreton, *Le culte de Napoléon 1815–1848* (Paris: Albin Michel, 1960), especially 353–87.

28. Guilhermy, *Monographie* 106, and his *L'église impériale de Saint-Denis et ses tombeaux* (Paris: Charles Fichot, 1867), 26–35, and also Paris, Bibliothèque nationale, nouv. acq. fr. 6122, fols. 154–55; see as well Jules Jaquemet, *L'église de Saint-Denis, sa crypte, ses tombeaux, ses chapelles, son trésor* (Paris: Putois-Cretté, 1867), 13–14, 76–89, and l'Abbé Testory, *L'église de Saint-Denis et les tombeaux royales* (Paris: De Rochette, 1870), 66. On the work of Viollet-le-Duc, see also Pierre-Marie Auzas, *Eugène Viollet le Duc 1814–1879* (Paris: Caisse Nationale des Monuments Historiques et des Sites, 1979), especially 76–79, and *Viollet-le-Duc*, ed. Bruno Foucart et al. (Paris: Editions de la Réunion des musées nationaux, 1980), 184–85.

29. Poisson, *Evocation* 3:72–77; Billard, *Tombeaux* n. 2 on 169–70; and Paris, Bibliothèque nationale, Cabinet des Estampes, Pe 103 quarto (Maurice Pascal, "Corps des rois de France Louis VIII, Henri IV, Louis XV, Turenne 1793. Basilique de St Denis," material related to the visit of Pascal to Saint-Denis in March 1895), fols. 7–14. For the sale of 23 and 24 November, see the notice from the *Constitutionnel* of 24 November 1846, quoted in the notes of the Baron de Guilhermy, Paris, Bibliothèque nationale, nouv. acq. fr. 6121, fol. 173v.

30. Jean Feray, "Le trésor des ultimes funérailles royales à Saint-Denis," *MH. Monuments historiques* 104 (September 1979):69–77, and, in the same volume (78–83), A.-J. Donzet, "L'aménagement de la crypte de Saint-Denis." For the history of the monument of the Duc de Berry in the years between its creation and 1973, see François Macé de Lépinay, "Un monument parisien éphémère. La chapelle expiatoire du duc de Berry," *Bulletin de la Société de l'histoire de l'art français*, 1973:283–89. A number of important dossiers relating to recent projects involving the tombs of Saint-Denis are housed in Paris, Archives de la Direction du Patrimoine, all in the section Seine-Saint-Denis, Basilique: 1237, 3e Dossier Travaux 1936 à 1940 (lighting of tombs, 1938); 1237, 4e Dossier Travaux 1941 à 1945 (war-time measures, 1941, 1942, 1945); 1237, 5e Dossier Travaux 1946 à 1949 (cleaning of tombs, 1946–47); 1236, Généralités, 5e Dossier 1947 à 1956 (royal crypt, 1945–52, and especially the reports of two tours of inspection, 6 February 1952 and 21 December 1953); Objets d'Art (plaques to identify tombs, 28 February 1948); 1239, Travaux divers antérieurs à 1959, Devis 767 / 1952 (tomb project of Formigé, 1952; lighting of tombs, 1953–58); 1238, 6e Dossier Travaux 1953 à 1958, Devis 621 / 1953 (tomb project of Formigé, 1953); Devis 601 / 1955 (tomb project of Formigé, 1955), Devis 1218 / 1955 (tomb project of Formigé, 1955), Devis 535 / 1956 (plan for royal crypt, 1956), and Devis 823 / 1959 (plan for royal crypt, 1959).

Persons in Groups is a collection of eighteen papers from the sixteenth annual conference of the Center for medieval and Early Renaissance Studies. These papers illustrate various approaches to the subject of social behavior as identity formation. Theoretical and methodological papers are offered by the social psychologist Peter Marsh, the anthropologist Sydel Silverman, and the historian Ronald Weissman. Other scholars explore five specific fields: behavior in the theater is discussed by Jennifer Goodman, Mark Franko, and Timothy Murray; behavior in the political arena is studied by Samuel Edgerton, Stephen Orgel, and Robert Seaberg; the social realm is the subject of Eugene Green, Christiane Klapisch-Zuber, and Diane Owen Hughes. Peter Brown, Jean-Claude Schmitt, and Janet Halley emphasize formal behavior in the religious sphere. The book concludes with historical perspectives on social identity formation presented by Sharon Farmer and Elizabeth Brown. The papers of the contributors are placed within a theoretical context which extends beyond medieval and Renaissance times to the present day, and which embraces a broad spectrum of fields and viewpoints.

Richard C. Trexler is a Professor of History at the University Center at Binghamton, State University of New York. He has been a Fellow at the Villa I Tatti, Florence, and in 1984–85 holds a Guggenheim fellowship, and a fellowship at the Center for Advanced Studies in the Visual Arts, the National Gallery of Art. He is the author of numerous articles and several books in Renaissance studies, including *Public Life in Renaissance Florence* (New York, 1980).

mrts

medieval & renaissance texts & studies
is the publishing program of the
Center for Medieval & Early Renaissance Studies
at the State University of New York at Binghamton.

mrts emphasizes books that are needed —
texts, translations, and major research tools.

mrts aims to publish the highest quality scholarship
in attractive and durable format at modest cost.